FABLE III

FABLE II

ALBION ATLAS

Introduction

All they wanted was a little warmth, maybe some food, and a promise that they wouldn't have to spend another winter on the cold streets of Old Town. It wasn't too much to ask for considering their predicament, but these two orphans had no way of knowing the man they hoped would prove their savior had long since gone mad with a hunger for power. Ever since learning about the Spire and the wish that destroyed all of Albion millennia ago, Lord Lucien had dedicated his every waking minute to rebuilding it. He knew there would be challenges, that one from the bloodline of Heroes might eventually attempt to stop him, but even he couldn't foresee the form that Hero might take. So when a pair of orphaned children entered his life one fateful night, possessing powers he had not accounted for, he did not hesitate to act. He reached for his gun, squeezed off two shots, and gave birth to a hatred and thirst for vengeance that would haunt him until the very end.

Fable II is a tale of a young Hero's quest for vengeance and the seemingly all-knowing gypsy by the name of Theresa who harnesses this young conqueror's determination and gives it direction. Theresa alone knows what it will take to stop Lord Lucien from erecting the Tattered Spire and she knows our Hero can't do it alone. Although they may be the anomalous fourth Hero whom Lucien didn't expect, they will need the Heroes of Strength, Will, and Skill by their side nevertheless. The task of felling Lord Lucien and his world-ending Tattered Spire will require the strength of all four of these Heroes as sure as it will take many years and involve much bloodshed and many sleepless nights. But no matter how steep the price, the Hero cannot afford the consequences of inaction. Not for Albion, and certainly not for the memory of his beloved sister.

ABOUT THIS GUIDE

You hold in your hands the ultimate reference book for the expansive world in which **Fable II** takes place. Here you'll find all you need to know in order to be the greatest Hero possible in every imaginable way, from swordplay to relationships, magic to home decorating, and gambling to love-making. The 'Quest Guide' portion of this book details all of your options for every situation in the game and lets you know beforehand exactly how a chosen outcome will affect your morality and purity, two very important facets of life in Albion. Knowing that not everyone wants or needs step-by-step assistance in questing, we've compiled the 'Albion Atlas'. This collection of maps is designed to serve as a spoiler-free guide to every chest, dig spot, Gargoyle, and Silver Key in the game world, not to mention much, much more. Lastly, it wouldn't be a Signature Series guidebook if we didn't include a thorough Achievement Guide as well—flip to the fold-out poster for detailed instructions on unlocking all 50 Achievements and boosting that Gamerscore of yours!

We at BradyGames thank you for purchasing what we feel is a special strategy guide for a special game and hope it serves you well. Happy questing!

Characters

You are the unquestioned star of *Fable II* and it is entirely up to you to decide what your Hero character will look like. Will they be male or female? Attractive and pure or ugly and evil? Thin or fat? These are decisions you'll make through the course of your adventure both directly and indirectly. Nearly everything you do and every choice you make affects your Hero's appearance at least in some small way. Be sure to read 'The Hero's Way' chapter of this book for a full discussion of the many ways in which the Hero's appearance is shaped through normal everyday actions and decisions. In the meantime, read on to learn a bit about the people you'll be meeting during your quest.

MAJOR PLAYERS

Lord Lucien

Lord Lucien was the wealthiest man in Bowerstone and a man everyone looked up to. That is, until his wife and daughter died tragically. Consumed by misery, Lucien threw himself into researching the Old Kingdom, and the citizenry stopped seeing him outside the castle walls. He was a man who many respected, but as he began to decipher the ancient Spire's secrets, his mind grew twisted and grief became madness. He's gone hopelessly mad and now poses a threat to Albion not seen in millennia.

Theresa

Little is known about this mysterious gypsy woman, other than she alone seems to understand how to stop Lucien's plan for world domination. She was there that day in Old Town to convince Rose to buy the music box and she was there to nurse you through your injuries in the days that followed. Theresa rarely ventures outside the Chamber of Fate in the Guild Cave, but her powers and your possession of the Bower Lake Tomb Seal allow her to communicate with you wherever you go. Whether or not she can fully be trusted is something you'll have to take a chance on...

Hammer

Sister Hannah is a member of the pacifist monks at the Temple of Light in Oakfield, but has within her deep reserves of strength. Her large stature has led many of the others at the Temple of Light to mockingly call her Hammer, a name she bristles at, but unbeknownst to her, history may indeed have a need for her muscles just yet. When she isn't daydreaming about a glorious life as a warrior, she can be found touring Albion's many pubs.

Garth

Garth is perhaps the most advanced Will user in all of Ablion, a trait that has forced him to seek out a life of solitude in Brightwood Tower. Unfortunately for Garth, people just aren't used to seeing magic anymore and tend to be fearful of any sudden outbursts of powers outside the realm of their simple ways of understanding. Garth's very existence is only a rumor to most people and he intends to keep it that way.

Reaver

Reaver's abilities with a pistol are as legendary as his ego is large. He's a man of grand claims and even bolder actions and makes no effort to hide either while living a life of luxury in a mansion in Bloodstone. Always looking for the path of least resistance through life, Reaver will do anything to make a quick bundle of gold. He thinks nothing of shooting someone in cold blood if they cross him—or if he's just mildly perturbed. Take care when dealing with him.

FAMILIAR FACES

Barnum

Barnum is blessed with the unfortunate combination of being one of the most dim-witted and most gullible people in all of Albion. His endless quests to get rich quick are all but certain to land him in financial ruin, yet you can't fault him for trying. Nor should you ever give up on him...

Derek

Derek was but a proud, if not unfortunate, city guard back in the days of your youth. Remember that day he asked you to retrieve the missing Search Warrants for him? You did give them back to him, right?

Arfur

If there was ever a man in Albion for whom everyone shared a communal disgust, it is Arfur. This crook would do anything for a gold coin, so long as it wasn't legal. His incessant propositions to Rose are enough to make you grit your teeth to this day. For the sake of Old Town, we can only hope you didn't sell him the Search Warrants.

Sam & Max

Sam and Max are but a pair of aristocrat brothers who share a great curiosity for the dead. Or, to be more exact, the *undead*. They've been getting themselves into trouble ever since they've come across the Normanomicon. Will they ever learn their lesson?

Belle

Nobody knows where Belle came from, but she's made herself a fixture at Fairfax Gardens and is in charge of the seemingly endless archaeological dig taking place there. Visitors to the area report that she is only willing to speak with those who don't mind assisting her in her research.

Jeeves

Jeeves is Lord Lucien's personal butler, but wouldn't stick around if things became dicey. He may hold the information to some of Lucien's belongings if you ever need to find them.

The Hero's Way

Just as the Hero in *Fable II* must learn to grow into their role as Albion's savior, so too must you learn the ways of the game world. Whether you're new to the *Fable* universe or are a longtime fan, there are plenty of new features and gameplay elements around which to wrap your head. This chapter is designed to help you do just that. Your copy of *Fable II* came with a comprehensive user's manual that does an excellent job detailing the controls and basic gameplay concepts. Rather than repeat the information in the user's manual, this chapter's goal is to expand on that information and provide you with everything you need to shape the Hero and the world of Albion exactly as you wish.

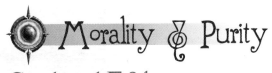

What sets *Fable II* apart from other games is the degree to which your choices affect the appearance of your character and how other people react to you. Nearly everything you do in the game, ranging from your initial choice of playing as a male or female to the food you eat and the combat techniques you employ, impacts your appearance. Much of it—yes, even your diet—also impacts your moral standing. Since word travels fast in Albion and everyone will be forever making their opinion about you known, you must plan accordingly. Read on for tips about living a moral and pure life or, if it suits you, an evil and corrupt one. Or perhaps somewhere in between...

Morality & Purity

Good and Evil

Understanding the distinction between morality and purity is of fundamental importance in *Fable II*. Morality (i.e. Good and Evil) is defined in Albion as an evaluation of the choices you make that affect others. The decisions you make that help or hurt others impacts your moral rating and tilts your rating either towards Good or Evil. Your Hero will be adorned with either a halo or demon horns should his morality rating tilt 100% to either extreme.

 Rapidly Good: Being good takes a bit longer, but you can quickly accrue positive moral points by giving money to beggars, donating large sums at the Temple of Light, earning gifts from villagers, and by completing Slave Rescue quests. The fastest way, provided you have enough money to do it, is to donate to the Temple of Light in 1000 Gold increments.

Rapidly Evil: The fastest way to become Evil is to begin killing people indiscriminately and committing crimes like vandalism, theft, and attacks with Will (non-fatal assaults). This is especially easy to do in Bowerstone Old Town, provided you give the search warrants to Arfur during the Childhood phase of the game (this leaves Old Town as a lawless place filled with people few will miss). Making Sacrifices at the Temple of Shadows is also extremely effective.

Purity & Corruption

Whereas moral dilemmas are those that impact other people, choices of purity and corruption only impact you. Some say these are a true measure of one's righteousness, as anyone can choose to respect the lives of others. Oddly enough, it can be harder sometimes to show ultimate respect for yourself. It can be hard to determine if a choice you're making falls into the category of morality or purity, but perhaps the best way to keep it all straight is to think of altruism and selfishness. If the actions you're taking can be considered either selfless or self-serving, then you can be sure that they will affect your purity rating.

 Path to Purity: Playing the Lute increases purity, as does eating healthily. Avoid meats, alcohol, and any low-grade snacks and instead consume vegetables, tofu, water, and fruit juices. Lowering the rent at properties you own or the prices of goods at shops also increases purity with every person who comes into contact with your property. Wearing a condom is yet another way to earn additional purity points.

Life of Corruption: All non-vegetarian food types and alcohol provide corruption of some kind. Gain high corruption by eating Rancid Beef Jerky or Canned Mutton Product, both of which have a -20 effect on purity. Increasing rent and the prices of goods in shops you own also lowers purity. Commissioning statues and showing off your trophies gains you corruption points for every point of renown they yield—it's a sign of conceit. Cheating on your spouse, having unprotected sex (or paying for sex) also earns corruption points.

Moral Standing

The morality and purity meters in the Personality page of the Logbook start at neutral and extend 1000 points in each direction. It's entirely possible to reverse a trend in one direction. For example, if you start out by Good and accrue 250 Good points, you'll need to then earn 1250 Evil points to push the Hero to 100% Evil. Everyone starts out inhabiting the morally grey area in the center and is viewed as "The Opportunist". This classification changes based on the position of the two needles as follows:

CLASS	EVIL	GOOD	CORRUPTION	PURITY	DESCRIPTION
The Debaser	< 25%	< 25%	> 25%	-	You are too preoccupied with your own pleasure to care much about the fate of others.
The Decadent	-	> 25%	>25%	-	You would go out of your way to help others, but you're just as concerned with helping yourself—usually to food, drink and assorted pleasures.
The Demon	> 25%	-	< 25%	< 25%	Your every action is guided by malevolence. You care little for anything else.
The Fanatic	> 25%	-	-	> 25%	Your devotion to the purity of your body is only matched by your dedication to pure evil.
The Ghoul	> 25%	-	> 25%	-	You are as degenerate as you are evil. The world has seldom seen such a dark being.
The Opportunist	< 25%	< 25%	< 25%	< 25%	You inhabit a morally grey area doing what you feel like, when you feel like it.
The Philanthropist	-	> 25%	< 25%	< 25%	Your every action is guided by selflessness and the belief that you can make the world a better place.
The Purist	< 25%	< 25%	-	> 25%	The principle that guides your life is purity of mind and body, without too much concern for banal matters like "morality".
The Saint	-	> 25%	-	> 25%	You are as pure and benevolent a being as Albion has ever seen.

DEVELOPER TIPS

The following tips come from the developers at Lionhead Studios and Microsoft Game Studios.

- If you hand the warrants to Arfur in Childhood, the Slums will have no law in later chapters. The region is then perfect for a crime spree.

- Remember, no witnesses equals no crime!

- Can't be bothered to charm people who have a potential gift for you? Just kill them, and you'll get it anyway. Obviously this doesn't work for shop discounts!

- Buy a big house and decorate it with trophy mounts. Sell the house for a huge profit, then when the owners are out, pop back in and steal back "your" trophies.

- If you want multiple spouses, keep a healthy bank balance and they'll be more likely to turn a blind eye to each other.

Physical Appearance

Clothing

As in the real-world, the clothing you wear impacts the way others think about you, at least as far as a first-impression is concerned. Every piece of clothing, makeup, hairstyle, and even a tattoo brings with it certain effects that affect a Hero's appearance. Some items make you look more aggressive, others increase your perceived friendliness, and yet others might make you look more attractive or posh. Although it's possible to be unattractive and still make friends, most of the villagers in Albion will be more inclined to like you and offer you gifts if they consider you attractive—it just makes your task that much easier.

Combat Techniques

The color and quality of your clothing isn't the only thing that affects your appearance. Your use of different combat techniques also changes the way you look. Increasing the level of the Physique ability results in your Hero gaining bulk and you'll get taller by increasing the Accuracy ability. Building up your Hero's catalog of spells and increasing the respective levels in those spells forces your Hero to obtain "Will Lines". Conversely discarding levels in these spells can remove, or lessen, Will Lines on your Hero. None of these are necessarily bad traits, nor do they have a negative effect on how villagers react to the Hero, but it happens nonetheless.

A Hero's Best Friend

One of the biggest additions to *Fable II* is the fact that you now have a dog accompanying you in your travels. And what a great companion this dog is to have! Not only does the dog lend an emotional touch to the gameplay—nobody likes to hear a dog whimper or see one limp—but he also helps out considerably when searching for treasure and even jumps in to help during combat! There are also a number of quests that can only be completed with the help of your dog, thanks to his incredible ability to sniff out buried items.

Understanding the Barks

Since your trusted canine companion can't speak to you, you have to listen for the different pitch of his barks in order to understand what he's trying to tell you. Your dog makes three main types of noises and you should immediately stop and pay attention to what he's trying to tell you regardless the sound you hear. The dog's loud sharp bark means that he has found treasure and wants you to follow him. Your dog is capable of sniffing out chests, Silver Keys, and dig spots. Your dog will emit a low, scary growl when enemies are nearby; prepare for combat! Lastly, the dog limps along and whimpers when he's been hurt. He won't be able to assist you until you tend to his wounds with the Heal expression.

Dogs of War

Your dog can help you in battle by finishing off downed enemies, provided he has reached a high enough level of combat. Your dog begins life as a Level 1 fighter, but you can level him up all the way to Level 5 by finding higher level "Dogs of War" books. Many can be purchased in Bowerstone Market at the Fiction Burns shop, but others can be obtained from traveling booksellers, or by scouring the countryside for treasure and buried loot. However, all Dogs of War & Treasure Hunting books become available to buy in the shop over time.

Once you've trained your dog to a suitable combat level, put him to use by attacking enemies with Flourishes and with the Vortex spell. Both of these attacks knock enemies to the ground, thus making them vulnerable to your dog's bite! Just beware that the more you dog tries to participate in battle, the more he's likely to get hurt. Heal him as soon as the fight is over if necessary.

Tricks and Treasure Hunting

Your dog can learn a lot more than just ankle-biting! Just as he begins life as a Level 1 combatant, he also starts out as a Level 1 treasure hunter. This means he can only sniff out dig spots that are close to the surface. There are five levels of dig spots and, not by coincidence, there are five levels of treasure hunting ability for your dog to reach. Locate the different "Treasure Hunting" books to increase your dog's ability to locate the deeper dig spots. Some of these books are buried in dig spots (in Bower Lake, no less!), but others must be purchased at the Fiction Burns shop in Bowerstone Market, or via traveling booksellers.

Treasure hunting is a plenty good reason to bring along a dog on your adventure, but we all know the real reason for having a dog is to teach him to do tricks! There are nearly a dozen various "Dog Tricks" books scattered across Albion that teach your dog different tricks. Just as in real life, the dog will only perform one of these tricks if he sees his master making a particular expression. Tricks range from chasing his tail to targeted urination and each trick is linked to at least two Hero expressions.

A big part of life in Albion revolves around your daily interactions with other villagers. Each of these people has several personality traits that make them unique (career, family status, sexual orientation, class, etc.), but their initial opinion of you is largely based on your renown, your title, and your appearance. The more famous and attractive you are, and the more impressive your title (e.g. "The Chosen One" versus "Chicken Chaser"), the more cooperative these people will be. You'll likely find that renown and popularity can increase exponentially once you get on the right side of villager opinions.

Villager Opinions

Every person in Albion has his or her own personality traits, likes and dislikes, as well as an opinions on you in three different spectrums: Hate/Love, Fear/Funny, and Ugly/Attractive. Many of these villagers have a particular threshold that when reached, will make them give you a gift or fall in love with you (desiring marriage). Whatever the facet, you need to move the needle to the right or left of the gift or heart icon, depending what side of neutral it's at. In other words, some people actually prefer fearing you or thinking you're ugly so you need to move the needle to the left of that threshold. The opposite holds true for those who want to think more positively of you.

The best way to change a villager's opinion of you is to see what their likes and dislikes are and either lead them to their favorite place, give them a gift (especially those of high value), or make expressions in front of them that they like. The Hero will learn dozens of expressions over the course of his quest and each of these can significantly raise or lower a person's opinion of you. The following table details the effects these expressions have on people.

Expressions and Effects

EXPRESSION	TYPE	RELATIVE POWER	SUCCESS	FAILURE	DOG TRICK
Blow Kiss	Flirty	3	Love	-	Wave
Come Back to my Place	Flirty	5	Love	Hate	Beg
Heroic Pose	Flirty	1	Love	Funny	Bunny Hop
Pickup Line	Flirty	1	Love	Hate	Beg
Seduce	Flirty	3	Love	Hate	Roll Over
Whistle	Flirty	2	Love	Funny	Bunny Hop
Worship	Flirty	4	Love	Funny	Roll Over
Belch	Fun	3	Funny	Hate	Hide Nose
Dance	Fun	1	Love	Hate	Bunny Hop
Fart	Fun	1	Funny	Ugly	Hide Nose
Hat, Headband, Moustache	Fun	3	Funny	-	Backflip
Laugh	Fun	4	Love	Funny	Bunny Hop
Sock Puppet	Fun	5	Funny	Scary	Chase Tail
Victory Arm Pump	Fun	2	Love	Hate	Chase Tail
Beg	Rude	3	Hate	-	Beg
Chicken	Rude	1	Hate	Funny	Play Dead
Kiss my Ass	Rude	5	Hate	Funny	Targeted Urination
Middle Finger	Rude	4	Hate	Funny	Targeted Urination
Play Dead	Rude	3	Hate	-	Play Dead
Point & Laugh	Rude	1	Hate	Funny	Targeted Urination
Vulgar Thrust	Rude	2	Hate	Funny	Chase Tail
Bloodlust Roar	Scary	1	Fear	Funny	Growl
Extort	Scary	5	Fear	-	Growl
Feign Attack	Scary	4	Fear	-	Growl
Growl	Scary	2	Fear	Funny	Growl
Scary Laugh	Scary	4	Fear	Funny	Growl
Slap	Scary	1	Fear	-	Growl
Threaten	Scary	3	Fear	-	Growl
Apologize	Social	2	Love	-	Roll Over
Dismiss	Social	-	-	-	Wave
Follow	Social	-	-	-	Wave
Gift	Social	-	Love	Hate	Wave
Lute	Social	-	Love	Hate	Bunny Hop
Thumbs Down	Social	-	Hate	-	Wave
Thumbs Up	Social	1	Love	-	Wave
Trophy	Social	1-5	Renown	-	Backflip

Criminal Intent

Naturally, there are going to be times when you need to or just simply *want to* break the law. There are a host of crimes you can commit in Albion, but you have to be prepared to face the consequences, and the resulting drop in favorability with the villagers, if you commit them. Most criminal activity is met with someone calling for the city guards. They will arrive on the scene and immediately attempt to arrest you. This is when you have to make a choice: pay a fine (ranging from 10 to 500 gold per crime), do community service (clear enemies from an area), or resist arrest. Choosing to resist arrest makes you the target of every city guard in the region and you'll have to either put up a fight and make your potential punishment that much worse, or run and hide in a different region.

DEVELOPER TIPS

The following tips come from the developers at Lionhead Studios and Microsoft Game Studios.

- ⊛ Increase your attractiveness as early as you can, that way you are more likely to get given gifts from adoring fans. Sleep in the gypsy caravan at the start of Early Adulthood for the attractiveness boost.

- ⊛ Getting married is a great way to get a healthy dowry and bonus renown.

- ⊛ The Lute expression is incredibly powerful when it comes to making people love you.

- ⊛ Always make sure that you are targeting the correct person when you're about to give a gift, especially in a crowd. It can be tricky to pick the right person in a crowded situation so be careful.

- ⊛ Upping rent lowers your purity and lowers the opinion your tenants have of you. Offset this by lowering the prices in a shop you own as this affects everyone in the village, not just your moaning tenants.

- ⊛ Building up fines can result in a big, bulk payment. Technically, the actual fee due at the time of arrest can be limitless.

⊙ Sex, Love, and Child-Rearing

As time goes by it's all but certain that you will eventually want to marry and, perhaps, have children. Players wishing to live a chaste life, or one defined by prolonged loneliness, are certainly able to do it, but as your renown grows, so does the number of people declaring their love for you. Although it can be a bit more difficult to find someone to fall in love with you early in the game, when you're a bit of a nobody, it's much easier after returning from the Crucible, especially if you're attractive.

Depending on the villager's opinion of you, getting married may only take handing him/her a ring and then setting up one of your properties as a "Marital Home". On the other hand, if the target of your affection isn't already in love with you, you will need to convince them to love you. Your first step in doing so is to study their personality traits, likes and dislikes, and make sure your gender is aligned with their same sexual orientation. Then take them on the perfect date. Use the Follow expression to bring them to their favorite location, give them their favorite gift (or any nice gift for that matter) and make them laugh or do something they like. Once the red heart appears above their head, signaling they love you, all you need to do is give them a ring. Any ring will do with paupers, but you better splurge for a nicer ring if you're about to propose to someone from the middle or upper classes.

There are several benefits of having a spouse, but they do come with a price. For starters, getting married gains you a sizable renown increase and also provides a boost to your morality and purity. There's also the added benefit of receiving periodic gifts from your spouse. On the other hand, you have to give your spouse an allowance (use the real estate sign on the house) and you also need to maintain a happy household, else they'll leave and take your renown bonus with them! Nobody likes to be left alone for too long, so be sure to visit them every now and then and always bring a gift and do a little dance. As in life, a marriage with laughter is a happy one.

There's a Demon Door in Oakfield that's particularly interested in seeing a proposal… (Turn to page 154 for a full explanation.)

When it comes to having sex with your spouse, all you need to do is have them follow you to the bedroom, give him/her the Come Back to My Place expression and approach the bed and press the A Button. Choose to have protected sex for a purity bonus or have unprotected sex if you want to risk having a child. Note that there is no pregnancy period—the baby will be born within moments. Having children is a fun way to increase the size of your family, but it becomes even more important that you provide a sizable allowance, visit frequently, and always bring a gift for your child!

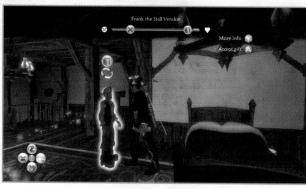

Of course, you don't necessarily need to have a family if all you're after is a little sexual release. There are plenty of prostitutes in the seedier sections of Albion and any one of them will be more than willing to satisfy your urges in exchange for a small fee. Just make sure to use a condom, else you might get a disease. And speaking of condoms, using a condom gives you enough of a purity bonus that it can exceed the corruption points earned for hiring a prostitute! Talk about a win-win situation!

TRAVEL AND TREASURE

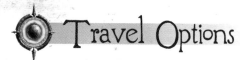

Travel Options

None of the areas in Albion are necessarily adjacent to one another—you cannot physically walk from one town or region to another. Instead, as you leave an area the clock is automatically advanced a set number of hours dependent on the distance you need to travel. Some areas are only a mile or so apart, whereas others, despite "connecting" are 70 miles apart and require upwards of 15 hours of walking. Since you never actually travel the countryside between areas, it's both possible and desirable to fast-travel by selecting the area you wish to head to from the Regions list in the Logbook. Time will certainly advance based on the distance between the areas—and you may run out of time on particular jobs, sales, or quests—but this saves you from having to use regional exits and travel from area to area.

The downside to doing all of this fast-travel is that you may glance over an area and miss valuable treasure or other collectibles that you haven't yet found. We recommend using the fast travel system for quickly traveling back to areas that you've already explored thoroughly, but continue on foot to the regional exit in areas to which you're new.

It's important to note that not all travel has to be done on foot. You can travel by carriage between Bowerstone Market and Oakfield and by ship between Westcliff and Bloodstone. Both methods of travel are 5x faster than traveling by foot.

ECONOMY AND REAL ESTATE

Earning and spending money is a big part of your quest through Albion and, lucky for you, there's no shortage of ways to build your wealth, nor things to spend it on. There are dozens of merchants across the land that will gladly sell you nearly every item and weapon you can think of. A good deal of the money you gain in the game world comes from finding chests and dig spots, but you can also take a number of different jobs and assignments to earn money as well. Each of these options are discussed in full detail in the 'Pub Games, Jobs, and More' chapter later in this book. One of the best ways to earn money is by owning property and charging rent.

Property Management

Every purchasable property in Albion has a real estate sign near the door that details a number of aspects about the property. Chief among them is the Base Value of the property and the current asking price. Although the Base Value of a property cannot be altered, the price you ultimately pay is a function of how well decorated the building is, the local town's economy, and even the owner's opinion of you. Ideally, you'll want to buy in a town with a crummy economy and get the owner to like you (or fear you) so that you can get a good deal on the property.

If the property you buy is a home, you can immediately move in and set it as a marital home if you choose, or you can rent it out. If it's a business such as a merchant stall or a tavern, you do not have the option to move in, but you can adjust the prices of the goods. Lowering rent and the prices of goods is a sign of generosity and gains you purity points with every person who comes into contact with that property. In contrast, raising the rent or prices of goods increases your corruption rating. Rather than increase the rent, we suggest you improve the quality of the décor in a given house. The rent automatically increases, but you won't lose purity points since the tenants don't mind paying more money in rent if the furniture is of a higher quality.

Sales & Shortages

Pay attention to the Sales screen in the Logbook so you know when certain shops are offering discounts on products. This is a great time to stock up on items, whether you need them or not, since there may very well be a shortage in the coming season. Just as shops often provide steep discounts (sometimes up to 75%) other shops will occasionally suffer a shortage and be willing to pay far more for an item than they normally would. The wily trader can make a fortune by taking advantage of the shifts in supply and demand!

DEVELOPER TIPS

The following tips come from the developers at Lionhead Studios and Microsoft Game Studios.

- Spending too much on shopping? You'll find that shopkeepers respond both to flirtation and intimidation. To get the best possible discount, use a bit of both.

- Still find your favorite shop's prices too high? Buy the shop outright, you'll get an excellent deal on its wares as its owner.

- Use carriages and ships to travel to sales that would run out if you had walked.

- Committing crimes lowers a town's economy; this is a great way to lower house prices before you buy.

- To raise the price of any property you have in the region, raise the town's economy. You can do this by buying and selling items and by doing jobs.

- Shops respond to the region's economy. Raise it to improve their selection of items.

- Invest any spare money in housing before going adventuring. You will then have a steady income while you quest. If you also set the rent low you can get a stream of purity, helping to keep yourself looking good!

- The stalls in Bowerstone Market are a great way to start a property empire as they are cheap, already populated, and enable you to have a discount on their various goods.

- When buying a house, make sure you take everything from all the cupboards before you rent it out. Also sleep in the bed first if it offers a bonus.

Health & Scarring

The red meter in the upper left-hand corner represents your Health. The game is not over when this meter is emptied. Instead, the Hero knocks back the enemies around him and gets back to his feet. The only drawback to this is that you can't collect the Experience Orbs that were nearby and that the Hero gains a few scars. Having Resurrection Phials in your possession at the time of being knocked down eliminates these nasty drawbacks and instantly revives your Hero.

Although the penalty for being knocked down is rather minimal, you should avoid running out of health so as to keep the battles moving along and to prevent any experience loss. Shops, chests, and dig spots contain numerous potions and food items that will replenish your health when consumed. You can also regain lost health by taking a nap.

Earning and Spending Experience

As you travel through the world of Albion, you can expect to encounter hundreds of blood-thirsty monsters and money-grubbing bandits who want nothing more than to see you dead. Yes, combat plays a rather large role in *Fable II* and to that extent it also plays a significant role in helping you get stronger and earn experience.

Your Hero has three primary options in combat: melee weaponry, ranged weaponry, and Will. These three attack options are not mutually exclusive; you can use them in quick succession and even together to perform powerful combination attacks. However, they do yield separate color-coded Experience Orbs. All attacks generate green, general purpose Experience Orbs, when the enemy dies, but the more you attack with melee weapons the more blue Experience Orbs you'll gain. The same holds true for ranged weapons and Will, but for yellow and red Experience Orbs, respectively. Each of these different types of Experience Orbs is used to purchase new and ever more powerful abilities. These abilities are broken into three classes: Strength (blue), Skill (yellow), and Will (red).

DEVELOPER TIPS

The following tips come from the developers at Lionhead Studios and Microsoft Game Studios.

- Cast Raise Dead to keep enemies off your back while you dispatch them with ranged combat, you'll find aimed shots will pass straight through your undead allies.

- Kill enemies as swiftly and in as few hits as possible to maximize bonus experience.

- To really pump a foe full of damage, cast Time Control, Flourish them and pop them in the air, then fill them full of lead before they hit the deck.

- Use the Zoom ability with ranged combat. Target the reticule on an enemy and hold, hold, hold for maximum damage!

- Rolling is a great compliment to shooting, as you'll complete any reload you've started mid-roll.

- Use Sub-Targeting for different effects: To neutralize an enemy shoot the weapon out of their hand. To slow them down, aim for the groin. To do max damage, aim for the head!

Strength

The three Strength Ability categories are Brutal Styles, Physique, and Toughness. It's important to upgrade your Hero's Toughness and Physique right away so that you can last longer in melee battles while you get a feel for the combat system and moving around during battles. Next up, focus on saving up your Strength Experience for Blocking and Flourishes. Chain Attacks will ultimately prove useful, but not before an additional one or two upgrades to Physique and Toughness.

BRUTAL STYLES

STYLE COSTS			
Style Costs	Flourishes	Chain Attacks	Counters
300	3000	18,000	72,000

Brutal Style 1: Blocking

Hold the X Button to block all incoming strikes, from any direction. You'll take a step back, but you'll be safe.

Brutal Style 2: Flourishes

Hold the X Button to charge up for a Flourish. When you feel a rumble, release the X Button to deliver a blow powerful enough to smash through an enemy's block, or send unblocking enemies flying through the air! This will knock them to the ground, where your dog will be able to attack them. Be warned: if you're attacked while charging for a Flourish, you'll automatically block, and then have to start charging again.

Brutal Style 3: Chain Attacks

By timing your strikes perfectly, you can chain strikes together, speeding them up and increasing their damage. Watch for the subtle clues that let you know the exact time window in which to press the X Button. In addition, while reloading ranged weapons, if you tap the Y Button at the moment you hear the reloading sound, you'll reload instantly.

Brutal Style 4: Counters

Just as an enemy is about to strike you, tap the X Button while pointing the Left Thumbstick in his direction to Counter his move. He'll be spun around and left dazed for a finishing move!

PHYSIQUE

Increases the damage you inflict with melee weapons.

PHYSIQUE COSTS AND DAMAGE INCREASES		
Level	Cost	Damage Multiplier
1	600	1.25
2	6000	1.50
3	36,000	1.90
4	144,000	2.30
5	432,000	3.00

TOUGHNESS

Increases the length of your health meter.

TOUGHNESS COSTS AND HEALTH METER INCREASES		
Level	Cost	Life
1	450	+100
2	4500	+200
3	27,000	+100
4	108,000	+100
5	324,000	+100

Skill

The three classifications of Skill Categories are Dexterous Styles, Accuracy, and Speed. Although Accuracy and Speed are indeed important, you should focus on learning all of the Dexterous Styles as quickly as possible. The Aimed Ranged Attack skill will allow you to begin targeting the 50 Gargoyles scattered throughout Albion and the ability to Zoom and Sub-Target the heads of distant enemies is extremely useful. Mix in the occasional Speed or Accuracy upgrade if you have a lot of general experience, but don't upgrade them fully before learning Sub-Targeting.

DEXTEROUS STYLES

STYLE COSTS			
Roll	Aimed Ranged Attack	Zoom	Sub-Targeting
300	3000	18,000	72,000

Dexterous Style 1: Roll

While facing an opponent with your weapon unsheathed, tap the A Button to roll in any direction. You won't take any damage while rolling, so use it to stay alive in tough spots!

Dexterous Style 2: Aimed Range Attack

Hold the Y Button to enter Aim mode, which allows you to manually aim using the Left Thumbstick. Once your reticule is close to an enemy, it will stick to them for easier targeting. Flick the Left Thumbstick while you're locked onto an enemy to instantly switch to other nearby enemies.

Dexterous Style 3: Zoom

Holding the Y Button longer while aiming will zoom you closer to a locked enemy. The more you zoom, the more powerful your shot will be.

Dexterous Style 4: Sub-Targeting

While holding the Y Button to aim, hold the Left Trigger to bring up the Sub-Targeting cursor. You can use this to choose which part of the enemy's body to aim at. Use the Left Thumbstick to switch between body parts. Experiment with different enemies to see what you can hit!

ACCURACY

Better accuracy will allow you to increase the damage you do with all guns and crossbows.

ACCURACY COSTS AND DAMAGE INCREASES

Level	Cost	Damage Multiplier
1	600	1.25
2	6000	1.50
3	36,000	1.90
4	144,000	2.30
5	432,000	3.00

SPEED

Increases the speed of all your strikes, and how quickly you reload your ranged weapons.

SPEED COSTS AND HEALTH METER INCREASES

Level	Cost	Speed Multiplier
1	450	1.10
2	4500	1.15
3	27,000	1.20
4	108,000	1.25
5	324,000	1.30

Will

There are eight different types of spells that you can use your Will Experience to purchase and each spell has five different levels. Each of these spells can be used effectively in combat (provided the enemy isn't resistant to them), but there are three that stand out from the crowd. By focusing your early upgrades on Inferno or Shock, Time Control, and Raise Dead you can effectively make your way through most every situation. Then, once you've gotten more comfortable with the battle system and are ready to experiment with other techniques, consider adding Force Push and Vortex. Blades and Chaos certainly have their place as well, but there are few enemies that Inferno or Shock can't handle, especially if used in conjunction with ranged weaponry.

FORCE PUSH

A solid wall of energy will push back all enemies around you, giving you more room to maneuver. You can also target single enemies.

SPELL COSTS

Level 1	Level 2	Level 3	Level 4	Level 5
300	1800	10,800	43,200	129,600

TARGETED & SURROUND STATS

Level	Targeted Damage	Targeted Collision Damage	Surround Damage	Surround Collision Damage
1	12	18	8	12
2	75	45	50	30
3	450	90	300	60
4	900	180	600	120
5	1800	360	1200	240

VORTEX

Summon mighty elemental forces to create powerful whirlwinds that sweep your enemies up and send them flying. Target individuals for massive damage, or use an area affect to affect more enemies for less damage.

SPELL COSTS

Level 1	Level 2	Level 3	Level 4	Level 5
400	2400	14,400	57,600	172,800

TARGETED & SURROUND STATS

Level	Targeted Duration	Targeted Damage	Max Targets	Surround Duration	Surround Damage	Max Targets
1	2.0 seconds	15	1	1.0 seconds	10	2
2	3.0 seconds	270	1	2.0 seconds	180	2
3	4.0 seconds	540	1	3.0 seconds	360	3
4	5.0 seconds	1080	1	4.0 seconds	720	4
5	6.0 seconds	2160	1	5.0 seconds	1440	5

INFERNO

Send forth a ball of trailing flames at an enemy, or scorch all those around you by summoning a ring of fire.

SPELL COSTS

Level 1	Level 2	Level 3	Level 4	Level 5
350	2100	12,600	50,400	151,200

TARGETED & SURROUND STATS

Level	Targeted Damage	Surround Damage
1	20	13
2	120	80
3	480	320
4	1440	960
5	2880	1920

SHOCK

Damage your enemies with a blast of electric energy. Shock also stuns the unfortunate recipients. One of the most powerful crowd control abilities, a surround Shock leaves enemies spasming and unable to attack, setting them up perfectly for finishing moves.

SPELL COSTS

Level 1	Level 2	Level 3	Level 4	Level 5
450	2700	16,200	64,800	194,400

TARGETED & SURROUND STATS

Level	Targeted Damage	Targeted Duration	Surround Damage	Surround Duration	Max Targets
1	25	1.0 seconds	17	1.0 seconds	3
2	450	1.5 seconds	300	1.5 seconds	4
3	900	2.0 seconds	600	2.0 seconds	5
4	1800	3.0 seconds	1200	3.0 seconds	6
5	3600	4.0 seconds	2400	4.0 seconds	8

BLADES

Summon mystical blades to fly at your enemies.

SPELL COSTS

Level 1	Level 2	Level 3	Level 4	Level 5
450	2700	16,200	64,800	194,400

TARGETED & SURROUND STATS

Level	Targeted Blades	Total Damage	Surround Blades	Damage per Blade
1	3	30	3	10
2	4	180	4	45
3	5	720	5	144
4	6	2160	6	360
5	8	4320	8	540

RAISE DEAD

Summon the spectral shadows of fallen creatures to fight by your side.

Flourish Invulnerability

SPELL COSTS

Level 1	Level 2	Level 3	Level 4	Level 5
500	3000	18,000	72,000	216,000

TARGETED & SURROUND STATS

Level	Targeted Shadows Summoned	Targeted Duration	Surround Shadows Summoned	Surround Duration
1	2	8	2	8
2	3	12	3	12
3	4	18	4	18
4	4	25	4	25
5	5	35	5	35

TIME CONTROL

Slow down time to gain an advantage over your sluggish enemies. You can also target a single enemy using the Left Thumbstick to rush towards him for a surprise attack.

SPELL COSTS

Level 1	Level 2	Level 3	Level 4	Level 5
600	3600	21,600	86,400	259,200

TARGETED & SURROUND STATS

Level	Targeted Distance	Damage Multiplier	Damage Duration	Target Stun Duration	Surround Duration
1	10.0 meters	1.20	2.0 seconds	0.0 seconds	4.0 seconds
2	10.0 meters	1.25	4.0 seconds	1.0 seconds	6.0 seconds
3	10.0 meters	1.30	6.0 seconds	2.0 seconds	9.0 seconds
4	10.0 meters	1.40	8.0 seconds	4.0 seconds	12.0 seconds
5	10.0 meters	1.50	10.0 seconds	6.0 seconds	15.0 seconds

CHAOS

Summon a Mask of Madness to scramble the minds of your enemies and you never know what might happen. Maybe they'll attack their friends, or maybe they'll scrub the floor to get those stains out. Cast your spell wide to catch more enemies in your web, or target a single one for a much longer effect.

SPELL COSTS

Level 1	Level 2	Level 3	Level 4	Level 5
600	3600	21,600	86,400	259,200

TARGETED & SURROUND STATS

Level	Targeted Duration	Surround Duration
1	5.0 seconds	3.0 seconds
2	10.0 seconds	6.0 seconds
3	15.0 seconds	9.0 seconds
4	20.0 seconds	12.0 seconds
5	25.0 seconds	15.0 seconds

CO-OP

DEVELOPER TIPS

The following tips come from the developers at Lionhead Studios and Microsoft Game Studios.

- The quality of your Henchman's weapons depends on how experienced you are as a Hero. If you've been playing Co-Op for a while, you may want to have the Henchman go to the Configuration screen, and re-enter the game, to see if his weapons have been upgraded.

- If the Henchman isn't using a save game, his abilities will be a copy of the Hero's abilities. Having the Henchman leave the game and re-enter it will refresh him with all of the Hero's current abilities.

- Since the Henchman and the Hero can have completely separate ability sets, it's a good idea to focus on taking complementary abilities.

- Casting Vortex and Inferno at the same time with your Henchman can create a veritable *firestorm* of destruction.

- If you play as a Henchman while signed into a Profile, you may use the existing Hero on your profile as a basis for the Henchman. This means that you will have all of the abilities that your Hero has. If you really want to blow someone away, try playing the early parts of the game with a fully developed Henchman!

Childhood

Our story begins in Old Town, a small forgotten neighborhood in the bustling city of Bowerstone. Two children - orphaned and homeless - stare through the falling snow at the warm glow of a distant castle. The elder child, Rose, feels enormous pressure as she searches for a way to secure shelter and food as winter marches in. You are Sparrow, her younger sibling. Sparrow isn't your real name, of course, it's just a title she's given you. You'll come to possess a number of titles over the years, but Sparrow isn't a bad way to be known, especially for a little kid like yourself.

BOWERSTONE OLD TOWN

Childhood

Winter is here, and life on the streets of Bowerstone Old Town is tough. You and your sister Rose are just doing your best to survive.

Follow Rose through Bowerstone Old Town to the crowd gathered around Mystical Murgo's caravan. He has a Music Box for sale that he says is capable of granting a single wish to whoever owns it. Rose doesn't believe in magic, but a mysterious woman named Theresa challenges her beliefs on the matter and convinces Rose to take a chance.

Snooping Around

Rose has no choice but to leave her diary out in the open in the shack you and she share. Head in the opposite direction of the glowing trail to locate it. Stealing other people's personal belongings will typically net you Corruption points—and will usually require a bit more stealth—but Rose's Diary can be swiped without penalty. It's always a good idea to venture off away from the glowing trail to see what you might find. Those who follow the glowing trail without deviation will get to their target much sooner, but they'll also be far less prepared for the trials that follow.

The Chicken Kicker — 5 Points

 Kick a chicken a good distance, or see one getting kicked.

Approach any of the chickens you see running around and give one a good hard kick with the A Button. Kick it good and far—at least 10 yards—to unlock this Achievement. It might take a few kicks to get one to travel the necessary distance, so keep on trying. And don't worry about earning any corruption points, as everyone knows kicking chickens is just good old-fashioned fun!

Go with Rose to seek out work and earn the five gold pieces necessary to buy the Music Box. There are plenty of people in the area who need a favor done for them. You and Rose need only convince them to reward your efforts accordingly. Complete the quests described here to earn the five gold pieces, then return to Murgo and purchase the music box.

Albion's Most Wanted

Derek: Earn a gold coin by finding the arrest warrants for Albion's most ruthless criminals.

 Good: Collect the five arrest warrants and give them to Derek.

Evil: Sell the five arrest warrants to Arfur.

Reward	Renown	Good	Evil	Purity	Corruption
1 Gold Coin	-	5	-5	-	-

The guard's five arrest warrants blew off down the alley near the photographer. Complete *Barnum's Image Capturing Device*, then head down the alley where the crowd was lined up. This alley leads to the arrest warrants.

SAVE THE DOG

An older boy, Rex, has cornered a stray dog and is about to beat it with a wooden sword. Rose tries to interfere, but gets head-butted by Rex and knocked to the ground. Rush towards the boy and press the X Button to draw your sword. Repeatedly tap the X Button while Rex is highlighted red to strike him over and over. Hit him five times to get him to leave the dog alone.

Saving the dog from certain torture earns you Good +4. This is an unavoidable act of kindness that you must endure, regardless of how evil you ultimately want to be.

Continue down the hill from the dog to find the **Warrant for Arson**. Locate the **Warrant for Sneakiness** near the steaming grate by the stairs straight ahead. Continue past the warehouse towards the stacked crates to find the **Warrant for Burglary** on the ground to the right of the couple arguing (Pete and Betty) over the bottle of booze. The **Warrant for Guntoting** is obtained after completing *Tramp's Treasure*. You'll find the **Warrant for Assault**, which the dog from earlier has found for you. Now that you have all five warrants, head back the way you came and give them to Derek.

EVIL ALTERNATIVE

GIVE THE WARRANTS TO ARFUR

Arfur will meet you in the alley near the photographer and offer to buy the warrants from you—he's clearly afraid of the guard getting these warrants back. There's no way a crook like Arfur should come to possess these warrants, but then again a gold coin from him is just as good as one from Derek. The choice is yours, but do know that this decision may have far-reaching implications.

Quest End

Barnum's Image Capturing Device

Barnum: *Help out Barnum by posing for a picture.*

 Good: Pose for a nice picture with a respectable expression.

Evil: Ruin Barnum's photo with a rude pose.

Reward	Renown	Good	Evil	Purity	Corruption
1 Gold Coin	-	-	-	-	-

Barnum has invented what just might be Albion's first camera and he wants you and Rose to strike a pose for him. Hop up onto the stage and strike either a respectable pose to make for a nice picture, or unleash a nasty, offensive pose to ruin his photo. Whether you succeed or fail doesn't matter, Barnum will give you a **gold coin** regardless.

CHILDHOOD INNOCENCE

Your choices at this young age don't have any immediate effect on your reputation or your standing in terms of purity and goodness, but that doesn't mean they won't come back to haunt you later. Those wanting to follow a path of righteousness would be wise to establish some good habits now. On the other hand, those who can't wait to wreak havoc on the world and be a thorn in Albion's side can begin their evil ways at this ripe young age.

ACHIEVEMENT

The Show-Off	5 Points

Impress a villager with a perfect expression, or see another Hero do so.

Head to any town, get a villager's attention, and perform an expression for them that can be extended. Hold the expression—it doesn't matter which one—until the meter turns green and release it in the sweet spot to succeed.

Quest End

The Beetle Hunt

Balthazar: *Clear Balthazar's warehouse of beetles, or smash his stock.*

Reward	Renown	Good	Evil	Purity	Corruption
1 Gold Coin	-	2	-1	-	-

The warehouse where Balthazar keeps his stock has been overrun by gigantic beetles, and he's scared to death of them. He wants you to head inside and use your popgun to shoot the beetles roaming around the upstairs. Ignore Arfur's tempting offer and head up the stairs and press the Y Button to draw your popgun. Press the Y Button as each of the beetles becomes highlighted in red. Kill all five beetles to receive your reward.

 Good: Kill the beetles on the second floor of the warehouse.

 Evil: Destroy the barrels and crates on the lower floor.

EVIL ALTERNATIVE
SMASH THE STOCK INSTEAD

Arfur says that Balthazar is late on some protection money and rather than beat him up, Arfur wants you and Rose to smash his stock. If you'd rather get paid for breaking a bunch of crates and barrels (and for ruining a man's livelihood) stay downstairs and use the sword to smash each of the items that turn red. Continue busting up the crates and barrels until the completion percentage reaches 100%. For a bit of extra fun, head upstairs and wipe out four of the five beetles. You can do this as long as you keep one beetle alive, and killing is fun, isn't it? Arfur will toss you the gold coin as promised, but Balthazar will be more than a little distraught.

Quest End

Tramp's Treasure

Pete: *Recover Pete's stolen bottle.*

Reward	Renown	Good	Evil	Purity	Corruption
1 Gold Coin	-	3	-3	-	-

EVIL ALTERNATIVE
GIVE THE BOTTLE TO PETE

Pete was the one who first offered you the gold coin for the bottle—and it was his bottle of wine, after all—so give him the bottle. Sure, he's an old man with an alcohol dependence, but that's not your problem! Besides, old men are funnier when they're drunk. Bottoms up old timer!

 Good: Retrieve the bottle of wine and give it to Betty.

 Evil: Ignore Betty's pleas and give the bottle to Pete.

The couple across the street from the warehouse is having a bit of an argument. The old man, Pete, wants you to retrieve the bottle of liquor from the thieving beggar that stole it from him. Head back down the street past the warehouse to locate Magpie's stash of stolen goods. Sneak up to him while he's sleeping and grab the bottle. Return to Pete and Betty and give the bottle to Betty to help her in her struggle to rid Pete of his alcohol addiction.

Quest End

The Love Letter

Monty: *Deliver a letter to Monty's beloved.*

 Good: Give Belinda the letter.

 Evil: Give the letter to Belinda's Mom.

Reward	Renown	Good	Evil	Purity	Corruption
1 Gold Coin	-	1	-1	-	-

Approach the man near the guard to listen to his conversation with the woman on the balcony of the house. It's a moment straight out of *Romeo and Juliet*, only the fair maiden's mother interrupts the romance and tells her to get inside and wash the floor. Monty is deeply disturbed by his beloved's mother and needs you to deliver a love letter on his behalf. He'll make sure you get your last gold coin required to buy the music box.

Walk up to the house and press the A Button to knock on the door. Belinda's mother answers the door and agrees to fetch a gold coin for the postage. Run upstairs and deliver the letter to Belinda as promised so Monty and Belinda can run away together. Your task fulfilled, Belinda pays you one gold coin.

The Love Letter
Give Belinda the letter?
Accept Ⓐ

4 of 5 gold pieces

EVIL ALTERNATIVE

GIVE THE LETTER TO BELINDA'S MOM

Rose's ploy to distract the mother actually has her looking for a gold coin. Rather than give the letter to Belinda, you can stay downstairs and hand the letter over to her mother. You'll still get the gold coin you need and you'll be able to break a couple of hearts in the process. This isn't a very nice thing to do, but it does have a rather comical outcome. Follow the mother outside as she goes looking for Monty in order to get maximum enjoyment out of this devious act.

ACHIEVEMENT

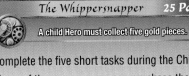
The Whippersnapper **25 Points**

A child Hero must collect five gold pieces.

Complete the five short tasks during the Childhood phase of the game so you can purchase the Music Box. Follow the glowing path through Bowerstone Old Town to each of the people in need of favors. Perform the tasks they ask to receive a gold piece from each of them.

Quest End

Childhood Continued

Thag's Cave

Use the five gold pieces you've earned to buy the **Music Box** and return to the area looking out across the city towards Castle Fairfax—it's time to see if wishes aren't just the stuff of fairy tales! Approach the crate and use the Music Box so Rose can wish for the two of you to be swept away to a life inside the castle. Follow Rose to the shack you call home. Get some sleep.

Men from the castle come during the night and wake everyone from their sleep. They've been sent by Lord Lucien to bring you and Rose to Castle Fairfax at once. Could the Music Box have worked? Could Rose's wish have finally come true? Meet with Lord Lucien to see for yourself…

Early Adulthood

Ten long years have passed since that fateful night at Castle Fairfax where you were forced to watch, helplessly, as Lord Lucien shot your sister Rose. Theresa found you in the street that night—you were badly injured, but Heroes like you don't perish easily—and took you home with her. She gave you shelter, nursed your wounds, and allowed you to live out your childhood alongside the carefree children of the gypsy camp at Bower Lake. Theresa has long said there would come a day when you would leave the safety of the camp and set out to avenge Rose's death. That day has come. Lord Lucien may have fled Castle Fairfax a decade ago, but he's still out there... Somewhere. You can feel it in your bones and in your heart you know you must kill him.

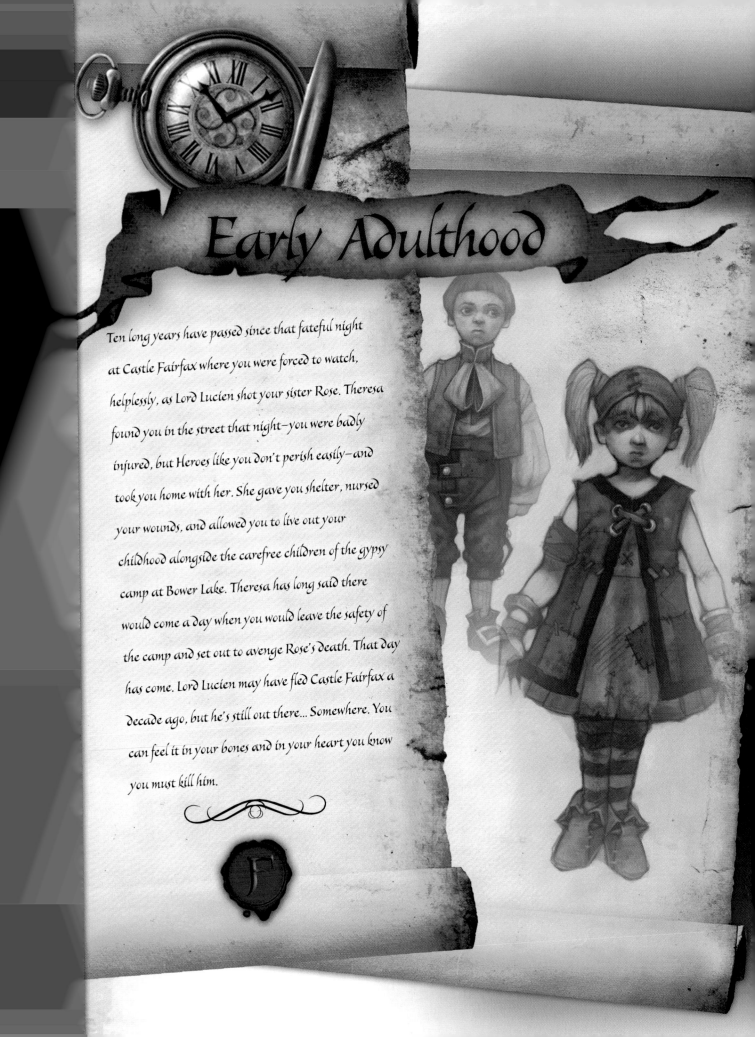

BOWER LAKE

The Birth of a Hero

Discover your destiny as you return to Albion.

Theresa joins you at the viewpoint overlooking Bower Lake and tells you it is time to leave. Run through the gypsy camp to your caravan and collect the items she's left for you in the chest. She's provided you with a **Rusty Longsword, Light Splintered Crossbow, Placebo Health Potion, Dog Elixir, Collar of Holding,** and a **Spade**. Use the Collar of Holding to name your dog—you won't be alone on this journey!

Caravan for Rent

You might not have any money just yet, but that's about to change. Approach the real estate sign on the side of your caravan and select the "Rent Out" option. It might take a few days for a tenant to move in, but you'll gain seven gold every five minutes (in real-time) once one does. Buying and renting properties is the fastest way to earn money in Albion. Best of all, you'll even earn up to a maximum of 100 rent payments while you're away from the game, although these payments accrue at a slower rate than when you are actively playing the game.

Follow the trail back through the gypsy camp to the main gate where Theresa awaits. Walk with her out onto the rope bridge to learn about the tomb on the island in Bower Lake. Theresa gives you the **Bower Lake Tomb Seal** and instructs you to swim out to the island and make your way through the cave under the tomb. This is your first step in becoming a proper Hero.

THE ALBION ATLAS

As an aspiring Hero you should now know that you are free to do what you want, when you want to do it. There is a lot to discover in this great world, and the shores of Bower Lake are a great place to start. Use the 'Albion Atlas' portion of this book as a reference and search for the many chests, dig spots, dive spots, and Silver Keys to be found here. You should always veer off the glowing trail and have a look around, especially when first entering a new area.

Consult the Bower Lake portion of the 'Albion Atlas' to learn the whereabouts of the **Rusty Flintlock Pistol**, **Rusty Cutlass,** and the first two books in the **Treasure Hunting** series. You can head to the tomb far better prepared than Theresa expected!

 ACHIEVEMENT

The Archaeologist — 5 Points

Dig up something the dog has discovered, or see another Hero do so.

Nearly every region in Albion has a number of buried items that your dog will sniff out. Follow him to these dig spots and use the Spade (press Down on the Directional Pad when the icon appears) to dig up the buried item. Note that there are five levels of dig spots and that you will need to enhance your dog's treasure hunting ability by finding the *Treasure Hunting* books in order for him to detect them all. Dogs can only sniff out dig spots that are rated equal or less than their current treasure hunting ability.

Take some time exploring the Bower Lake area to locate some of the chests and to find the books that can further improve your dog's treasure hunting ability. When you're ready to continue on, dive into the lake and swim out to the island in the center. Grab the **Silver Key** behind the tomb (you'll need these to open silver key chests), then go inside. Leap off the ledge inside the tomb to dive into the water of the Guild Cave far below.

ACHIEVEMENT

The Pooch Pamperer — 5 Points

Play fetch with your dog, or see another Hero's dog play.

Your dog should locate a dig spot on the side of the dirt path as you leave the bridge and make your way down to the lake in the very beginning of the Early Adulthood phase of the story. Don't take a detour; stick to the path. Use the Spade to dig into the ground he is pawing at to retrieve the **Rubber Ball**. Obtaining this item automatically teaches you the Fetch expression. Play fetch with the dog to unlock this Achievement and to keep your dog happy and unafraid. Just make sure not to throw the ball too softly or too hard, else he might not chase after it.

DOG TREASURE HUNTING

If you get the Treasure Hunting book by Brightwood Road prior to entering the tomb, you will find multiple dig sites inside the Guild Cave that you wouldn't normally find.

LIONHEAD STUDIOS

Sub Area

Guild Cave

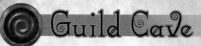

The Guild Cave is home to the Chamber of Fate, a special place in this once thriving academy. You must head to the far end of this cave to prove that you indeed possess the makings of a Hero. Keep your sword on the ready, and hack and slash your way past the swarms of giant beetles that emerge from the musty ground beneath your feet. Hold the Right Trigger to absorb the Experience Orbs the defeated enemies yield. This experience will be used later to learn abilities, once you have earned the privilege.

Giant Beetles

Giant beetles attack in swarms and do most of their damage by slamming into their prey while flying around. These dive-bombing insects move slowly and don't inflict much damage, but they can bring down an inexperienced Hero if given the opportunity. They are extremely susceptible to all manner of attacks and can be defeated with a single slash of even the weakest of swords.

Some beetles, known as facehuggers, leap and latch onto their prey's face, doing damage over time. Mash the buttons on the controller to force them off. Some giant beetles tend to hang back and attack from afar by spitting a toxic purple substance. These projectile attacks aren't terribly common and are also quite easy to avoid, especially once you have learned the Roll ability. These spitballs inflict more damage than the physical attacks so keep your eyes peeled for giant beetles lurking in the distance. Use your ranged weaponry to defeat them as soon as they're spotted.

Explore the area beyond the gate on the left-hand side to find a chest, then continue along the main path. You'll soon come to a yellow flit switch that operates another gate. Use your ranged weapon to shoot the switch to open the gate and continue on to a gate on your left leading to a chest. Grab the Rusty Mace and head back to the main path. The path winds its way to a water-filled cavern. Swim around the area and explore the lower ledges where the skeletons of earlier tomb raiders now lay, and collect their letters. Continue along the upper path to the next cavern and use your crossbow or pistol to battle past the giant beetles on the bridges to get across the area. Shoot the flit switch up ahead then strike it with the sword when it repositions itself. Shoot it a second time after that to open the gate.

The room to the left contains numerous old bookshelves (some still contain books that you can take and sell later) and a pair of chests. Crash through the barrels and crates to reach the chests located here, then continue along the main path to the Chamber of Fate. Pause and take a moment to listen to Theresa's tale about the Guild and a past Hero. Step into the light on the dais to begin the transformation into a Will-using Hero. Follow Theresa's instructions and use the experience you've gained slaughtering the hapless giant beetles to acquire your first Will ability. Hit the red flit switch with whichever spell you acquire to open the Cullis Gate and step through to return to Bower Lake.

Ability Purchases

The Hero can spend experience for abilities in any of three categories: Strength, Skill, and Will. We detail everything you'll ever need to know about experience and abilities in 'The Hero's Way' portion of this book. For the meantime, use your experience to acquire the Shock spell and any of the Strength abilities—we recommend Toughness.

BEWITCHING REWARDS

Make sure to find all three skeletons. Each contains a note and a part of a tale. Regardless of the order in which you find the skeletons, the third always provides the final note. Finding all three notes reveals a before unseen dive spot in the pool of water near the sunken columns of the wooden bridge. You'll find a **Bewitching Augment** below.

Sub-Area End

Bandits

Bandits are the lowest form of human enemy you'll encounter. These sword-wielding lowlifes prey on innocent, helpless travelers and imprison many of them as slaves. Although they travel in packs, they typically lack the tactical coordination and intelligence necessary to develop any semblance of group strategy. As a result, they often attack individually.

The Hero can make quick work of the bandits with melee, ranged, and magic attacks. Practice mixing up your attacks to generate a higher bonus and to earn a greater variety of Experience Orbs. Although you can try to draw several bandits in close to hit them with a single area-effect Shock spell, you'll find it quicker to dispatch them with targeted spells or more traditional attacks.

The Bandit

Guard: *Travel to the bandit camp and defeat the bandits terrorizing Bower Lake.*

 Good: Defeat Thag and use the key to free the slaves.

 Evil: Defeat Thag, but either give the key to the slaver or leave the area without freeing the slaves.

Reward	Renown	Good	Evil	Purity	Corruption
Thag's Head	100	30	-30	-	-

Theresa would like you to meet her in Bowerstone Market but the road leading west out of Bower Lake is currently blocked. The guards have barricaded the road leading in and out of the region on account of the bandits that have been terrorizing travelers. You must head to the bandit camp and defeat them in order to open the road so you can continue on to Bowerstone Market.

Follow the road to the bandit camp in the northwest corner of Bower Lake and approach the slave caravan in the center of the camp to lure the bandits out of hiding. Defeat the waves of attackers with a variety of attacks and ready yourself for the battle with Thag. Take a moment to drink any potions you have if necessary and back away from the house near the slaves to put some distance between yourself and Thag.

THAG
BOWER LAKE BANDIT LEADER

Weaknesses	Resistances
-	Chaos, Vortex, and Force Push

HP

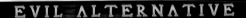

400

Thag is the leader of the bandits and, as such, is far tougher in every way. He's bigger, he's smarter, and he's way more aggressive! All your attacks can be used against him, but it's best to not let him get too close since he's pretty deadly with a sword. Stay on the run and hit him with any ranged weaponry you have as well as with a barrage of targeted magic spells. His primary attack is to move in close and strike with his sword, but he's also capable of taking a running start before attacking. Use the fact that Thag fights alone to your advantage by backpedaling away from him without worry of being surrounded.

Defeat Thag with a steady assault of ranged and magic attacks to put an end to his reign of terror. Strafe around the perimeter of the area while holding the L Trigger to maintain a target-lock on Thag. Fire away at him with your crossbow or the Rusty Flintlock Pistol. Force Push doesn't work well against Thag, but you can quickly cast Inferno or another magic spell to buy some time if he gets too close.

EXPRESSIONS LEARNED

You might be wondering what you're going to do with the **Thag's Head** trophy. Well, for starters, you can use the newly-learned Trophy expression. This allows you to show off your prize to all who will watch (doing so gains you renown, but costs you corruption). Additionally, defeating Thag also earns you the Dismiss and Follow expressions.

Go inside Thag's cabin to loot the chest near his bed. **Thag's Cage Key** unlocks the door to the slaves in the caravan outside. The slaver attacks if you free the slaves. You can kill him without repercussion and gain the 100 gold he would have given you for the key. It's a win-win situation!

The slaver bought the prisoners from Thag and feels he deserves to be able to keep them. And ownership is 90% of the law, right? You can choose to give Thag's Cage Key to the slaver (he'll give you 100 gold for it), but it will put a pretty significant dent in your morality. There is an option for those who both want the 100 gold and don't want to gain or lose any purity points. Give the slaver the key, take the gold, then kill him and take back the key. You'll need to turn the safety off your weapons to attack him, but it's a small price to pay for Evil +30.

Of course, once you have the key you can still free the slaves, thereby getting a net morality change of zero, and still make off with the 100 gold.

Quest End

The New Hero   **50 Points**

The terror of Bower Lake must be defeated.

After completing the journey through the Guild Cave in Bower Lake, Theresa summons you to meet her in Bowerstone Market. The road is barricaded on account of bandit activity; you must head to the bandit camp in Bower Lake and clean out the thugs. Defeat the low-level Bandits that attack first to lure their leader, Thag, out of his den. Defeat Thag and lay claim to this Achievement.

ACHIEVEMENT

The Hunter   **5 Points**

Kill a sweet, innocent, fluffy bunny rabbit (remember, safety's off!)

This Achievement can be obtained immediately after leaving the Gypsy Camp at the start of Adolescence. Hit the Right Bumper to bring up the Expression Wheel and turn off the safety on your weapons. Now look for a rabbit hopping around and shoot it with your crossbow or gun. It only takes one shot to kill it.

ACHIEVEMENT

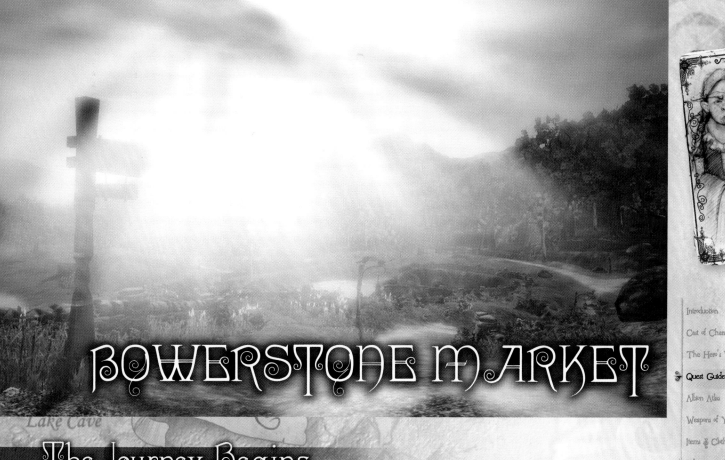

BOWERSTONE MARKET

The Journey Begins

Travel to Oakfield and talk to the abbot.

Bowerstone Market is a vibrant town filled with people of all walks of life, from the beggar on the bridge to the wealthy owners of the numerous mansions in town. Theresa has summoned you here for an important meeting, but there's no hurry to meet her. Spend some time scouring the area for treasure and getting your bearings in this rather large town. When ready, head to the clock tower in the middle of town. Theresa will use her powers to tell you she's been delayed. Spend the next five minutes working at the Blacksmith to earn some extra money, which you should use to buy upgraded weaponry from his shop. Consider purchasing the Light Yew Crossbow and Iron Longsword, both of which have a 30.0 damage rating.

A BARD'S ORATORY

You'll pick up a follower on your way into town—a bard. He'll follow you everywhere you go and sing simple rhymes about your activities and the buildings you visit. You can give him the Dismiss expression to make him stop, or you can allow him to continue to trail you. The Bard will naturally attract a crowd so put this to your advantage and show off the Thag's Head trophy for extra renown.

Return to the clock tower in the center of town once Theresa has arrived and walk with her down the alley to a secluded area overlooking the sea. Theresa informs you of Lucien's plans, the history of the Tattered Spire, and what you must now do. Your quest isn't going to be easy, but you must locate the three Heroes before Lucien does: the Pilgrim, the Mage, and the Thief. She gives you five **Fate Cards** to study and instructs you to head to Oakfield and seek out the abbot residing there.

The Journey Begins
Find the abbot in Oakfield.

The Hero of Many Names   5 Points

Change your Hero's title, or see another Hero change theirs.

All aspiring Heroes begin their life with the title of "Sparrow" and it's perfectly natural for you to eventually want a change. You can purchase new titles from the Town Crier in any town to unlock this Achievement. Note that nearly every one of these titles can be obtained for free, provided you first meet the qualifying condition.

BOWERSTONE OLD TOWN

The Journey Begins (Continued)

Head north out of Bowerstone Market to Old Town. This area looks dramatically different depending on whom you gave the arrest warrants to so many years ago. If you gave them to Derek, the guard, then you'll see Old Town as a trendy neighborhood filled with well-kept houses, manicured lawns, and a thriving retail industry. Those who gave the warrants to Arfur will not be so lucky. Under Arfur's care, the town of the Hero's childhood has plummeted into despair and dereliction. And you have only yourself to blame (or thank).

Potions Aplenty

Even if you don't have the benefit of Derek's 50% special discount, Bowerstone Old Town is still a good place to score some extra experience. Not only do many of the dig spots and chests contain potions, but you can even find an Epiphanic Blueberry Pie too! Use these items to gain a wealth of experience and use it to upgrade your Skills, particularly the Dexterous Styles. Learning the Aimed Ranged Attack ability before heading to Rookridge will make your travels much easier and allow you to begin hunting down Gargoyles.

Have a look around Old Town, load up on potions, buy some new clothes, and consider purchasing a stall or two if you can afford it. This is a great place (assuming it's not the Bowerstone Slums) to invest in a business. It also has a number of dig spots, chests, and Silver Keys to find. Additionally, if you gave the warrants to Arfur and Old Town has been turned into slums, there will be a number of Assassination jobs you could participate in. Either way, continue north out of town towards Rookridge when ready to proceed.

DEREK'S SPECIAL DISCOUNT

Those who gave the five arrest warrants to Derek will see their good deed pay off more than they could have ever hoped! As sheriff, Derek has instructed all of the merchants in Old Town to extend his special 50% discount to you. It's his way of thanking you for the being such a good kid way back when.

ROOKRIDGE

The Journey Begins (Continued)

Rookridge is a mountainous region of Albion and is home to bandits and giant beetles alike. The path is straightforward from Bowerstone Old Town, but there are treasures lying off the main road so look around.

The Road to Oakfield

> **Bandit:** *Take whatever you find from the bodies, he's not going to tell anyone.*

Reward	Renown	Good	Evil	Purity	Corruption
-	-	-	-	10	-10

Pure: Don't loot the bodies.

Corrupt: Loot the bodies.

CORRUPT ALTERNATIVE

STEAL FROM THE DEAD

Why worry about the dead? You're not going to hurt their feelings, after all! And it's not like they'll need their valuables in the afterlife. Help yourself to the treasures they were carrying. Pilfer the corpses to find the **Erudite Apple Pie**, **50 Gold**, and **Milk Chocolate**.

You'll encounter this tramp on the road leading through Rookridge. According to the tramp, the caravan and its occupants were like this when he got here. He swears he didn't have anything to do with their poor, unfortunate demise. But, in his mind, dead people don't need their jewels and money. He might be willing to steal from the dead, but that doesn't mean you have to sink to his level. Ignore your temptation to make a quick buck and keep on moving. That is, if you're feeling particularly pure.

Quest End

The sound of gunfire sounds as you get closer to the mountains. There is a row of bandits on the ledge to the east. Take cover behind the rocks and use your ranged weaponry to take them out from afar; there are too many to risk an ambush. Having the Aimed Ranged Attack ability will really come in handy here. You'll eventually come to a bandit camp in a small clearing near a Demon Door. Continue to hang back and use your ranged weaponry to clear out the foes before moving in for a closer look.

Proceed to the broken bridge and follow the bandit's advice and dive into the water below. Swim downstream to the beach on the right where you'll find a dig spot, a Gargoyle, and a distraught man named Herman. You'll need to navigate the cave on this beach in order to continue through Rookridge.

THE GARGOYLES

The first time you shoot down a Gargoyle with a ranged weapon (will need the Aimed Ranged Attack ability), you'll get a **Gargoyle Map** and The Gargoyles side-quest becomes active. This quest doesn't have any effect on your morality or purity ratings, nor your renown but it can lead to great treasure! See the 'Albion Atlas' for the Gargoyle locations in every Region and be sure to check out the map for the Gargoyle Cave, accessible via Bowerstone Market. See additional info about the Gargoyles in the 'Achievement Guide' portion of this book.

Sub Area

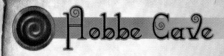

Hobbe Cave

Lead Herman into Hobbe Cave and start down the path after his missing boy. There are a number of dig spots and other treasures in this moderately large cave, so listen for your dog's bark. The path through the underground hollow is rather straightforward, with only one or two branches leading away from the main path.

Hobbe

Hobbes are small cave-dwelling creatures that rely on their fangs, claws, and maces to beat interlopers to death. Rumors say they turn small children into hobbes, but a few think they just eat them. Either way, they are certainly nothing with which to trifle. Hobbes attack with vicious aggression and typically attack in groups. They are capable fighters, known to block melee attacks with surprising skill. There are hobbes with rudimentary magic attacks as well, and others with explosive area effect attacks. As such, it is best to beat them back with ranged attacks and magic spells. Area-effect spells are particularly useful given their tendency to surround their prey. Hobbes come in multiple sizes and the larger hobbes are especially nasty. Take out the smaller hobbes first so you can concentrate on the larger ones without distraction.

Battle past the hobbes to the room with the spiraling walkway and begin the ascent. Leap from the walkway onto the ledge below to access the secret room in the corner to find an easy-to-miss chest and dig spot. Continue up the walkway and onward to the storage room where many more hobbes lie in wait. Use your Shock spell and ranged weaponry to defeat them and keep moving deeper into the cave. Herman soon finds what he thinks is his son and dies by a hobbe with his son's voice—there's nothing for you to worry about, just keep moving. Follow the path up and around the narrow rocky ledge to the exit. You'll emerge in a small structure on the other side of the broken bridge.

Have a Nice Fall!

You can make quick work of the hobbes on the rocky spiraling ledge near the cave exit by knocking them off into the abyss. The best way to do this is with the Force Push ability, but standard magic and melee attacks can do the trick too. Soften them up with a magic blast to get them off balance, then strike with a Flourish attack to send them flying! Not only will you still be able to collect the Experience Orbs, you'll also get a nice XP bonus!

Sub-Area End

You will emerge from Hobbe Cave in a stable next to an abandoned coach house. Slay the nearby bandits that taunted you from across the bridge earlier and continue the trek up the path towards Oakfield.

OAKFIELD

The Ritual

Escort Hannah, the abbot's daughter, to the Wellspring of Light.

THE FATE OF OAKFIELD IN YOUR HANDS

Have a good look around Oakfield upon arriving here and think about how you would like it to look in the future. You'll have the opportunity to choose sides in a war between the Temple of Shadows and the Temple of Light—as with Bowerstone Old Town, the choice you make will have far-reaching implications!

You'll be in and around this town for a while, so consider earning some money as a woodcutter and buying a house or a stall or two. The paths are a bit tricky to negotiate at first, so don't be surprised if you get twisted around. The path to the Temple of Light, where the abbot is located, requires you to cross the river, then double-back to the southeast to follow a faint forest trail into the hills. You must approach the Temple of Light from the east, above the large ponds near the waterfall.

The Temple of Light is home to a devoutly pacifist order of monks placed in charge of an incredibly special celebration involving a golden acorn. Tradition states that two monks must go into the Wellspring Cave together to fetch the sacred water the sapling will need to grow, but the abbot at the temple wants to ignore the tradition and, instead, send a skilled combatant to protect his daughter as she fetches the water. After all, it doesn't matter how many monks you send into the cave if they refuse to defend themselves.

The abbot appreciates your willingness to help escort his daughter through the cave, but this is too much responsibility for an unfamiliar nobody like yourself! You have to gain an additional 400 renown by completing other quests before he'll entrust his only daughter to your protection.

The Sculptor

Sculptor: Model for the sculptor?

Reward	Renown	Good	Evil	Purity	Corruption
-	100+	-	-	-	-10

 Pure: N/A

 Corrupt: Pay to have additional statues of yourself made.

Follow the trail along the north bank of the river to the sculptor's residence. She's hacking away at a giant stone block in the barn and needs a model who can hold a pose long enough for her to make a statue. Hop onto the modeling platform and hold any extended expression you like until she gives you permission to release it. You'll have to hold it long after the meter's green sweet spot appears. Release the expression as the white dot approaches the green area to avoid having the statue be embarrassing.

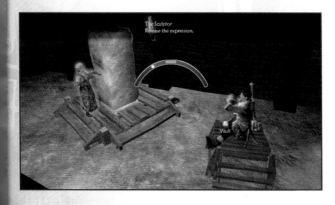

CORRUPT ALTERNATIVE

PUT YOUR EGO ON DISPLAY

Having a statue made in your likeness in Oakfield is a nice gesture, but nobody cares what these farm-town hicks think! Having statues in the city is what really matters! The sculptor will happily chisel additional statues of you to place throughout Albion, provided you first find an empty plinth (and "activate" it), then return to Oakfield and pay the sculptor a hefty sum. Having additional statues of yourself made will indeed gain you extra renown and increase your popularity in other towns, but it's also a behavior that only the most narcissistic of Heroes would indulge in.

STATUE PLINTHS

Region	Sculpting Commission
Oakfield	Free (50 Gold for repeat)
Brightwood	75 Gold
Westcliff Camp	100 Gold
Bloodstone	150 Gold
Fairfax Gardens	500 Gold

You'll gain increasing amounts of renown each time you commission a statue in a new town and successfully perform the expression. Your first statue only gains you 100 renown, but additional ones can gain you hundreds more renown, depending on your success at holding the expression.

Statue Do-Overs

Did that statue of you farting come out a little *messy*? Did you pull a muscle extending the Victory Arm Pump for too long? The sculptor will sculpt whatever pose you're in when you end the expression, but that doesn't mean you have to live with the results! Head back the next day and commission another statue to replace the one you had made.

A Bridge Too Far

Barnum: *Will you fight the bandits in Rookridge?*

Good: -

Evil: -

Reward	Renown	Good	Evil	Purity	Corruption
Dash's Goggles & Barnum's Thesaurus	250	-	-	-	-

Head to The Sandgoose pub and talk to Barnum on the second floor. It's been a long time since that winter morning when he took your photo with Rose, but he's still up to his old get-rich-quick schemes. This time, he's gone and purchased the bridge in Rookridge in hopes of making toll money. Of course, he won't be able to make any money until the bandits have been eliminated and the bridge can be repaired.

Load up on fruit and potions in Oakfield, then return to Rookridge to battle the bandits. Follow your dog up the path from the bridge to the old abandoned Rookridge Inn where they are hiding out. Rush up the stairs to the closet on the left-hand side of the landing and use it for cover. Take aim with your ranged weapons and pick off the bandits as they come down the stairs.

SNIPE DASH FROM THE INN

If you want to take a shot at Dash while he's on the bridge, try to build your Dexterous Styles up to two stars before accepting this quest. Exit the inn onto the balcony and turn to the left and target towards the bridge where Dash is standing. A few shots from here will weaken him enough to make the end of the battle easier for your Hero.

Quest End

Introduction

Cast of Characters

The Hero's Way

Quest Guide

Albion Atlas

Weapons of Yore

Items & Clothing

Pub Games, Jobs & More

Enemies of Albion

CHAPTER 1
Childhood

CHAPTER 2
Early Adulthood

CHAPTER 3
Late Adulthood

CHAPTER 4
Happily Ever After

Exit the inn on the second floor walkway and prepare to be challenged by the bandit leader, Dash. Dash fancies himself a fast runner and will

set off running farther into the mountains. Chase after him carefully as his many bandit thugs are lying in wait around every turn. Keep your health topped off and use a combination of magic and gunfire to thwart the bandits as they attack. The Force Push spell is particularly effective, given their tendency to surround the Hero at close range. Continue the chase until you come to a small clearing where Dash has been cornered atop a stone monument by the dog. Draw your ranged weapon and fire on him to complete the quest. Return to Barnum at the pub in Oakfield.

Till Death Do Us Part

Speak to the ghost of a jilted lover and become its instrument of vengeance.

👍 **Pure:** Destroy the rejection note and marry Alex.

☹ **Evil:** Give Alex the rejection note.

Reward	Renown	Good	Evil	Purity	Corruption
-	100	-	-10	10	-

Return to Rookridge and follow the path to the viewpoint where the statue is located. There is a ghost standing near the statue and he's clearly upset. He was all set to marry a woman named Alex, but she left him at the altar, so he killed himself. He has spent years trying to think of a way to exact revenge on her for breaking his heart and now he has the perfect plan. He wants you to get her to fall in love with you. Seduce her (use the Seduce expression from the book the ghost provides you) and make

her want to marry you, then when she's fallen hopelessly in love with you, give her the **Rejection Note** the ghost has written.

GENDER NEUTRAL NAMING

The ghost in this quest will always be the same sex as the Hero and the target will be of an opposite sex. The unisex name "Alex" serves the story well in this instance and the only difference between playing as a man versus as a woman is that the male version of Alex is in the pub, instead of near the bridge. Figures.

Alex is located in Bowerstone Market, near the main bridge. Head there at once and strike up a conversation with her. Instruct her to follow you to the clock

tower in the center of town to get the passion flowing (it's her favorite place), then use the Seduce expression learned from the book to really woo her. This is all it takes to get her to fall in love with you.

At this point, those wanting to do what's right should have her follow you to Oakfield where, instead of rejecting her, you can give her a ring in front of the Demon Door near the water. This will not only complete the quest, but it also provides access to the Homestead (and earns you a bunch of extra renown). Behind the Demon Door in Oakfield is a small plot of land with a quaint country home, a mill, and even a few chickens! Take Alex to the house (Serenity Farm) and make it your marital home. Grab the **Hammerthyst** from the chest at the mill, then return to Rookridge to speak with the ghost.

EVIL ALTERNATIVE
BREAK HER HEART

The ghost didn't spend so many years crafting a Rejection Note just so you can swoop in and steal his former fiancé! Meet Alex in Bowerstone and guide her to the clock tower to woo her. Check her likes and dislikes and do what you can to get her to fall in love with you. Once she does, take a deep breath, look into her eyes, and give her the Rejection Note. Return to the ghost at Rookridge to let him know you've accomplished the task.

Quest End

The Temple of Shadows

Gain entry to the Temple of Shadows.

Reward	Renown	Good	Evil	Purity	Corruption
-	-	-	-25	-	-

Good: -

Evil: Eat the Crunchy Chicks.

Return to Rookridge from Oakfield and cross the lengthy stone bridge to the massive temple in the northwest corner of the region. Speak to the shadow-worshipper standing outside the gate to learn about the temple's initiation procedure. In order to get into the Temple of Shadows, you have to eat five Crunchy Chicks. He'll hand you the five baby birds and you simply have to tap left on the Directional Pad to toss them back one at a time.

3 of 5 chicks eaten

Treasure Inside!

You have to be a little immoral to get into the Temple of Shadows at this point, but you're going to have to at least gain access to this area if you're going to ever get all of the Gargoyles and Silver Keys. There are two Gargoyles and one Silver Key located behind the gate of the Temple of Shadows. You don't need to go so far as to offer up sacrifices, but you at least need to get in the door. Do-gooders should attempt the *Defender of Light* quest later.

Quest End

Sacrificing to the Shadows

Sacrifice villagers at the Temple of Shadows.

	Good: -
	Evil: Sacrifice villagers and monks to earn Loyalty Points.

Reward	Renown	Good	Evil	Purity	Corruption
-	-	-	-50	-	-30

The shadow-worshippers may be a pretty sadistic bunch of folks, but they're not averse to having a good time. That's why they leave the fate of their sacrifices up to the Wheel of Misfortune. Will it be decapitation? Will it be impalement? Only the wheel knows! Leaving the method of death up to chance isn't the only bit of fun the shadow-worshippers have; they also have a rewards plan! That's right, Shadow Loyalty Points are awarded for every sacrifice made to the Wheel of Misfortune. Bonus points are awarded for making sacrifices at night and those who sacrifice monks from the Temple of Light will earn even more! As a new member, you stand to earn a special prize if you can accumulate 2000 Shadow Loyalty Points at the Wheel of Misfortune.

Sacrificing villagers to the Wheel of Misfortune is brutally straightforward. All you need to do is convince villagers to follow you, then travel (either by foot or by using fast travel) to the Temple of Shadows. Lead the villagers to the circular area on the floor in front of the Wheel of Misfortune, then pull the lever on the right to start the Wheel. The villagers will be instantly killed by whatever heinous method the wheel selects. You'll take serious hits to your morality and purity with every sacrifice, but it's a small price to pay for a chance to win potions and more!

Depending on how much renown you have when tackling this quest, you'll likely only be able to lead up to four followers at once. The best thing to do then is to head to the Temple of Light and convince the monks there to follow you. Gather up as many monks as you can from the Temple of Light, then head to the Temple of Shadows to sacrifice them. You shouldn't have much trouble convincing them to follow you, provided you do a lot of dancing, arm-pumping, and flirting. It will take you several trips to the Temple of Shadows to accumulate all 2000 reward points, but you can earn over 600 reward points per trip by sacrificing four monks at night.

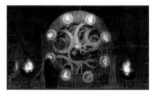

The fun doesn't end once you've earned your 2000 points! Now you can attempt to earn the legendary **Maelstrom** sword by making an amazing sacrifice during the hour between midnight and 1 AM. The best way to ensure success is to convince a villager to marry you (make sure you lead them to a marital home to make it official) and have him or her follow you to Oakfield. Once there, you may choose to add three monks from the Temple of Light to the group and kill some time with the Bard in The Sandgoose building up some extra renown while you wait for the clock to advance to morning. Fast-travel to the Temple of Shadows with your four sacrifices—yes, even your spouse—and wait in the lobby for midnight to come around. Rush down the hall to the Wheel of Misfortune and pull the lever to complete the quest.

Fast-Travel Time Manipulation

It takes 13 hours to travel from Oakfield to the Temple of Shadows, but you're going to spend some time performing the sacrifice and wooing your next batch of lambs. This makes it difficult to ensure that each of your sacrifices is performed in the dead of night. Fortunately, you can mix in some fast-travel to Bowerstone Market or Bower Lake to switch up the time of day so that your trip to Rookridge from will get you there at night. Experiment with different destinations (or by sleeping for 6 or 12 hours) to ensure you arrive at the Temple of Shadows after dusk.

Quest End

The Archaeologist

Belle: *Collect an artifact for the archaeologist?*

 Good: Locate all 13 artifacts and the entombed treasure to which they lead.

 Evil: Kill Belle.

Reward	Renown	Good	Evil	Purity	Corruption
The Archon's Dream	-	300+	-50	-50	-30

Speak to the woman near the archaeological dig site in Fairfax Gardens (proceed east out of Bowerstone Market) to learn of her quest to receive missing artifacts. There are currently just three such artifacts and you'll gain renown for each one you retrieve. Belle gives you a **Research Note** containing a clue to the whereabouts for every artifact. All you have to do is get to the right region, then follow your dog to the dig site. Use the spade to dig up the artifact and return it to Belle to receive the next Research Note.

Artifact Details

Artifact	Renown	Location
1	75	Bowerstone Old Town
2	100	Rookridge
3	125	Bowerstone Cemetery

MORE DIGGING TO BE DONE...

Belle only has three Research Notes for you at this point, but there will be many more later. Return to Belle periodically throughout your adventure to see if she has any other quests for you. There are a total of 13 artifacts to find, including the three available now. Check your Quest list periodically for updates from Belle. You can find a full listing of the artifact locations in the 'Pub Games, Jobs, and More' chapter.

EVIL ALTERNATIVE

NOBODY'S ERRAND-BOY!

Belle had you running all over Albion for years and now that you've wrestled the prized gem from the tomb beneath Fairfax Gardens, she expects you to hand it over. What for? Draw your sword, turn the safety off, and let her have it. The Archon's Dream will fetch a pretty nugget on the black market!

Quest End

Now that you have more than enough renown to impress the abbot, return to the Temple of Light atop the hill in Oakfield and speak with him. Listen to his plan as you walk along the path with the old man and agree to escort his daughter through the Wellspring Cave. Follow the trail back down the hill to the cave; you'll hear his daughter Hannah singing long before you see her.

Sub Area

Wellspring Cave

Hannah has to carry a heavy jug through Wellspring Cave and fill it at two different fountains. You're there to lead her through safely. Make your way through the spiraling entrance cave to the circular room in the center. There are three switches on the floor, each controls the gate nearest to it. Proceed through the left-hand gate first and locate the switches near the statue. Hannah holds the jug under the water fountain while you stand on the other switch to make the water flow.

Hollow Man

The hollow men of Wellspring Cave are unlike any creature the Hero has seen. They float nearby as twinkling lights, then plunge into the ground and erupt as ghastly reanimated corpses. Hollow men carry sickles, other crude melee weapons, and attack at close range. They are a slower form of enemy, but can be extremely dangerous as they tend to attack in large groups.

Hollow men are extremely susceptible to fire damage so make full use of the Inferno spell when battling them. A Level 2 Inferno cast targeted at a specific enemy will kill it on the spot. Melee and ranged weapons work as well, but neither are nearly as effective as fireball targeted at their dried up skin and loose, sagging clothes!

Lead the way through the second gate and take your place on the switch atop the platform while Hannah fills the jug from the next fountain. Hollow men appear in the room in groups of three and it's up to you to protect Hannah from them. Charge up Level 2 Inferno spells and target the hollow men one at a time with the Left Thumbstick while firing the spell to hit them directly.

Return to the central chamber and proceed through the third gate to the final fountain. A large gang of hollow men attacks on the way to the fountain. Pay close attention to the headless hollow man. He's tougher than most and will take a bit of effort to bring down. Draw them away from Hannah and allow them to surround the Hero while you charge a Level 2 Inferno spell. Cast it as an area spell to burn everyone in the vicinity. Continue to the proper location and stand on the switch so Hannah can bless the waters. This time, unfortunately, there is an interruption; Hannah must rush back to the Temple of Light at once!

Sub-Area End

The Hero of Strength

Follow Hannah back to the Temple of Light.

	Good: -
	Evil: -

Reward	Renown	Good	Evil	Purity	Corruption
Golden Oak Leaf	1000	-	-	-	-

Lord Lucien has sent one of his agents to the Temple of Light to inquire about an unusually strong woman. While this indeed takes a horrible turn of events, this tragedy has awakened Hannah's underlying rage. She renounces her father's pacifist philosophy and even her own name, adopting the more Heroic "Hammer." Behold, the Hero of Strength has been found! Meet with Theresa after the funeral to learn about your next task—tracking down the Hero of Will.

Quest End

ACHIEVEMENT

The Hero of Strength	100 Points
Complete the Hero of Strength.	

Meet with the abbot in Oakfield to learn about the escort mission he would like for you to perform. Gain the 500 Renown the abbot requires, then you must escort Hannah through the Wellspring Cave so she can collect the water she needs. Use level 2 Inferno spells to protect her from the Hollow Men that attack. Follow Hannah back to the Temple of Light when the time arises to discover the Hero of Strength.

Make donations to the Temple of Light.

	Good: Donate gold to the Temple of Light.
	Evil: -

Reward	Renown	Good	Evil	Purity	Corruption
-	-	2-75	-	2-75	-

One of the easiest ways to accumulate morality and purity is to make generous donations to the Temple of Light. As you might expect, the more you donate the more benevolent you will appear. But there is a minimum donation required to receive any gain, and also a sweet spot after which the return on your investment is lessened. In short, you want to donate 1000 Gold at a time in order to receive morality and purity increases of +25 at a time, which offers the best bang for your coin. You can gain +25 per every 1000 Gold if you make your donations separately, instead of one lump sum donation. Use this technique to gain +125 morality and purity per every 5000 gold you donate. In contrast, a single 5000 Gold donation will only net you +75 morality and purity.

Temple of Light Donations

Donation (Gold)	Morality	Purity
49 or less	0	0
50 to 249	2	2
250 to 999	10	10
1000 to 2499	25	25
2500 to 4999	50	50
5000 or more	75	75

Once you've donated a cumulative total of at least 500 gold to the Temple of Light, you'll be asked to give again as the sun reaches its zenith to earn the honorary role of being the Harvest Benefactor. Making a sizable donation of at least 10,000 Gold between 12:00 and 1:00 pm will earn you **The Rising Sun** legendary weapon. You'll be able to make subsequent donations to the Temple of Light for as long as it is in business so give often and give generously.

Quest End

The Summoners

Sam and Max: *Kill 100 hollow men in the cemetery and retrieve the Book of the Extremely Dead.*

Reward	Renown	Good	Evil	Purity	Corruption
Hollow Man Head	250	-	-	-	-

◯	Good: -
😈	Evil: -

DEVELOPMENT SECRET

If you think Sam and Max look a little bit different than everyone else, that's because they aren't from Albion. These characters are modeled after Simon and Dene Carter. Dene (with the ponytail) is the Creative Director on the game and his brother Simon is the Technical Director. Not only did Simon not know about this easter egg until he saw it during a play-test, but there was a bug early in the development process that left his character pants-less. Rumor has it that fixing that bug was assigned top priority!

Sam and Max have used the Normanomicon to accidentally summon the dead and now they need your help to undo their misdeeds. Travel to Bowerstone Cemetery and follow the glowing path to each of the five hollow men hotspots. Waves totaling 20 hollow men attack at each area. Look for the tell-tale white lights signaling their arrival and quickly rush to the center of the spawn area and begin charging an Inferno spell. Unleash a Level 2 or higher Inferno spell to make quick work of the lumbering undead. Continue blasting them with flames until the area has been cleared and you can move to the next area. Destroy all 100 hollow men and retrieve the **Normanomicon** from the crypt near the hilly path. Return it to Sam in Bowerstone Old Town.

Quest End

BRIGHTWOOD

The Hero of Will

Find the Hero of Will.

Return to Bower Lake and use the Cullis Gate atop the hill to join Theresa and Hammer at the Chamber of Fate. Theresa needs you to head to Brightwood in pursuit of Garth, the silent mage you saw in the halls of Castle Fairfax all those years ago. Lucien's men are also looking for Garth so you had better move fast!

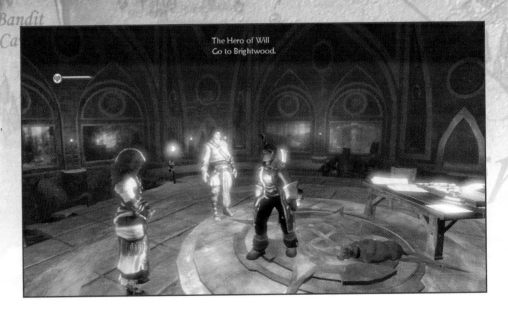

The Hero of Will
Go to Brightwood.

Brightwood is reachable via the road on the east side of Bower Lake. Proceed through this hilly region towards the stairs leading up to Brightwood Tower and watch as the Spire guards make their grand entrance, teleported into battle by the unearthly Shard.

Spire Guards

The Spire guards are an elite set of footsoldiers in Lord Lucien's army. They're also sent out to do his bidding, which explains their presence here in Brightwood. They also oversee, direct, and mistreat the slaves working in the Spire. Spire guards are capable swordsmen with a knack for defense. Equipped with a cutlasses, the Spire guards are capable of attacking with brutal efficiency.

The basic Spire guards don't have any particular weaknesses or resistances, but they are quite a bit harder to damage than other human enemies thanks to their training and thick armor. Stay on the move (perform rolls to avoid their sword slashes) and alternate between Flourishes and gunshot blasts. Use Force Push to keep them from getting too close and to buy yourself time to unleash a high-level magic spell.

Fight your way past the Spire guards with a mix of Flourish attacks and magic and venture inside the tower. There is a commotion upstairs—you're too late! A massive fire blocks your path, forcing you to stand by and watch as Lucien's fearsome-looking Commandant captures Garth. Theresa knows there was nothing you could do to prevent Garth's abduction, but she's already formulating a new plan. Return to the Chamber of Fate to meet with her.

CHOOSING SIDES IN BRIGHTWOOD

Two enormously different but related quests become active after leaving Brightwood Tower. *Cold Comfort Farmer* asks you to take sides with the farmer and avenge his wife's death. On the other hand, *Red Harvest* asks that you side with the bandits and eliminate the farmer and the farmer's guards in the region. You can only choose one of these two quests. They offer the same amount of renown for completion, so it's simply a matter of whether you want to be good or evil. Your decision here will affect the availability of subsequent quests later in the game.

Cold Comfort Farmer

Farmer Giles: *Bring Ripper to justice?*

Reward	Renown	Good	Evil	Purity	Corruption
-	750	30	-	-	-20

😀 **Good:** Return Ripper to the farmer alive.

👎 **Corrupt:** Kill Ripper.

Visit the farmer's small cabin in the woods of Brightwood to hear his sorry tale and agree to hunt Ripper down and bring him to justice. The farmer doesn't want you to kill Ripper though; he wants you to capture him alive. Follow the glowing path to Ripper's camp and prepare for battle against his many guards. Run to the far side of the camp and locate and equip the **Iron Clockwork Rifle** if you haven't already acquired a steel one. Use this to put down as many of the bandits as you can from a safe distance, then switch to a magic attack. A Level 2 or 3 Blades spell can rip the bandits to shreds!

Ripper will attack last, once all of his men have been defeated. He's a big guy, armed with a rifle and cutlass, but he's not difficult to beat into submission. Use a steady stream of Flourish attacks to get him to surrender. Choose to spare him afterwards in order to gain a +30 boost to your morality.

Quest End

Red Harvest

	Reward	Renown	Good	Evil	Purity	Corruption
Arfur: Help Ripper's bandit crew expand its operations in Brightwood.	-	750	-	-50	-	-

 Good: -

Evil: Complete the quest.

Meet with Arfur on the docks in Bowerstone Market to learn about the need to expand the burglary business in Brightwood. He'll tell you all about a business acquaintance named Ripper who needs a job done. Head to the bandit camp in Brightwood and use the Whistle expression three times to meet with Ripper. Once you do, he'll direct you to Giles' farm in Brightwood with instructions to kill Giles, take his key, and return it to Ripper.

Farmer Giles has already lost his wife to Ripper and has assembled an army of gun-toting protection near his house. Listen for the first gunshot aimed in your direction and take cover behind the tree nearest the path. Use the tree for protection while you put your rifle or crossbow to use against the dozen bodyguards. Kill every last one of them (-30 morality per kill) then finish the battle by defeating Giles when he exits the house. Use Raise Dead and melee attacks to make quick work of him and retrieve **Giles' Cellar Key**.

What you do now is up to you, but we recommend using the key to unlock the basement door. There's a portcullis that keeps half the Farm Cellar off-limits for now, but you'll find **Giles' Manuscript** in a chest near the sacks of potatoes. Go ahead and read it to see why Ripper and his crew were so intent on getting into the cellar. Speaking of Ripper, you had better turn around…

Quest End

The Bargain

Recover Lucien's diary.

Meet Theresa at the Chamber of Fate to get your next task. Theresa believes that the best way to find out what Lucien is up to is to get the diary that he left behind when he vanished that night ten years ago. Lucien's butler Jeeves is believed to have kept the diary. Head to The Cow and Corset pub in Bowerstone Market and look for him in the room upstairs. Jeeves will sell you a map to the diary's location for 1000 gold, an offer for which you have no alternative. Give Jeeves the money in exchange for the **Map to Lucien's Diary**.

Money Back Guarantee!

So long as you don't mind losing some morality points, there is a way to get your money back from Jeeves: Kill him. Make sure nobody else is around though, otherwise someone will undoubtedly call the guards on you.

Return to Bower Lake and cross the bridge over the river to the hill with the three tree stumps on it. This is where Jeeves buried the diary—and also where a forest troll now lives! Use an evasive-minded approach to defeat the forest troll while blasting it with Inferno or Blades spells to pop its weak spots. Once the forest troll has been defeated, move to the dirt patch where it stood and dig up **Lucien's Diary** and bring it to Theresa.

Forest Troll

The forest troll is unlike any creature you've seen in Albion thus far. It is a massive creature that spins in place heaving rocks and debris at its prey. It is also capable of sending a massive shockwave outward across the ground; it doesn't radiate outwards in all directions, but is a targeted attack rather than area of effect.

Getting close to the forest troll is simply out of the question. The beast is far too strong to attempt a melee attack. It's possible, but the reward doesn't justify the risk. Instead, keep on the move circling around the forest troll while watching for it to attack. Move out of the way of the attack, then stop and either shoot one of the weak spots on its body with your ranged weapon or, better yet, cast a Level 2 or higher Inferno or Blades spell. The spell ruptures the red sore-like weak spot that was targeted and inflicts heavy damage. Another option is to use Raise Dead to summon a distraction force of zombies, then move towards the forest troll and attack with a high-level area-affect spell to damage multiple weak spots at once!

Westcliff

In order to rescue Garth, you'll need to gain access to the Tattered Spire. Theresa has learned that the winners of The Crucible in Westcliff are being recruited by Lucien to be Spire guards, so this is where you must go to continue your journey. Return to Brightwood and fight your way past the bandits to the road leading to The Bandit Coast on the south end of the region. Hammer will be waiting for you. Hammer is all too anxious to let her massive hammer fly and you'll

be glad you have her by your side when you get to the bandit-ridden coast up ahead. Battle your way up the path past the numerous bands of bandits to the bridge leading to their primary camp. The two of you should have little trouble massacring the bandits with simultaneous melee attacks. And best of all, you needn't worry about having to keep her healthy!

CHECK THE TOMB!

The main path forks along the coastal cliffs. Take the left-hand path to access a tomb with an exceptionally strong **Troll Strength Potion** in it, as well as another Gargoyle.

Hammer will smash through the blockade on the far side of the bridge and a number of bandits and highwaymen immediately rush out to defend their camp. Hammer will rush in to start pummeling as many foes as she can. This gives you the opportunity to stand back and cast magic or use your ranged weapons. The battle gradually shifts to the center of their stronghold and one highwayman emerges from the shadows. Charge your magic and let them get close before unleashing it on the lot of them.

Highwayman

Highwaymen are far tougher than most everyday bandits and are equipped with both a sword and a pistol. They travel in packs and are fierce combatants. Fortunately, the Hero should have more than enough firepower to deal with them before their first encounter. Highwaymen aren't as susceptible to Force Push or Chaos spells, but a Level 3 Inferno spell will all but wipe them out; just hope Hammer gives you enough time to charge it!

Once the area has been secured, spend some time in the fort before moving on to Westcliff. There are a number of chests and dig spots here, as well as a Gargoyle to shoot. Gain a free health replenishment by napping on the bedroll in the caravan near the gate Hammer smashed, then wake up and head north through to Westcliff.

WESTCLIFF

Road to Westcliff (Continued)

Balverine

Balverines are among the most terrifying creatures in Albion. They appear as though they're half man and half wolf, but are far stronger and faster than either species alone. Balverines use their giant hands and long nails to claw and tear at their prey with rapid swipes. Balverines are not only ferociously aggressive, but they are capable of leaping high into the air (completely out of sight) and landing behind their opponent for a surprise attack.

The best way to fend off a balverine attack is with Inferno magic, their fur is awfully susceptible to singeing, but there are other ways too, of course. For starters, try using a fast melee weapon and chain attacks. The balverine will leap into the air to break your attack. Quickly roll out of the way to avoid having it land behind you. Get up and renew the chain to finish it off! A Level 1 targeted Time Control is extremely effective against balverines. If you're quick, you can cast it almost instantaneously, rush behind one during its claw-swipe attack, and you get a bonus to damage on your next hit.

The road from the Bandit Coast to Westcliff leads to a narrow path in a mountainous section of the region. Balverines attack frequently along the path so be on guard. Soften them up with a quick shot of Inferno, then unleash some chain attacks with a fast-striking melee weapon.

The duo soon comes to a woman in need of help. Her husband lies dead at her feet; she's lost her son and needs you to accompany her to the Howling Halls where he's believed to have been taken. Push on past the balverines and across the wooden bridge and through the fog-filled swamp to the entrance to Howling Halls.

Sub Area

Howling Halls

The underground temple known as Howling Halls is home to an army of balverines. You have been tricked! The lady you escorted suddenly leaps into the air (surprisingly like a balverine herself) as waves of balverines attack! Work with Hammer to fend off the initial waves of balverines. These balverines can make quick work of the non-Heroes of the world. Part of the balverines' success comes from the giant spike-laden pit in the center of the main hall. Hammer uses her massive sledge to topple the pillar in the center of the room to form a bridge over the pit. You have to protect her from your earlier charge who is now a white-furred balverine while she does. Hit the beast with an Inferno spell, then attack with a Flourish and chained attacks to keep it on the defensive. It jumps around like the others, so be ready to roll out of the way.

Cross the pit on Hammer's bridge and continue through the dilapidated room up ahead to the circular stairwell in the distance. Don't miss the Gargoyle after you cross the bridge. Climb the stairs to the second floor, grab the silver key, then exit back to Westcliff. Journey along the path to Westcliff Camp up ahead and speak to Mad-dog about entering The Crucible.

Sub-Area End

You need to enter the Crucible battle arena, fight your way through eight progressively harder rounds of combat, and come out alive to gain passage to the Tattered Spire. Head to Westcliff Camp and speak to Mad-dog to sign up.

CRUCIBLE PREPARATIONS

You'll be able to visit a merchant to replenish your stock of food and potions after the third round and again after the sixth round, but you're going to need more than that to survive this test. Visit the shops in Westcliff Camp and purchase all of the food they sell to have as many sources of health replenishment as possible. We also recommend splurging on the Master Katana. Sell any jewels or other valuables if necessary, but definitely buy yourself the best weapon you can afford before entering the Crucible. Lastly, make sure your Inferno and Blades spells are up to Level 3 or 4 and begin investing your Will experience in either the Blades or Raise Dead spells.

Don't even think about using Time Control in the Crucible if you're trying for record times. Although the timer appears to slow during the battle, the extra time incurred is spontaneously added on after the Time Control effect ends, and you realize you've saved no time at all! It actually hurts you!

The Crucible

Compete in the Crucible to earn passage to the Spire.

Reward	Renown	Good	Evil	Purity	Corruption
Crucible Trophy & 10,000 Gold	-	-	-	-	-

Good:	-
Evil:	-

The Crucible pits you against several waves of every enemy type you've encountered thus far (along with some stronger variants). Most rounds consist of three waves of enemies. Successive waves only appear once the previous wave has been completely defeated so don't waste any time! Speaking of time, each round also has a time goal; beat that time and score eight Perfect Rounds during a follow-up visit to the Crucible and win a legendary weapon (so don't sweat it if you can't do it with your current abilities)!

AUGMENT YOUR WINNINGS

Before you enter the Crucible ensure you get the maximum benefit by equipping your weapon with a gold or experience augment, or even both!

LIONHEAD STUDIOS

Your primary concern needs to be simply surviving the onslaught of enemies in each round, but there are prizes to be had for doing it quickly as well as for doing it with flair. Beating the target times earns you Perfect Rounds which can lead to a big prize in the end.

However, there are smaller gold bonuses available to those who excite the crowd, even if it means finishing in a slower time. The audience loves it when competitors use the environment to kill enemies so look for switches, traps, and pits to use against the enemies. The crowd also likes to see a competitor fight with style so mix up your attacks, use combinations that could increase the experience earned, and do whatever you can to juggle enemies or defeat numerous enemies very swiftly. Read on for tips!

Round 1

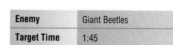

Enemy	Giant Beetles
Target Time	1:45

Giant beetles are susceptible to Inferno and the crowd loves to see whole infestations go up in flames with a single attack. Rush to the center of their spawn area and unleash a Level 3 or higher Inferno spell to wipe them out. There are three waves of giant beetles so make sure you get every last one of them. The third wave is a bit stronger and more spread out so make use of the katana's swiftness and finish them off by hand.

Round 2

Enemy	Hobbes
Target Time	1:50

The arena with the hobbes has two switches that, when stepped on, cause a number of damaging spikes to rise from the square-shaped ring of floor panels in the center. The crowd loves seeing hobbes impaled on these spikes, but the spikes don't do enough damage to the heartier hobbes to make it a very useful tactic. Instead, soften the hobbes up with your most powerful spell, then switch to melee attacks and, if possible, either the Blades or Raise Dead spell.

Round 3

Enemy	Hobbes
Target Time	2:25

This round also contains hobbes, but these hobbes are a mix of magic-users and ones with a penchant for self-destruction. The arena contains several explosive barrels that can be targeted and shot to aid in weakening the hobbes in the vicinity. Additionally, you could also use melee attacks and Force Push to knock some of the hobbes into the pit in the center of the area (this also excites the crowd). Best of all, buy yourself some time while one of the hobbes rushes

forward with a keg of dynamite about to explode. Lead this kamikaze hobbe towards the others, then cast Time Control to slow them all down. This will give you time to roll away from the blast while the rest are trapped in explosion.

Round 4

Enemy	Hollow Men
Target Time	2:30

The three waves of hollow men that attack can be laid to waste with a series of spells and attacks. First cast Chaos or Raise Dead to distract them. This is important since many of the hollow men here have rather large cleavers and axes and are capable of doing considerable damage. While they are sufficiently distracted, ready up a powerful Inferno spell to finish them off. Hollow men are vulnerable to Inferno and should fall in time.

Round 5

Enemy	Bandits
Target Time	2:10

This arena is conducive to long-range combat, so grab your best crossbow or rifle and start targeting the explosive barrels on the floor and atop the wooden bridge. Shooting these barrels won't only kill any bandits standing nearby, but will also raise the crowd's excitement. Hold your ground near the starting point and snipe from there, but watch for bandits that rush the stairs leading to your position. Quickly cast Raise Dead or Inferno to deal with them, then return your focus to the bandits in the distance. There will often be a small group on the opposite end of the arena, beyond the

bridge, that won't attack unless you come to them. If the next wave of enemies isn't introduced after you kill all the ones you can see, rush down to the floor and go after those atop the hill.

Round 6

Enemy	Highwaymen
Target Time	2:00

This is a really fun arena to play on, even though the enemies are quite vicious and incredibly well-armed. The arena has three large pits into which enemies can be knocked and it also has several explosive barrels that can be used to do the shoving. But that's not all! As highwaymen rush you, bandits attack with guns from the perimeter of the circular arena. Unbeknownst to them, there are flame-throwers mounted along the wall right behind them. All you have to do is step on the switch on the rocky bridge nearest the side you wish to set aflame and they'll instantly be set ablaze. Stand on the switch to keep the flames coming and to burn them right off the edge and into the pit!

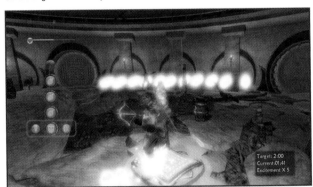

Round 7

Enemy	Balverines
Target Time	2:35

Balverines may be vicious, but they are also highly flammable! Ready a Level 4 Inferno spell and wait for the wave of hairy critters to get near. This spell will instantly eliminate the majority of balverines that attack. Finish off any stragglers with your katana, then ready another Inferno spell and wait for the next wave. Repeat this foolproof plan of attack until the round is cleared and you can collect your prize.

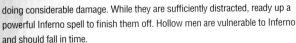

Round 8

Enemy	Rock Troll
Target Time	1:50

The final round of the Crucible pits you in a one-on-giant battle against a rock troll. The rock troll is similar to the forest troll you fought at Bower Lake, only it's a bit tougher, has more weak spots to hit, and throws larger rocks! Other than that, it's almost identical. This is a great battle to use Blades if you have it; it automatically targets the rock troll's weak spots while you use your ranged weapon and take out a few more. Use the large rocks in the arena for cover from the rock troll's projectile attacks, then hop out from hiding and hit him with another Blades attack. The only way to damage the troll is by attacking its weak spots; remember the ones on its back—they can be hard to hit. Just be quick about it since the rock troll will summon hobbes into the arena.

Excitement X 2
Target: 1:50
Current:01:14

Quest End

ALL CHEER FOR LIONHEART!

Success in the Crucible doesn't just bring fame, fortune, and a one-way trip on a slave ship, but it also brings the right to be called Lionheart! Head to any Town Crier to acquire this new title for free.

Now that you've impressed Mad-dog and the others and have won a spot on the next ship bound for the Tattered Spire, it's time you complete the rounds and tidy up any unfinished business. You'll be back—eventually—but it might be a while. Make the rounds and finish any incomplete quests you were working on before heading to the beach in Westcliff to join the ship.

Westcliff Development

Barnum is looking for a business partner to invest 5000 gold in his new scheme and, as usual, has a harebrained plan to get rich.

| | | Good: - |
| | | Evil: - |

Reward	Renown	Good	Evil	Purity	Corruption
-	1500	-	-	-	-

Barnum is standing atop the hill near the pub and believes he's come up with just the right idea to get rich. He wants to turn Westcliff Camp into a theme park destination! All he needs to get started on this grand idea is a small investment from you. Be sure to invest in Barnum's plan before leaving Westcliff for good, else you might miss a golden opportunity to score a lot of renown! Barnum will send for you when his plan comes to fruition.

Quest End

Westcliff Shooting Range

The finest shooters in Albion test their skill at Westcliff range. Can you win the top prize?

| | | Good: - |
| | | Evil: - |

Reward	Renown	Good	Evil	Purity	Corruption
-	-	-	-	-	-

The Westcliff Shooting Range is at the end of the path in Westcliff Camp. This mini-game of sorts provides an idyllic backdrop for unloading all of your frustrations on cardboard cutouts of bandits and civilians. With this being a town run by bandits, you can rest assured that you'll be targeting the citizen images.

The shooting range competition consists of three rounds. The first round is near the cabin on the left. The second is on the bridge straight ahead. The third is near the stockade on the right. Each round lasts a minute and you have to score as many points as you can to earn points (you must also score at least 15 points in each round to move on to the next round). You earn 3 points per headshot, 1 point per body shot, and you lose points for hitting a bandit. There are four civilian target styles:

- Man in vest
- Old Lady
- Woman in Dress
- Merchant in Blue

Avoid shooting the skeleton bandits.

There is no denying that the shooting range is plenty difficult. Don't make it harder for yourself by using a weapon that is slow to reload or that has a slow firing rate. You should also upgrade your Speed ability to Level 3 or higher if trying to get one of the best prizes. Other than those tips, all we can tell you is to practice.

Shooting Range Prize Chart

Place	Points Required	Prize
1	175 points	Red Dragon Pistol
2	150 points	Hero Doll
3	125 points	Cure-All Health Potion
4	95 points	Table Wine
5	65 points	Worn Double Bed
6	45 points	Dog Treat

Introduction
Cast of Characters
The Hero's Way
➤ Quest Guide
Albion Atlas
Weapons of Yore
Items & Clothing
Pub Games, Jobs & More
Enemies of Albion

Head Shots

You should always aim for the head of the civilian cutouts during the first two rounds, but the targets tend to drop a lot faster in the third round so you may not have enough time to line up the perfect shot. If you can get the headshot in the third round then take it, but if you're having trouble lining your shots up in time just go for the chest wound instead. It's better to get numerous 1-point shots off than risk not getting any points while trying to earn 3.

Quest End

Defender of the Light

Monk: *Defend the Wellspring Cave from the Temple of Shadows?*

 Pure: Save the Temple from the attack.

👎 **Corrupt:** -

Reward	Renown	Good	Evil	Purity	Corruption
Temple of Light Seal	750	-	-	20	-

Return to the Temple of Light in Oakfield and speak to the monks about the attack taking place in Wellspring Cave. They need you to head there at once and clear out the Shadow Worshippers before they taint the springs and ruin the Golden Oak's water supply. Follow the glowing path back to the Wellspring Cave entrance and go to the first fountain room at once.

The Shadow Worshippers consist of a gang of bodyguards sent to protect an evil monk working to cast a spell on the fountain. Slaughter the bodyguards just as you would bandits or highwaymen, then target the monk and lay waste to him with a Blades spell or with your ranged weapons. Head to the second spring room and eliminate the Shadow Worshippers there as well, then proceed to the third room and do the same. The monk in the final room is none other than Cornelius Grim, the leader of the Temple of Shadows. He'll use his black magic to summon a gang of hollow men to aid in his defense, so keep back and ready an Inferno spell. Slay Cornelius as soon as you can to save the Temple of Light's water supply.

CHAPTER 1
Childhood
➤ CHAPTER 2
Early Adulthood
CHAPTER 3
Late Adulthood
CHAPTER 4
Happily Ever After

FAILURE TO ACT

Evil triumphs when good Heroes do nothing. If you fail to champion the cause of righteousness, you may find the consequences of inaction quite steep.

LIONHEAD STUDIOS

Quest End

The Oakfield Massacre

Cornelius Grim: Massacre the population of Oakfield in the name of the Temple of Shadows?					

 Good: -

Evil: Massacre Oakfield.

Reward	Renown	Good	Evil	Purity	Corruption
Temple of Shadows Seal	750	-	600+	-	-

Are you truly evil? That is the question you have to ask yourself before accepting this quest. This devilish proposition will be asked of you after proving yourself in the Crucible, and only if you have made prior sacrifices to the Temple of Shadows. If you indeed fancy a chance at shooting the proverbial fish in a barrel, then look no further. Accept the mission at the Temple of Shadows, then head to Oakfield and speak to Wicked Wilbur to learn the details.

Population: 15

Your assignment is simple: Execute all the villagers and guards in Oakfield. The majority of them will congregate near the bridge over the river, in the tavern, and on the road leading up to the woodcutter's barn. The glowing path will help guide you to any stragglers (don't forget about those sniveling monks at the Temple of Light!), but some will return to the tavern out of fear so check back there frequently. The guards won't fall quite as easily as the typical villagers, but this only means they might require two shots from your crossbow instead of just one. Enjoy the slaughter you evil, evil, thing.

That's Mr. Fearmonger to You!

If you're undecided about whether or not you want to participate in this quest, do understand that you will likely unlock several scary expressions and even a free title or two during the course of this quest. You'll drop 20-30 points in morality every time you kill a villager—this means you can gain over 600 points in evilness during this one quest!

Quest End

No Going Back!

Entering The Tattered Spire will forever close the ability to play through a few quests, specifically the *Cold Comfort Farmer/Red Harvest* and the *Defending the Light/Oakfield Massacre*. So, take a moment to choose which of these quests you'll take on and complete them before heading to the Spire.

THE TATTERED SPIRE

The Spire

*You are now one of Lucien's guards in the Spire,
where Garth is being held captive.*

Head to the beach near Westcliff Camp once you're ready to perform your Heroic duty and board the ship to go to the Tattered Spire. Doing so won't be easy, as you need to leave your items, weapons, and dog behind on the beach. There's no need to worry about a thing though; Hammer will watch over everything while you're gone.

The journey to the Tattered Spire doesn't take long and, before you know it, you're standing alongside the other new guards, listening to Lucien speak. His lecture is one wrought with madness and it quickly becomes clear that you may never leave this place.

A week passes and you've been summoned to the Commandant. Your clothes are different and you're now wearing a collar that ensures your obedience. Explore the guard's quarters on this floor and locate some goodies, then proceed down the hall to the stairs leading up to the prisoners' area. Bob is there to lead you further. But more importantly, the last cell on the right contains Garth, the Hero of Will. There's nothing you can do to free Garth at this time, but the day will come eventually.

Continue onward to your meeting with the Commandant, at which time he explains the level of obedience he expects from Spire guards like you. The collar around your neck will not only paralyze you with pain whenever you disobey, it will drain experience too! The Commandant gives you ten seconds to follow his direction and step towards him. Use the Directional Pad to either thank the Commandant, insult him, or just stand by and do nothing. The choice is yours.

THE FINGER OF CHOICE

The Hero temporarily gains access to the Middle Finger expression upon meeting the Commandant. You can use this expression to resist following the Commandant's command to step towards him, but it will cost you significant experience, particularly if you resist him all three times he beckons for you to approach him.

Prisoner Watch

Watch over the prisoners while the other Spire guard goes to eat.

 Good: Feed the prisoners.

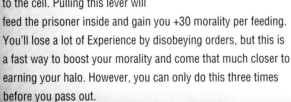 **Evil:** Let the prisoners starve.

Reward	Renown	Good	Evil	Purity	Corruption
-	-	30 (x3)	-30	-	-

It's now been 38 weeks since you first arrived at the Tattered Spire. You're gaining responsibility, but the Commandant is still wary of your obedience. You've just been summoned to the detention area and asked to watch the prisoners while a fellow Spire guard takes a break. The guard wants you to starve the prisoners, but you don't have to. Each prison cell has a large rusty lever to the right of it that controls the food supply to the cell. Pulling this lever will feed the prisoner inside and gain you +30 morality per feeding. You'll lose a lot of Experience by disobeying orders, but this is a fast way to boost your morality and come that much closer to earning your halo. However, you can only do this three times before you pass out.

You have lost 1720 experience.

02:15

EVIL ALTERNATIVE

LET THEM STARVE!

Of course, you don't have to feed the prisoners. Sure, they might be able to work a bit harder if they weren't so malnourished, but that's not your problem. You're just following orders. And, besides, it's fun to watch them beg. Go ahead and admit it. Just don't complain when you lose 30 morality points for every three minutes that go by in which you don't feed them.

Quest End

Prove Your Loyalty

Commandant: *Take the sword and kill Bob.*

 Good: Attack the Commandant.

Evil: Either do nothing or kill Bob.

Reward	Renown	Good	Evil	Purity	Corruption
-	-	50	-10/-50	-	-

137 weeks have passed since you arrived via the ship from Westcliff and the Commandant has once again summoned you to his chamber to test your loyalty. Bob is splayed out on the floor and the Commandant gives you a Master Cutlass to use in killing Bob. For those following the path of righteousness, this is the moment you've been waiting for. Use the sword to attack the Commandant instead! Sure, you'll fail miserably in your attempt and lose more experience, but you'll gain a wealth of morality points in the process. You can also stand by and let the timer count down without taking any action. This will cost you 10 morality points, but you won't lose as much experience and won't have to kill Bob.

Take the sword. Ⓐ

EVIL ALTERNATIVE

WITH PLEASURE, SIR COMMANDANT

If the Commandant is going to give you the honor of killing Bob, then why should you resist him? Take the Master Cutlass over to where Bob lies and press the X Button to strike him dead. This will please the Commandant significantly and not cost you any experience. You'll lose 50 morality points for the action too, bringing you that much closer to the devilish cretin you aspire to be!

It's too bad though, that so many years have to pass before you get another opportunity like this one…

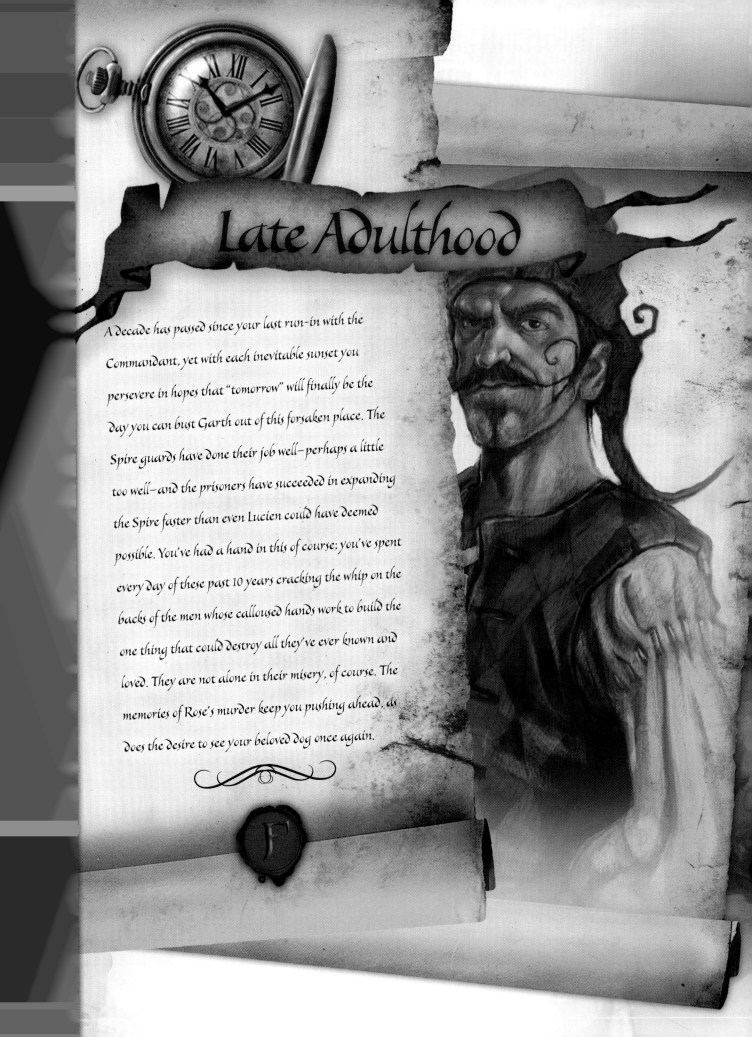

Late Adulthood

A decade has passed since your last run-in with the Commandant, yet with each inevitable sunset you persevere in hopes that "tomorrow" will finally be the day you can bust Garth out of this forsaken place. The Spire guards have done their job well—perhaps a little too well—and the prisoners have succeeded in expanding the Spire faster than even Lucien could have deemed possible. You've had a hand in this of course; you've spent every day of these past 10 years cracking the whip on the backs of the men whose calloused hands work to build the one thing that could destroy all they've ever known and loved. They are not alone in their misery, of course. The memories of Rose's murder keep you pushing ahead, as does the desire to see your beloved dog once again.

THE TATTERED SPIRE

The Spire (Continued)

The Hero of Will

You have been in the Spire for 10 years. You can't leave without Garth.

Good: -	
Evil: -	

Reward	Renown	Good	Evil	Purity	Corruption
Broken Spire Collar	5000	-	-	-	-

Report to the Commandant to learn about the missing guard. Follow the glowing path back through the Spire to the body and take the **Steel Cutlass**, **Steel Clockwork Pistol**, and **Cure-All Health Potions** from it. Garth has built up enough strength to destroy the collar and kill the guard, and now he needs to destroy the collar you're wearing too.

Use your weapons to fight past the throngs of Spire guards as you work your way back to the Commandant's room. Use your spells to compound the damage and to instantly kill wave after wave of Spire guards. Proceed to the Commandant's room and look out the window at the new arrivals; you'll need those ships to get out of here!

COMMANDANT
SPIRE GUARD COMMANDER

Weaknesses	Resistances
Bullets	Chaos, Vortex, and Force Push

HP

| 2000 |

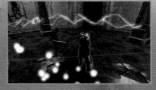

The Commandant can't harm you in his normal manner since Garth was able to destroy the security collar around your neck, but that doesn't mean you're in for an easy fight! The Commandant attacks alongside a steady stream of Spire guards that serves to distract and backstab you while you pursue their leader. The Commandant doesn't just let his men do all the dirty work, he fights for himself too! He'll wield his massive sword whenever you move within reach of it, but he'll primarily attack with magic. Be ready to roll out of the way whenever standing in front of him to avoid the row of spikes he makes rise from the floor.

The Spire guards protecting the Commandant don't share the resistances of their leader and can be kept at bay with Force Push. Use this spell to keep the Spire guards from attacking while you focus on the Commandant. Hit him with your most powerful spells (use Cure-All Health Potions to replenish the health lost while you're charging the spell) and with plenty of gunfire. The Commandant is susceptible to bullets, so put the Steel Clockwork Pistol to use to get off a burst of shots on him. The battle area is surrounded by electric current, but there is plenty of room to roam around. So long as you don't waste too much energy fighting the Spire guards and avoid standing directly in front of the Commandant, you should come out okay. The Commandant starts to warp around the room as the fight rages on; use this time to ready a powerful Blades spell and hit him with it as soon as he reappears!

Use the Cullis Gate with Garth to head to the docks and fight your way through the swarms of Spire guards to reach the end of the dock. Don't stop and wait for the Spire guards to come to you though. Keep advancing across the length of the dock so you'll have the opportunity to make a last-minute sprint for the ships if things go bad. Congratulations, you're about to be a free Hero again!

Quest End

ACHIEVEMENT

The Hero of Will — **100 Points**

Complete the Hero of Will.

Locate the weapons on the missing guard then fight alongside Garth as you make your way to the Commandant's room. Defeat the Commandant in an epic battle against him and his top Spire Guards, then escort Garth across the docks. Sail back to Oakfield and reunite with Theresa and your dog on the dock.

OAKFIELD

The Cullis Gate

Return to your life back in Albion before finding the Hero of Skill.

Statue Cave

It was great to see and pet your dog again, but Theresa needs you to get to the Rookridge Inn to pay a visit to Hammer. She's been on a lengthy pub-crawl around Albion and can't wait to start looking for the missing Hero. Travel to Rookridge when it's comfortable for you. In the meantime, Hammer is returning to the Guild Cave and Theresa will summon you to join them when the time is right.

TIMES HAVE CHANGED

You've been gone for quite some time and you have to accept the fact that things may not be as you left them. Many of the regions, particularly the rural ones, have changed considerably in the 10 years since you've left. And some of these changes will be a function of the choices you made all those years before. Take your time and explore all the areas to which you've been, take part in the optional side-quests that appear, build up your wealth, and for goodness sakes, get some better clothes!

Hobbe Squatters

Tommy: *A group of hobbes has infested a cave that happens to be someone's home.*

Reward	Renown	Good	Evil	Purity	Corruption
Hobbe Leg	3500	-	-	-	-

Make your way to the Temple of Light and speak to a cross-dressing man named Tommy about the problem he's having with the hobbes who have taken up residence in his cavern. Agree to help him out by eliminating the hobbes in Echo Mine, located on the eastern side of Oakfield. Use a combination of Time Control and Inferno to destroy the hobbes milling around outside the entrance to the cavern, then head into Echo Mine.

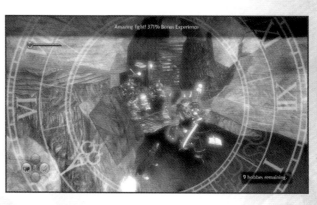

There are 15 hobbes running about the cave that you must defeat. Continue to use your spells and ranged weaponry to pick them off as they approach. Most hobbes attack in groups of three to five. Collect the pages from the diary and continue onto the bridge where you'll need to defeat the hobbe leader.

Take advantage of the time it takes for the hobbe leader to cross the bridge to begin pumping him full of lead. Use the Time Control spell as he gets near to slow him down, then ready a Level 3 or 4 Inferno spell to finish the hat-wearing magician before he can even think about casting magic bolts your way.

Return the way you came to the cave exit where you will find Tommy. Tommy didn't send you here to clear out the squatters; he sent you here to die! Naturally, you didn't spend 10 years of your life toiling away at the Tattered Spire so some powdered-wig wearing guy in heels could spill your blood. Let him have it, grab **Tommy's Cavern Key,** and exit Echo Mine.

Quest End

Blind Date

Farmer Giles: *Farmer Giles wants his son to get married. Can you find him a suitable partner?*

Good: Set Rupert up with a gay man.

Evil: Ignore Rupert's preferences and set him up with a woman.

Reward	Renown	Good	Evil	Purity	Corruption
-	3500	10	-10	-	-

Head to Brightwood and visit Farmer Giles (assuming you didn't kill him in *Red Harvest*) to learn about his son's dating problems. Farmer Giles desperately wants to see his son settle down and start a family, but he can't seem to get the boy to meet the right girl. Rupert, his son, is in the cornfield near the barn. A quick chat with him is all it takes to realize that he's actually interested in men, not women. Rupert gives you a photo of himself for you to use in finding him a suitable partner.

Head to Bowerstone Market in search of a gay man to show the photo to. There aren't that many men in Bowerstone Market who aren't already spoken for, let alone who are gay, but there is sure to be one out there who is not only gay, but quite impressed by the photo of Rupert. Show him the photo of Rupert and he'll give you the details for the blind date he wants to go on with Rupert. Take the details back to Brightwood and give them to Rupert who is inside the house with his father.

BRIGHTWOOD FARM FOR SALE!

Rupert was able to convince his father to move to the city with him and sell the farm. You can now purchase the Brightwood Farm to add to your real estate empire. The farm has a base value of 74,480 gold.

EVIL ALTERNATIVE
FATHER KNOWS BEST

Just because Rupert wants you to set him up with a gay man, doesn't mean you have to. Head to Bowerstone Market and find a single, straight woman. Preferably one that fancies herself a bit raunchy—she'll be easier to impress with the photo. Take the details she gives you back to Rupert and watch him cringe as he prepares for another date with a woman.

Quest End

Return on Investment

Those who lent Barnum the 5000 Gold he requested in *Westcliff Development* ought to make sure to return to Westcliff to see what he's done with the place. Your investment allowed him to completely transform Westcliff into a family-friendly vacation destination. Not only will you receive 1500 renown for your efforts, but Barnum is set to pay you back with interest! And thanks to that stay at the Tattered Spire, your money has grown to 15,000 Gold!

And speaking of Westcliff, there are plenty of improvements you should check out thanks to Barnum. Lots of new chests to get, a new bridge connecting the camp with the road to Bandit Coast, and the Shooting Range is easier than ever!

The Cullis Gate

Skip conversation (A)

Return to the Guild Cave in Bower Lake when you're finished taking care of business. The initial meeting between Hammer and Garth doesn't go as smoothly as Theresa had hoped, but everyone is ready to get to work searching for the Hero of Skill. There's a rumor that the Hero of Skill is in the port town of Bloodstone, but getting there requires traveling through the dreaded Wraithmarsh. Garth has a Cullis Gate at Brightwood Tower that could deliver the group to Wraithmarsh; head to Brightwood to meet up with Garth and Hammer.

BRIGHTWOOD

The Cullis Gate (Continued)

Lucien is on to your plans and has sent a full contingent of Spire guards to Brightwood in an attempt to keep you from using the Cullis Gate at the tower. Garth knows enough to not take the main entrance to the tower so he opts to lead the group on a trip across the river to the back side. This path is also crawling with Spire guards, but you should have little trouble with them thanks to the addition of Hammer and Garth. There is an abundance of dig spots and chests in this area of Brightwood so do keep your eyes and ears open for treasure.

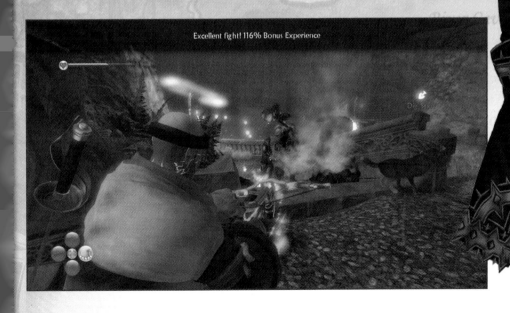

Excellent fight! 116% Bonus Experience

Devastating Will Combo

Arguably one of the best ways to dispatch groups of enemies is to quickly cast a Level 1 Time Control spell, then charge and cast a Level 3 Time Control spell while the first one is in effect. This lengthier dose of Time Control provides all the time you need to charge a Level 4 or 5 Inferno spell.

Battle your way up the stairs and across the terraces behind the tower and head inside. A Shard appears and attacks with deadly intent. Quickly target the white ball of energy that serves as its core to destroy it before it can complete its mission. Continue up the stairs to the Cullis Gate location.

Garth has to use all the power he possesses to charge the Cullis Gate, else you'll never be able to reach Wraithmarsh. It's up to you and Hammer to keep him safe from the throngs of Spire guards that will be deployed by the massive Shard. Back away from the center of the roof so you can see the Spire guards. Put your best ranged weapon to use against them as soon as they appear. Those with the Sub-Targeting ability will be able to drop the attackers with a string of headshots. All is not lost if you don't have Sub-Targeting yet, however; focus on using the Time Control spell to slow the enemies' movements and buy yourself time to unleash powerful Inferno or Blades spells. Of course, Raise Dead also throws a monkey wrench into their plans. Use the Cullis Gate as soon as its power reaches 100%.

WRAITHMARSH

Stranded

You are stranded in Wraithmarsh. You must find your way through to Bloodstone.

Garth and Hammer didn't make it through the Cullis Gate before it malfunctioned, but that doesn't mean you're alone. A crazed inhabitant of the marshes found your unconscious body and locked you up in a cage. Fortunately, the man quickly succumbs to the creatures of the fog and your dog retrieves the key to the cage. You're free once again, but the marshes are a dangerous place to be alone.

Explore the area north and south of the cage where you begin this leg of the journey, then head west towards the drowned farm. A banshee makes an appearance in the water in the center of this former town square. Put some distance between you and it, wipe out the banshee children, then target its head with your ranged weapon; banshees are particularly vulnerable to arrow damage, so ready your crossbow if you have one.

Banshee

Banshees are unlike other creatures you've encountered in that they float above the ground and use their powers to summon a cadre of shadow creatures to attack. The banshee itself will attack with a powerful Soul Suck attack if you stray too close, but they tend to let their minions fight for them. Wipe out the little critters with an area spell, then take aim at the main attraction.

Banshees are immune to the Chaos spell and tend to be unaffected by area spells thanks to their ability to float. You can inflict significant damage with melee attacks and targeted spells, but the absolute best way to handle a banshee is with a Master Repeater Crossbow. Stand back and wait for the banshee to cover her face with her hands. That's your signal that the banshee can be targeted. Use the crossbow, preferably with the Sub-Targeting ability, and fire a quick barrage of six arrows straight into its head—you don't even need to reload! It's possible to drop a banshee with a Master-level crossbow in just a few shots, provided you aim for the head!

Wade through the water of the drowned farm and briefly ignore the path on the left so as to inspect the former town of Oakvale up ahead. It's a sad sight for sure, not to mention a reminder of what could happen when one lets their thirst for power to get the better of them. Have a look around for a digging spot, then head back the way you came and take the path up the hill and across the bridge.

Fight your way past the hollow men, including an elder, that begin to enter the area as you make your way up the hill and across another large bridge. This one leads to a massive circle of tombs. The area is flooded both with water and with an approaching gang of hollow men of varying degrees of toughness. Stand back and hurl Inferno spells at them, then switch to your ranged weapon and take them out with carefully aimed headshots. Employ the same strategy for the banshee that appears in the marsh farther to the east.

Continue through the swamp to the next encounter with a troll. This particular troll has some pretty resistant weak spots on its body (resistant to Inferno and Blades spells in addition to Chaos) and it moves a bit quicker than other trolls you've faced. There are several ways to go about defeating this particular troll, including using Time Control and Vortex to destroy many of the weak spots in a single attack. Cast a Level 1 Time Control spell to buy yourself time to cast a Level 2 or 3 Time Control spell. Run behind the troll and unleash as powerful a Vortex spell as you can to rupture several weak spots at once. You can also use your ranged weaponry and the Sub-Targeting ability to pop the weak spots one at a time from a safe distance. Use the ruins on the ground for cover or head to the bridge. Defeat the troll and continue to the northeast to exit the area and travel to Bloodstone.

BRIDGE OVER TROLL-FILLED WATERS

When fighting the troll in Wraithmarsh, if you attack it from the bridge behind it, it will be unable to hit you with the ground snake attack at all. If you position yourself correctly, no attack from the troll will be able to hit you, including thrown rocks, as they simply shatter on the railings of the bridge. In addition, from the vantage point of the bridge, when the troll bends down to grab a rock, the weak points on its back are visible to be shot at.

BLOODSTONE

The Hero of Skill

Find Reaver and convince him to join your cause.

Congratulations on surviving the journey through Wraithmarsh. Theresa and Garth's belief that Reaver is hanging out in Bloodstone has been proven true. There is a mansion at the east side of town, in the hills, that belongs to him. There's no need to hurry over to him right away; he's not going anywhere. Take all the time you need to have a look around and to dig up the many pieces of treasure that lurk both on and off the shore of this harbor town. Head to Reaver's mansion after embarking on any of the optional quests that may provide additional renown.

Chest Hunting

Many of the buildings in Bloodstone have a side-entrance that leads directly to the second floor living space. You can often find chests located in the rooms upstairs, specifically behind a pile of breakable crates and barrels.

Reaver has been expecting you and has given considerable thought to the request you no doubt have of him. He agrees to join you and the others in your foolish attack against Lucien only if you manage to return **Reaver's Dark Seal** to its rightful owner in Wraithmarsh. Pick up the seal from the table and leave the way you came. It's clear from speaking to Reaver that the favor he asks of you is one fraught with considerable risk—you should indeed spend some time completing other quests before taking on this challenge.

Treasure Island of Doom!

Salty Jack: *An old drunk has seen the ghost of a pirate.*

Reward	Renown	Good	Evil	Purity	Corruption
Captain Dread's Sword	7500	-	-	-	-

 Good: -

Evil: -

Pay a visit to the tavern in Bloodstone and speak to the old sailor standing off to the left. Oblige him when he asks for you to buy him a beer and listen closely to his tale. Salty Jack will tell you all about the smuggler's cave and the pirate ghost he's seen. He needs you to investigate the cave and vouch for him. Exit the bar and follow the path around the south side of the harbor, around the rocky headland near the sea and into the Sinkhole cave.

ACHIEVEMENT

The Cliff Diver — 5 Points
Cliff dive 500 feet, or see another Hero do so.

There aren't many places where you can make a 500 feet dive so rather than attempt to jump off every cliff you see, let us tell you exactly where to do it. Head to Bloodstone and walk along the southern shore to the entrance to the Sinkhole cave. Enter this out-of-the-way cavern (you'll need to visit this area during the *Treasure Island of Doom* quest) and dive off the ledge straight ahead to earn this Achievement.

Enter the cave and dive off the platform into the water far, far below. Swim out onto the rocks and make your way along the path past the secret pirate ship hidden away inside this grotto. Climb the wooden walkways beyond the ship and head inside. Draw your ranged weapon and prepare for battle against a number of pirate ghosts. Continue on to the mess hall where a dozen or so pirate ghosts launch their attack. Use the Time Control spell to slow them down while you ready a high level spell like Inferno or Vortex.

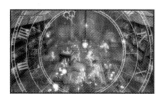

Continue through the galley to the locked door up ahead. Smash the crates on the side of the room and step on the switch beneath it to open the door to Captain Dread's bedroom. Use **Captain Dread's Key** on the nightstand to open the chest containing the **Lever**. Head back outside to the wooden walkway and use the lever to open the floodgates. This raises the ship off the rocks and makes it suitable for plying the waters once again. First things first; you have to defeat Captain Dread.

Board the ship and use a combination of Time Control, Inferno, and well-aimed ranged attacks to obliterate the three waves of ghost pirates that attack. Captain Dread will stand back and watch the mayhem, so ignore him until he begins to move around and attack. There are a lot of ghost pirates to contend with but they are vulnerable to Inferno and can be defeated quickly with the powerful fire spell.

CAPTAIN DREAD
LEADER OF THE PIRATE GHOSTS

Weaknesses	Resistances
Holy	Inferno, Blades, Chaos, Vortex, and Force Push

HP 4000

Captain Dread is immune to Chaos and resistant to damage from all other magic-based attacks. A level 4 or 5 spell will still inflict plenty of damage of course, but you won't get as much bang for your buck with them as you normally would. One spell that is still plenty helpful is Time Control and you should definitely put it to use in slowing Captain Dread down as you unload on him with your ranged weaponry.

The leader of the ghost pirates stalks his ship with a wrath unseen in other enemies. He's tall and he uses his long arms and tremendous strength to inflict heavy damage with the cutlass he wields. You must keep on the move to stay out of his reach and perform somersaults to dodge his attacks. Those who have obtained the Rising Sun signifying their philanthropy have an advantage in that their attacks inflict more damage than normal. Either way, the best attack is to use your most powerful ranged weapon and attack Captain Dread's head with the Sub-Targeting ability.

Defeat Captain Dread to acquire **Captain Dread's Map**; approach the wheel aboard the ship. The ship can sense the map you possess and automatically guides you to Lion's Head Isle. There are ten bags of 1500 Gold stashed throughout the secret island where Captain Dread hid his loot. Consult the map in the 'Albion Atlas' section of the book to find the ten treasures, then board the ship and sail it back to Bloodstone to prove that Salty Jack wasn't losing his marbles after all!

Quest End

Rescuing Charlie

Granny Miggins: *Granny Miggins is worried sick about her grandson, Charlie.*

Reward	Renown	Good	Evil	Purity	Corruption
Gold Burden Augment	5000	30	-50	-	-20

Good: Save Charles from the hollow men.

Evil: Kill Charles and tell Granny Miggins he died. Or be especially corrupt and impersonate Charles.

Make a special trip back to the gypsy camp in Bower Lake and speak with the old grandmotherly lady on the footbridge. She tells you all about her missing grandson, Charlie, and begs you to go looking for him. Since Charlie isn't the type to talk to strangers, or so she hopes, she gives you a note with her handwriting to prove that you're nobody to fear. Charlie is in the Tomb of Heroes, accessible via the dried up pond in the northeast corner of Bower Lake (the door to the Tomb of Heroes will not open until this quest is triggered).

Descend the stairs into the Tomb and advance through the darkened hall to the empty pool in the area straight ahead. Locate the items in the chests and continue around the bend to the man in the large hat near the sarcophagus. This is Charlie and, yes, he's a bit too old to be doted on by his grandmother. Help Charlie live out his adventurous spirit by protecting him from the hollow men that attack while he unlocks the sarcophagus in the tomb. Use a combination of magic spells and ranged and melee attacks. Buy yourself some time with Time Control and unleash a horde of your own ghostly spirits with the Raise Dead spell. This should give you the advantage you need to protect Charlie.

Help Charlie slide the cover off the sarcophagus, then escort him back through the tomb to his grandmother outside. You'll have to face a number of hollow men in the corridors leading back to the surface (the path you took to get in is blocked, so a longer, narrower route will have to suffice). Protect Charlie as best you can by weakening the attacking hollow men with an Inferno spell, then finish them off with your ranged weapons. Charlie has a small sword and does a decent job contributing to the fight, but he won't survive without your help.

Quest End

EVIL ALTERNATIVE

END OF MISERY

First, the "baby" Granny Miggins bothers you to rescue, turns out to be a 40-year-old man, then you find out the sarcophagus has already been looted. This whole situation has misery written all over it. Do everyone involved a favor and kill Charlie deep inside the tomb. Search the body to take his hat then, when you exit the tomb, Granny Miggins thinks you're her precious grandson and gives you the gift she had for him. Regardless of your choice, you'll still get the powerful augment. You'll just lose some morality and purity doing it this way.

Something Rotten

Joseph: *A strange and unpleasant smell is driving the Rookridge Inn out of business.*

Reward	Renown	Good	Evil	Purity	Corruption
Troll's Eyeball	3500	-	-	-	-

Good: -	
Evil: -	

The bartender at the Rookridge Inn says the water they're using is polluted and he wants you to look into cleaning it up. Exit through the second floor balcony and head up the path to The Wellspring to see what is in the cave fouling up the water.

As it turns out, there is a troll living in the watery bottom of the cave. Run down the path towards it to lure it from its slumber, then cast Time Control before it can start lobbing its rocks. Use your ranged weaponry in conjunction with Time Control and Vortex to blast apart its weak spots as quickly as possible. You don't want to give the troll too much time to attack, else the fight could begin to tilt in its favor. You're have stay near the water or at least on the lowermost portion of the ramp leading out of the cave, else the troll will hunker down and go back to sleep. You can't fight it from high up on the sloping path.

FOR SALE: ROOKRIDGE INN

The bartender was thankful that you were able to defeat the troll fouling up the water, but he doesn't want to run the inn anymore and is putting it up for sale. Cheaply. He's going to give you a pretty steep discount too since he likes you. You can buy the inn, The Lucky Heather, for under 2500 Gold!

Quest End

The Hero of Skill (Continued)

Returning the Dark Seal

Find the dark seal's owner in Wraithmarsh.

 Good: Sacrifice yourself to save the girl.

 Evil: Sacrifice the girl to save yourself.

Reward	Renown	Good	Evil	Purity	Corruption
-	-	50	-50	-	-

Return to the drowned farm area in Wraithmarsh and make your way along the old carriage road to the large stone building on the right. This is the Shadow Court where the rightful owner of the seal resides. Head inside.

Break On Through

The Shadow Court contains several cracked stone walls and boarded-up holes that can be smashed apart with a couple swings of your weapon. Keep your eyes peeled for these anomalies in the walls' appearance so you can find the secrets contained behind them.

Fight your way past the enemies in the Shadow Court and slip through the narrow passageways en route to the spiked floor. Use Time Control to slow the spikes long enough so you can run and roll across them safely. Step on the switch near the chest to turn the spikes off, grab the item from the chest, and continue on to the right. Defeat the throngs of shadow creatures that appear in this next room—Inferno and ranged attacks keep them at bay—and jump down the hole to the lower level.

You've finally reached the source of the constant sobbing, a woman standing alone in front of an altar of sorts. Three shadow spirits soon appear and demand that one of you be sacrificed as punishment for possessing the Dark Seal. It doesn't matter to them which of you are sacrificed, but whomever is left holding the Dark Seal will be aged prematurely and permanently. Since the woman had nothing to do with the favor you're performing for Reaver—and because you really want "The Paragon" Achievement—you should hold onto the seal and take whatever punishment comes with it.

Exit the Shadow Court via the spiraling stairs behind you. This leads to a chest behind a locked gate and the main door back out to Wraithmarsh.

EVIL ALTERNATIVE

SACRIFICE THE GIRL

Just because Reaver asked you to return the Dark Seal doesn't mean that you have to be the one who personally hands it over to them! Press the A Button to hand the Dark Seal to the woman and let her hold it as the spirit's countdown (you'll feel the controller vibrate) commences. Sure, the woman is quite young and it is a shame to sacrifice her youth, but you can't always be expected to do what's right.

No Going Back!

Just in case you don't hear Theresa's warning, we'll reiterate it here. Returning to Reaver in Bloodstone sets actions in motion that cannot be reversed, nor will you be able to break away to do other things once they begin. If you have any unfinished business at this time, we recommend you do it now. We suggest completing the following quests before going back to Reaver… or forever hold your peace.

Quest End

Love Hurts

The lonely gravekeeper in Bowerstone Cemetery is conducting a strange experiment.

Good: Allow the gravekeeper to marry his love.

Evil: Break the poor guy's heart.

Reward	Renown	Good	Evil	Purity	Corruption
Rod of Life	8500	10	-10	-	-

Visit the gravekeeper in the mansion at the north end of Bowerstone Cemetery to find out about his troubles. He's a bit hesitant to speak to strangers, but he'll eventually ask you for help in collecting the body parts of the deceased Lady Grey; he's trying to bring her back to life. Agree to help him and fast-travel to Hobbe Cave at Rookridge to look for the first body part: the lower body. Follow your dog past the swarming hobbes to the dig spot and use your spade to dig up **Lady Grey's Lower Body** and the **First Witchspotters Note**. Return to the gravekeeper to find the location of the second body part. He's in the library.

The second body part is located in Twinblade's Tomb in Wraithmarsh. Travel to the Bloodstone Road corner of Wraithmarsh and enter the tomb in the northwest corner of the swamp.

Love Hurts
Retrieve part of the body from a tomb in Wraithmarsh.

Twinblade's Tomb doesn't contain much in the way of treasure, but what it lacks in collectibles it makes up for with hordes of hollow men and a plethora of gates and doorways controlled by flit switches and switch plates. There is only one path through the tomb, so it's all but impossible to get lost, but many of the doors are locked. You'll need to stand on the switch plate in the room or shoot the flit switch in order to open the door. Many of the flit switches require more than one shot and some require a melee strike. Just remember that the color of the flit switches matches up with the color of the X, Y, and B Buttons on your controller so you simply have to hit it with the corresponding attack.

The tomb also has a unique expression statue serving as part of its security system. Stand on the switch plate in the room with the green-glowing statue and match the statue's expression to open the door. In this case, you'll need to perform the Chicken expression. With that done, head up the stairs on the left and shoot the flit switch in the distance to unlock the door below. Use the Raise Dead and Inferno spells to thwart the attacks of the hollow men in the circular room and quickly shoot

the flit switch as it repositions itself on each of the statues. Use the switch at the end of the corridor to open the final gate where you'll find **Lady Grey's Upper Body** and the **Second Witchspotters Note**.

Return to the gravekeeper in Bowerstone Cemetery and hand over the second body part. You're two-thirds of the way through helping him; now he needs you to visit Lady Grey's Tomb in Fairfax Gardens to retrieve her head. Sure it's gruesome, but it's in the name of science! One of the gated areas in Fairfax Gardens is now open so head there at once and enter Lady Grey's Tomb on the north side of the area.

Locate the chests in the corners of the dark, sand-filled room you descend into, then take **Lady Grey's Head** and the **Third Witchspotters Note** from the casket on the altar. Hack and slash your way past the giant beetles lurking in the sand and head up the stairs at the far end of the tomb to exit outside the other tomb in Fairfax Gardens.

Return to the gravekeeper's mansion in Bowerstone Cemetery and meet him in his basement research laboratory. Hand over the third and final body part and watch in awe as he brings Lady Grey back from the dead. Unfortunately, the gravekeeper's experiment had one unexpected drawback—Lady Grey will fall in love with the first person she sees. And that person is you! You have to quickly exit the basement before her love for you becomes irreversible. Head upstairs to the main foyer so the gravekeeper can have his chance at love with Lady Grey. You'll be able to hear their conversation from upstairs and know how the quest ends.

EVIL ALTERNATIVE

SWEET LITTLE FRANKEN-BRIDE

You grew up hearing stories about the illustrious Lady Grey and here's your chance to make her yours! It's not your fault that the undead Lady Grey has fallen in love with you, so there's no reason for you to be the one to break her heart. Hasn't this woman suffered enough already? Ignore the gravekeeper's sorrow-filled pleas to exit the room and keep her as your bride.

Quest End

The Cemetery Mansion

Investigate the gravekeeper's cave in the cemetery.

Reward	Renown	Good	Evil	Purity	Corruption
-	3500	30	-30	-	-

Good: Keep the lost souls free from hell.

Evil: Condemn the lost souls to hell.

The Bowerstone Cemetery Mansion becomes available for purchase after completion of the *Love Hurts* quest and at a cost of 100,000 Gold. Purchase the building to gain the **Gravekeeper's Key** and **Gravekeeper's Note**, a note detailing the location of a nearby crypt. Use the key to unlock the gate near the scrap yard in Bowerstone Cemetery and head inside Shelley Crypt to see what treasures you might find.

Head down the path to the crypt to where the rows of web-covered sarcophagi are lined up. Explore the path to the north to find **The Stone of Myr'Bregothil**, an incredibly powerful augment. Securing the precious stone was easy, but now you have to find a way out! Smash through the cracked wall to find what can only be described as a former torture chamber. Lay waste to the hollow men that attack, gather up the treasure your dog inevitably sniffs out, and continue south to the room with the flit switch.

It might not seem like there is a way across this room full of pedestals and empty space, but a series of light bridges forms as you hit the flit switches. Strike the blue flit switch on the near side of the void, then shoot it when it repositions itself to create a segment of the bridge. Cross to the next pedestal and repeat the process again. Keep this up all the way across the void.

Continue along the path to the massive hollow man blocking the rocky bridge in the distance. He's there to represent the lost souls condemned to an afterlife of hell if the Stone of Myr'Bregothil leaves this sacred place. He's asking for you to kindly return the stone to him. If you're the good-natured type, then you should kindly hand the stone over. You may not get to keep such a powerful item, but the hilarious conversation between the hollow man and his fellow lost souls should be all the reward you need.

EVIL ALTERNATIVE

FINDERS KEEPERS!

What does the lost soul of a hollow man need such a great item for? You're the one who shelled out the 100,000 Gold for the mansion and you're the one who inherited the key to this place. Everything in it belongs to you! Besides, if you give in to one hollow man, pretty soon every hollow man in Albion will be thinking he can just stop you in your tracks and get a handout! Is that the kind of world you want to live in? Tell the hollow man to step aside, don't press the A Button, and keep the stone yourself.

You'll be able to sell the stone for a hefty sum of money once you get topside, but you're going to have to defeat this massive hollow man first.

HOLLOW MAN LEADER
PROTECTOR OF THE LOST SOULS

HP

| 4000 |

Weaknesses	Resistances
Good	Evil, Shock, Chaos, Vortex, Force Push

The hollow man leader fights similarly to other hollow men, only he's much bigger and can take far more punishment than the others. Since it's unlikely that you'll muster a strong enough blast with Force Push to knock him off the bridge, your best bet is to cast a Level 3 Time Control spell, then back away and charge up a high level Inferno spell. Finish him off with a couple of shots to the head. He's tough and he can do a lot of damage if he swings his massive cleavers at you, but you're safe so long as you can keep your distance.

Quest End

T.O.B.Y.

Toby: *Help Toby transform Bloodstone into a peaceful town?*

 Good: Run Toby out of town.

Evil: Kill Toby.

Reward	Renown	Good	Evil	Purity	Corruption
Mutton of Eternal Hope	4000	10	-30	-	

Pay a visit to the balding man on the second floor of the building on the hill in Bloodstone to learn about the Temple of Benevolent Yokels (T.O.B.Y.) led by the man they call Toby. Toby is deeply disturbed by the filth and immorality in Bloodstone and would like your help in retrieving several items for use in a ceremony that will help run the riffraff out of town. Follow his instructions (and the glowing path) to each of the three houses Toby describes and retrieve the food items he specified. The first two items, the Mutton of Eternal Hope and the Wine of Forgiveness, are located in dressers on the second floor of the houses he specifies. The third item, the Sacred Pie of Kindness, is in the cupboard on the ground floor.

Toby's next request is for you to bring him a prostitute so he can try and teach her the error of her ways. Of course, he wants you to leave him alone while he "talks" to her. Bring him the prostitute as he requests, then speak to the man in the street to learn the truth about Toby. It turns out he's actually a con-artist and pulls stunts like this all the time.

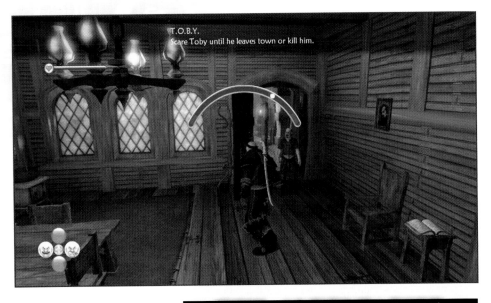

Head back to Toby's house and knock on the door until he answers it—it will take at least four or five knocks before he finally opens up. Step inside the house and use the scary expressions like Growl, Bloodlust Roar, and Slap to scare him into leaving town. The Threaten expression works well too, but you may not have been evil enough to earn it.

EVIL ALTERNATIVE

BUT WORDS WILL NEVER HURT HIM

You could spend a few minutes trying to scare Toby out of town with a bunch of growls and threats, but doesn't he deserve more than that? After all, this is the guy who had you running all over town like a trained dog. Guys like Toby don't deserve to be treated gently. Not in towns like Bloodstone and not by the likes of you. Grab your blade and fillet him on the spot. You owe it to yourself.

 Quest End

Evil in Wraithmarsh

Mrs. Spade: *The brothers Max and Sam have gotten into trouble again… And they've travelled all the way to Wraithmarsh to do it.*

Reward	Renown	Good	Evil	Purity	Corruption
Banshee Rags	4000	-	-	-	-

Good: -

Evil: -

Make your way to the Cow & Corset in Bowerstone Market and find Mrs. Spade in the room upstairs. She is in need of a Hero to go and make sure her sons Sam and Max are all right. She doesn't know exactly where they went, other than to say they're somewhere in Wraithmarsh. Fortunately, your dog is capable of tracking them once you get there. Follow your dog through Wraithmarsh to the entrance to The Well and climb down the ladder.

Run through the ankle-deep water towards the large cavern in the distance where Sam and Max have managed to get themselves surrounded by a gang of hostile hollow men. Put your Time Control and Inferno spells to use and help the brothers out.

They'll thank you by letting you know that they've made the mistake of summoning more deadly creatures with the Normanomicon. This time they summoned a banshee to Bloodstone! Head to Bloodstone at once and run out onto the dock to put a stop to the hysteria ravaging the town. Cast the Raise Dead spell along with Inferno or Blades to eliminate her army of shadowy children, then take aim on her head with your most powerful ranged weapon. Shoot the banshee repeatedly while she's covering her face to defeat her, then return to Bowerstone Market to bring Sam and Max back to their mother.

Quest End

Bloodstone Assault

Leave Bloodstone with Reaver.

Reward	Renown	Good	Evil	Purity	Corruption
Shard Shard	10,000	-	-	-	-

Good: -

Evil: -

Return to Reaver's Mansion in Bloodstone once you're ready to tackle Lucien. Reaver has discovered that you escaped from the Spire, and figured he could earn some coin by selling you out to Lucien. Unfortunately for him, Lucien needs Reaver as much as he needs you, and has sent forces to Bloodstone to capture the pirate king. Your only hope is to escape through the secret cavern known as Reaver's Rear Passage.

Free Cash

The chest of drawers right next to the entrance to Reaver's Rear Passage contains 1000 Gold and you don't even have to steal to get it. Just search the chest to pick up a cool 1000 gold!

Follow Reaver through his secret study and out onto the walkway in the cavern behind it. A wave of Spire guards attacks from the walkways on the right-hand side of the cave. Hold your ground alongside Reaver and use your ranged weaponry and the Sub-Targeting ability to pick them off with a bevy of headshots. Look for groups of enemies gathered together, release the L Trigger so you can aim manually, and target the barrels of explosives scattered about. Advance up the walkway the Spire guards were on to lay claim to the **Live Forever Health Potion** located there, then turn and eliminate the Spire guards flooding in from the other side.

Push on deeper into the cavern to the cavern with the two railcar trestles. Quickly target the explosives on the upper bridge to blow the massive stalactites off the ceiling and down onto the Spire guards below. Avoid detonating the barrels of explosive on the lower tracks as you cross the bridge into the cave at the other end. This passage leads you up several flights of stairs to the upper walkway where the Spire guards were moments ago. Turn and fire on the barrels in

the mine cars below (the ones you just ran past) to knock the Spire guards into the abyss. Reaver encourages you to keep on moving and that's precisely what you should do. Smash through the boards to exit out onto Smuggler's Beach where Hammer and Garth stand waiting. And where more Spire guards are coming...

GREAT SHARD
OLD KINGDOM SUPERWEAPON

Weaknesses	Resistances
Shock, Bullet, Arrows	Chaos, Vortex, Force Push

HP 7000

The Great Shard is capable of deploying up to ten Spire guards at once while keeping its vulnerable "eye" behind a bullet-proof shell. You can focus on slaying the Spire guards and lieutenant Spire guards, but that won't help you get any closer to defeating the Great Shard. And firing your ranged weapons at it won't do anything either.

Run up onto either of the raised ledges near the water and leave the Spire guards to Reaver and Hammer while you and Garth focus on the Great Shard. Await the moment when the Shard opens and reveals its weak spot, then unleash your full fury! The Great Shard continues to deploy tens of Spire guards to the beach, but you should only take your attention off the Great Shard if the Spire guards begin to attack you directly or if the Great Shard summons a smaller Shard into the fray. If this happens, use your Time Control spell to slow the action down, then beat them back with a high level Inferno spell or by casting Raise Dead.

Quest End

ACHIEVEMENT

The Hero of Skill — 100 Points
Complete the Hero of Skill.

Acquire enough renown to earn Reaver's cooperation in Bloodstone. Then, after you return the Dark Seal to its rightful owners at the Shadow Court for him, he will accompany you. Fight your way through Reaver's Rear Passage and defeat the Great Shard to finally introduce him to Theresa and unlock this Achievement.

The Weapon

Meet Theresa in Bower Lake and stand in the circle at Hero Hill.

Theresa has assembled the three Heroes atop Hero Hill in order to transfer the most powerful weapon of all to you, the fourth Hero. The process, though painful, seems to go according to plan. That is until Lucien arrives on the scene…

Spoiler Alert!

The remaining components of this quest guide provide instructions through to the very ending of the game. We suggest you close the book and read no further until you get to the final choice Theresa presents to you—you might want our help in making that decision. Nevertheless, we will cover everything that happens between now and then as spoiler-free as possible just in case you get into trouble.

Bottles remaining: 13

You wake to the sound of Rose's voice. You're both children again, but you're not in Bowerstone Old Town. No, you're on a picturesque farm, living in a beautiful house, and you haven't a care in the world. Follow Rose outside to the farm and practice your swordsmanship by defeating the 8 giant beetles that rise up out of the mud. Rose is such a great sister she even set up 20 bottles for you to shoot with your Toy Gun. The bottles are set up on walls, wagons, near the docks, and even in trees. Of course, you're just a kid having fun so you don't actually have to shoot them if you don't want to. You could always kick the chickens back into their pen if you feel like doing that instead.

Enjoy the day however you see fit, then head to bed when it gets dark and Rose calls you in to sleep. The sound of music interrupts your slumber. Ignore Rose's pleas to stay inside and head down the path, away from the pond, towards the sound of the music box. Take it in your hands, for it is the weapon of which Theresa spoke.

Retribution

	The Spire is fully operational. Lucien must be stopped.

Reward	Renown	Good	Evil	Purity	Corruption
A Letter from Rose	-	300	-300	500 or 0	-500

Pure: Choose "Sacrifice" or "Family".

Corrupt: Choose "Wealth".

Climb the steps to where Lucien is standing with Hammer, Garth, and Reaver. The three Heroes you've worked so hard to convince to join you are now being sucked empty of their powers; Lucien is between them, growing stronger on their Heroic strengths as you read this. Fortunately, you have the one thing that can take Lucien's power from him. Stand tall and press and hold the A Button to use the Music Box to capture Lucien's power from him. Once drained of his power, he is no longer a threat. One shot will kill him, but if you take him out immediately, you'll miss his last words.

Theresa presents you with one final task: you must make a wish. It's not an easy decision to make, but the choices and their consequences are listed here.

SACRIFICE: This is the most pure and selfless choice you can make. This will bring back the thousands of lives lost to the Tattered Spire, but it will not net you any wealth, nor will your loved ones (or even your dog!) return to life. You will not be able to complete any remaining quests that require digging, but the public will erect a statue in your honor.

FAMILY: Selecting "Family" brings any of your loved ones who have died—including your dog—back to life. This is still a "good" selection in terms of morality, but it is an impure decision on account of the thousands you are choosing to ignore. That said, you need your dog in order to finish any quests that involve digging and this is the only way to bring him back.

WEALTH: Only the most selfish of Heroes would turn their backs on their own family and thousands of others in favor of riches, but that is the option you have. Selecting "Wealth" will reward you with untold fortunes and the ability to buy whatever you want, whenever you want. But will it buy you respect? However, as with the Sacrifice option, your dog will not be brought back to life, and you will no longer be able to finish any quests that require digging.

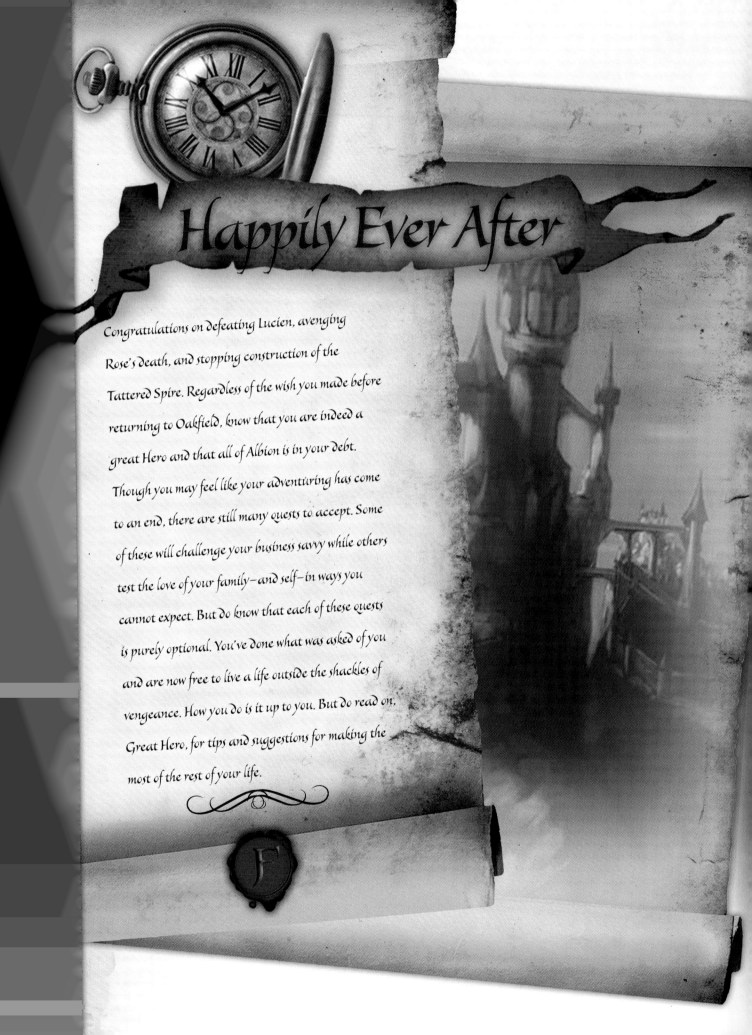

Happily Ever After

Congratulations on defeating Lucien, avenging Rose's death, and stopping construction of the Tattered Spire. Regardless of the wish you made before returning to Oakfield, know that you are indeed a great Hero and that all of Albion is in your debt. Though you may feel like your adventuring has come to an end, there are still many quests to accept. Some of these will challenge your business savvy while others test the love of your family—and self—in ways you cannot expect. But do know that each of these quests is purely optional. You've done what was asked of you and are now free to live a life outside the shackles of vengeance. How you do is it up to you. But do read on, Great Hero, for tips and suggestions for making the most of the rest of your life.

GREATER ALBION

If your quest to upend Lucien's plans has only served to whet your appetite for power, renown, and riches then you have come to the right place. There are plenty of tasks that remain for the Hero craving more of life's offerings, many of which are available to those from either end of the moral spectrum. Now that you have entered a state of older age and have more time to indulge your interests, consider embarking on the following journeys:

Real Estate Mogul: There are dozens of properties in Albion that you can purchase, including some special properties that, when bought, trigger unique quests (see below). Save up your money and start purchasing as many of these buildings as possible and slowly build an empire worth at least 2.5 million gold!

Side-Quests: One of the ways to continue to build renown and to earn the rights to more titles is to complete the various Archaeologist, Assassination, Bounty Hunter, and Slave Rescue/ Civilian Displacement quests. There are 13 Archaeologist quests and a limitless number of randomly generated quests of the other varieties.

Start a Family: You've probably already married at least once or twice, but is the marriage holding steady? If so, set to having children by having as much unprotected sex as you can. Consider expanding your exploits by starting a second family in another town, or by convincing several prostitutes to accompany you back to your house for an orgy. There are several family- and sex-related Achievements to earn and now is a great time to do so.

Collector: Have you found each and every Gargoyle or Silver Key? Have you unlocked each of the Demon Doors? There are a number of things to collect in Albion, and many more secrets to discover. Scour the land with an area-by-area search with this book's 'Albion Atlas' as your guide to find every hidden chest, dig spot, tomb, and so much more in the game.

True Gamer: Your freedom from the need to search for treasure and slaughter ruthless enemies means that you have more time to enjoy more leisurely pursuits such as gambling, gladiatorial combat, and the ever-popular cardboard shooting range. Or perhaps you simply want to kick back and enjoy the stress-free life of a woodcutter or bartender? Now is a great time to max out your job skills, boost your gambler rating, and win all the prizes at the Shooting Range and Crucible in Westcliff.

Mentor Others: There is arguably no better way to spend your later years in life than by being a mentor for someone much less experienced. Log into Xbox LIVE and offer your wisdom, experience, and talents to the other would-be Heroes in Albion by helping accompany them in their adventures. Though they will surely benefit from your experience and support, remember to let your prospective protégé suffer through their own mistakes and to only offer advice when it is requested.

Additional Quests

Complete the following quests to see everything that Albion has to offer. You may have encountered some of these during Adulthood.

Brightwood Tower

Garth's research has made his old home a dangerous place to be. Do you dare sleep in the tower?

	Good: -
	Evil: -

Reward	Renown	Good	Evil	Purity	Corruption
Son of Chesty	3000	-	-	-	-

Fight through the throngs of Spire guards near the entrance to Brightwood Tower and purchase the property (Base Value of 250,000 Gold). It's expensive, but the Spire guards no longer appear once you own Brightwood Tower. The previous owner, Garth, has left a note for you warning you of the strange dreams you can expect to have when sleeping in the bed at the top of the tower. Take **Garth's Journal** from the chest atop the tower, shoot the Gargoyle through the window, then sleep in the bed to be whisked away in a dream to Nightmare Hollow.

Your first visit to Nightmare Hollow takes place with you as a child. You're armed with all your current powers and weapons, but you're in the body of an eight year old. Head down the path to the central area and approach the chest in the middle of the clearing. This chest isn't an ordinary chest, it's a special chest that loves to play practical jokes on its "friends" and it now thinks you're its Super Best Friend. You need to follow Chesty through Nightmare Hollow as it disappears and reappears in five different places. Every time you discover its new hiding spot it will summon a wave of enemies as a joke. You'll need to defeat waves of giant beetles, hobbes, hollow men, banshees, and finally balverines. Only after slaughtering all of Chesty's "other friends" will you finally receive Chesty's prized contents: **Diamond of Sorrow** and **100,000 Gold**. The Diamond of Sorrow carries with it a base value of 100,000 Gold!

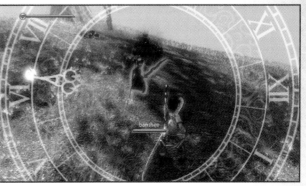

A Hard Night's Dream

Use the bed in the clearing near the final chest location to return to Brightwood Tower, then sleep in the tower's bed a second time. You'll return to Nightmare Hollow as an adult and will have full use of your expressions. Retrace your steps through the area towards the final chest location from your earlier visit and perform the Chicken expression in front of the Expression Statue to open the door to the cabin. Head inside to collect the **Emerald** from the chest. Just beware the banshee!

Quest End

BUY THE FARM!

Put the 100,000 Gold you just earned from Nightmare Hollow to use in purchasing Brightwood Farm from the Giles family. Get the Portcullis Key from the farmer's bedroom then access the Farm Cellar via the trapdoor in the barn. (If you killed Farmer Giles, then you will find the key in his grave.) Navigate the underground labyrinth with your faithful furry companion and dig up **The Enforcer**, the legendary blunderbuss!

The Hit

A contract has been taken out on your life.

	Good: -
	Evil: -

Reward	Renown	Good	Evil	Purity	Corruption
Lucien's Contract	7500	-	-	-	-

You'll no doubt notice after completing the *Hero of Will* quest that you are the target of an increasing number of ambushes. This is because a contract has been taken out on your life and small gangs of highwaymen have flocked to all of the areas where you might be in hopes of being the lucky bunch to bring you down. Of course, you're not aware of this contract at first. It's only after obtaining all four **Sketch Fragments** that you become aware of the contract, and where the Highwaymen's Guild is based.

This quest will not activate until after you've found the four Sketch Fragments and the only way to do that is by defeating at least four groups of highwaymen attackers while out traveling. Every specific group of highwaymen ambushers holds a Sketch Fragment for this quest. However, several ambushes include highwaymen that aren't associated with a quest. You'll have to roam the areas at Bower Lake, along the path in Bandit Coast, in Brightwood, at Westcliff, and in Rookridge.

Once you have all four pieces and know that the Highwaymen's Guild is based in Brightwood, fast-travel there and pay a visit to the Forsaken Fortress on the outskirts of the area. Forsaken Fortress is crawling with highwaymen, but it's their leader, Darius Zing, that you're really after. Use Time Control, Raise Dead, and what should be a pair of very powerful weapons to crash through the lesser highwaymen to get to their leader. Shoot spells at him and use Sub-Targeting to blast away at his head from afar. Chase him to the rear of the fortress and finish him off to complete the quest.

Quest End

Introduction

Cast of Characters

The Hero's Way

Quest Guide

Albion Atlas

Weapons of Yore

Items & Clothing

Pub Games, Jobs & More

Enemies

Castle Fairfax

Albion's most magnificent, and most expensive, property is available for sale.

Reward	Renown	Good	Evil	Purity	Corruption
Sex Change Souvenir	10,000	-	-	-	-

Good: -

Evil: -

It's not going to be easy, but you need to save up 1,000,000 Gold and purchase Castle Fairfax to gain access to the valuable contents within the castle (search the furniture for valuable money bags), not to mention this quest. Purchasing Castle Fairfax is also important for the incredibly valuable sleeping bonuses it gives you when you sleep in Lord Lucien's former bed.

Get Rich Quick

There are many ways to go about earning the riches needed to acquire the castle, but chief among them is maximizing your bartending ability and spending time working at one of the taverns. With a fully-maxed gold multiplier, at a Level 5 salary, you can earn as much as 1125 gold for every beer you pour! Another powerful way to earn money is to equip the Golden Touch augment and head to The Crucible. Slaughter wave after wave of enemies to gain 50 gold per kill. Together with bonuses earned from the crowd, The Crucible can yield plenty of gold in a short amount of time.

Take your time exploring the castle when you first enter it. Use the 50 Silver Keys to unlock the chest in the throne room, shoot the final Gargoyle in the library, and have a good thorough look around. When ready to continue with the quest, head down the eastern hall to the master suite and sleep in the regal bed. The butler will meet you when you wake to inform you of the bandits that are attacking the castle from a secret entrance in Fairfax Tomb.

The first wave attacks in the bedroom shortly after the butler tells you of the ambush. Ready your most powerful inferno spell and release it as soon as the bandits enter the room. Follow the glowing path down the hall to the throne room where the next wave is set to attack. Use a combination of Time Control, Inferno, and Sub-Targeting with either The Enforcer or The Perforator to eliminate the bandits and kill the bandit chief in the library. The butler then reveals the entrance to Fairfax Tomb, where you must go to finish the bandit extermination.

Sub Area

Fairfax Tomb

Descend into the secret tomb and pull the right-hand lever in the room ahead to open the gates to each of the small alcoves off the side of the main path. Put down the bandits that attack and take a few moments to follow your dog to the treasure and dig spots in these small side-rooms. Pull the left-hand gate to continue to the large room with the spiraling staircase. Blast your way to the bottom of the room and exit through the doorway opposite the stairs.

Use your Inferno spell and legendary weapons to crush the hobbes in this corner of the tomb and continue to the room with the flit switch. Shoot and slash the flit switch as necessary to unlock the door to the next area. The room with the row of sarcophagi has one of the trickiest flit switches in all of Albion. Hit it with magic, then run to the right and shoot it each time it repositions itself to guide it down from the ledge to where you can hit it at close-range.

Castle Fairfax
Pick up the potion. You can then drink it or leave the tomb. If you leave without drinking it, the potion will evaporate.

Pick Up

The final room contains several chests and the **Potion of Transmogrification**. If you've ever held the secret desire to have a sex-change, now is the time to do it or forever hold your peace (and your privates).

Sub-Area End

Quest End

Introduction
Cast of Characters
The Hero's Way
Quest Guide
Albion Atlas
Weapons of Yore
Items & Clothing
Pub Games, Jobs & More
Enemies

Blackmail!

Someone knows you're a bigamist!

Reward	Renown	Good	Evil	Purity	Corruption
-	1000	-	-30	10	-20

👍 **Pure:** Refuse to pay off the blackmailer.

😈 **Evil:** Kill or pay off the blackmailer.

It's pretty easy to live a double life, married to two different people, if you have the money to distract the spouses from your perpetual absence. That is, until someone decides to blackmail you! This quest will eventually become active during one of your visits home, after you've maintained two separate marriages for a while. Your spouse will tell you a letter had come from someone, a Blackmail Letter!

Head to Bowerstone Market and meet Kenneth, the blackmailer, under the bridge on the Bower Lake side of the river. If you're going to do the pure thing, you'll refuse to pay off the blackmailer

and take whatever punishment and embarrassment you have coming your way. That's the only right thing to do.

EVIL ALTERNATIVE

DON'T MESS WITH A HERO'S FAMILY!

Let us be honest here for a moment. If you were really concerned about doing what's right and pure, you wouldn't be married to two different people in the first place. So with that in mind, we suggest you kill Kenneth. Nobody should ever butt their nose into another family's affairs, and certainly not this Kenneth punk! Meet him under the bridge and slice his throat, then use the 2000 gold you would have given him and buy your wives and/or husbands some nice gifts. This way everyone is happy and your secret is safe. At least for now…

Blackmail!
Pay Kenneth 2,000 gold.
Accept

Quest End

105

The Rescue

Your child has entered a perilous cave.

 Good: Head to Hobbe Cave and save your child.

 Evil: -

Reward	Renown	Good	Evil	Purity	Corruption
Hobbe Staff Head	1500	30	-	-	-

Kids get into the darndest predicaments, and yours is no exception. Not long after your child turns nine years old (roughly 20 to 30 minutes of gameplay after his birth), you'll be notified by your spouse that the child has gone missing. He left a letter saying that he wants to be an adventurer like you and has run off to explore the Hobbe Cave in Rookridge. Visit your spouse to get the letter and to assure them that everything will be fine, then head off to Hobbe Cave.

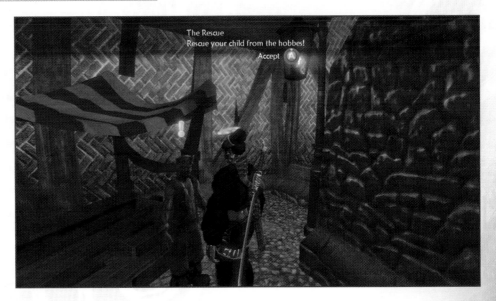

The Hobbe Cave has many, many more hobbes (were you expecting banshees?) in it than when you first visited it so many years ago before the bridge was rebuilt. Although the hobbes have indeed grown more numerous and far stronger, so have you. Unveil your mighty powers with a powerful Vortex spell and a lengthy chain attack, preferably with the Daichi! Push on deeper into the cave, following the glowing path, while using Sub-Targeting to blast away at the hobbes stomping towards you through the narrow cave.

The final hobbe in the dead-end portion of the cave has a Cage Key on its person, uh, self. Use the key to unlock the cage with your child in it, then lead them up the narrow walkway to the ladder exit. The footpath in the canyon has many hobbes on it and you need to keep your kid safe. Snipe from afar to reduce the number of hobbes you'll have to deal with, then charge up a powerful Force Push spell to knock the others over the edge.

Quest End

Albion Atlas

Our Hero's journey takes place in Albion, a sprawling expanse of land that includes a diverse array of towns, villages, and countryside. The struggle to defeat Lord Lucien will lead from the mountains to the sea, through underground caves, and to faraway island beaches. They say an explorer is only as good as their maps, and if that's the case you're going to be one excellent adventurer! This section of the book contains maps for every area in Albion, complete with details on item locations, Demon Doors, properties and merchants, and much more. Travel well.

Randomized Treasures

You'll find that many of the Chests, Dig Spots, & Dive Spots throughout Albion offer different items on separate play-throughs. Jewelry, dyes, potions, and food items are more likely to be randomized. The items presented in the Atlas are intended to provide a quick overview of what you may find while adventuring.

How to Use this Atlas

This atlas details all the information necessary to uncover the secrets of each town, tomb, countryside, and cave. However, upon looking at the vast amount of data and images, you may feel that this is a daunting section. Nothing could be further from the truth. Every element is intentionally designed to be the easiest method to present the locations of secrets, spotlight businesses and homes, jobs, pub games, and merchants in the area.

(1)	**AREA NAME AND**	THERE ARE FOUR TYPES OF AREAS INDICATED THROUGHOUT THE ATLAS: CAVES, COUNTRYSIDES, TOMBS, &
(2)	**AREA TYPE**	TOWNS. HOWEVER, SOME AREAS ARE JUST TOO MYSTERIOUS AND DEFY DESCRIPTION...
(3)	**AREA SYNOPSIS**	TAKE A SECOND TO LEARN ABOUT THE AREA. THIS PROVIDES A PROPER INTRODUCTION BEFORE YOU DECIDE TO RUSH INTO THE AREA.
(4)	**MAP REFERENCE TAB**	QUICKLY FIND THE AREA YOU WANT BY FLIPPING THROUGH THE REFERENCE TABS.
(5)	**COLLECTIBLE SYNOPSIS**	GET AN IDEA ABOUT HOW MANY GOODIES ARE IN THE AREA.
(6)	**AVAILABLE JOBS & PUB GAMES**	FEEL LIKE WORKING OR PLAYING? THIS TELLS YOU WHAT YOU CAN DO TO EARN SOME GOLD—OR LOSE IT.
(7)	**NEIGHBORING REGIONS**	THIS PROVIDES AN ACCURATE DESCRIPTION FOR THE TRAVEL TIME NECESSARY TO REACH ANOTHER REGION AND THE GENERAL DIRECTION IN WHICH THAT AREA LIES.
(8)	**AREA MAP**	THE MAPS PROVIDE CALLOUTS FOR EVERY SECRET AND HIDDEN ELEMENT IN THE AREA: CHESTS, DEMON DOORS, DIG SPOTS, DIVE SPOTS, GARGOYLES, & SILVER KEYS. THEY RELATE DIRECTLY TO THE ASSOCIATED TABLES IN THE AREA SECTION.
(9)	**QUESTS AND NOTES**	SOME AREAS HAVE QUESTS OR DATA THAT DESERVE TO BE MENTIONED IN THE ATLAS ITSELF. TAKE A MOMENT TO READ THESE BEFORE LEAVING (OR EVEN ENTERING) AN AREA.
(10)	**TREASURE OF THE LAND**	THIS IS THE SECTION THAT PROVIDES ALL THE DETAILS ON ALL THE HIDDEN ELEMENTS IN THE AREA. MOST HEROES ARE CONCERNED WITH THREE THINGS: COMBAT, QUEST, & TREASURE. THIS SECTION PROVIDES ALL YOU NEED TO KNOW ABOUT THE LATTER.
(11)	**CHESTS**	EACH CHEST ENTRY INDICATES HOW MANY SILVER KEYS (IF ANY) ARE REQUIRED TO OPEN THE CHEST, WHERE THE CHEST CAN BE FOUND, AND THE CONTENTS OF THE CHEST. WHAT MORE DO YOU NEED TO KNOW?
(12)	**DIG SPOTS**	YOU DOG KNOWS WHEN THERE ARE BURIED SECRETS WAITING TO BE DISCOVERED; THIS TABLE INDICATES WHAT'S TO BE FOUND. REMINDER: THE DOG MUST BE MAXED IN TREASURE HUNTING IN ORDER TO FIND ALL THE DIG SPOTS.
(13)	**DIVE SPOTS**	FELL LIKE A SWIM? TAKE A DIVE AND BRING UP SOME BURIED TREASURE OF YOUR VERY OWN.
(14)	**GARGOYLES**	THESE LITTLE BEASTIES HIDE THROUGHOUT ALBION AND ARE PARTS OF A REGION-SPANNING QUEST THAT'LL TAKE YOU MOST OF YOUR HEROIC CAREER. FOLLOW THE INSTRUCTIONS AND CHECK THEM OFF YOUR LIST ONE BY ONE.
(15)	**SILVER KEYS**	YOU'LL NEED TO REMAIN VIGILANT AND FIND EVERY LAST ONE OF ALBION'S SILVER KEYS TO OPEN CHESTS THAT CONTAIN INCREDIBLE TREASURE.
(16)	**DEMON DOOR**	EACH DEMON DOOR REQUIRES SOMETHING OF YOUR HERO AND THESE ENTRIES PROVIDE THE STRATEGY FOR YOU TO OPEN EACH. HOWEVER, DEPENDING ON YOUR MORAL TENDENCIES, THERE MAY BE SOME THAT YOU ARE BETTER OFF SKIPPING...
(17)	**MERCHANT DIRECTORY**	WITH A BRIEF SUMMARY OF THE AREA'S ECONOMIC STANDING AND POINTS OF INTEREST, THE MERCHANT DIRECTORY IS A SHOPPER'S NECESSITY. THE TABLE SHOWS WHAT WARES ARE AVAILABLE AND INDICATES THE HIGHEST QUALITY OF GOODS THAT CAN BE PURCHASED AT EACH ESTABLISHMENT.
(18)	**REAL ESTATE SNAPSHOT**	ONCE AGAIN, A SUMMARY PROVIDES ALL THE INFORMATION NECESSARY FOR THE SERIOUS INVESTOR. FOR THOSE INTERESTED IN BECOMING PROPERTY MAGNATES SHOULD TAKE SPECIAL NOTICE OF THE INFORMATION FOUND IN THIS SECTION.
(19)	**SPOTLIGHT HOME AND BUSINESS**	SOME REGIONS HAVE CERTAIN GEMS THAT SHOULD BE SNATCHED UP AS SOON AS POSSIBLE. ALONG WITH THE BASIC INFORMATION ON THE PROPERTY VALUE AND OWNER, THIS SECTION PROVIDES ANY BONUSES THAT CAN BE GAINED BY PURCHASING THE PROPERTY. LASTLY, THE DESCRIPTION OFFERS INSIGHT AND PURCHASING STRATEGIES THAT'LL COME IN HANDY TO ANYONE INTERESTED.

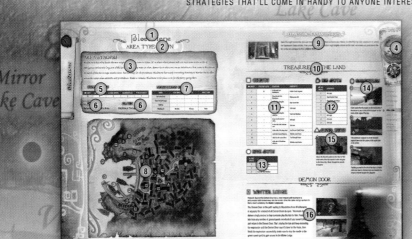

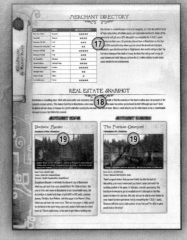

Archon's Knot
AREA TYPE: TOMB

AREA SYNOPSIS

Archon's Knot is a highly secretive tomb located in the Brightwood region. It is predominantly devoid of enemies, but contains a series of puzzles that will challenge your mind as well as your weaponry. This tomb can only be accessed after your Hero returns from the Spire and leaps off Brightwood Tower into a well that is otherwise out of reach. Ascend Brightwood Tower to the landing where the Cullis Gate is and leap from the tower at the gap in the railing to freefall into the well. Make your way past the spiked floors and locked gates (for which Archon's Knot is known) to exit high on the side of a mountain near a chest containing the Daichi, the single, best melee weapon in Albion!

COLLECTIBLES

🎁 CHEST	⚒ DIG SPOTS	⚓ DIVE SPOTS	🗿 GARGOYLES	🗝 SILVER KEYS
1	1	1	1	1

NEIGHBORING REGIONS

NAME	DISTANCE	TIME	DIRECTION
Brightwood	-	-	-

Untangling the Knot

If you thought finding Archon's Knot was tricky, wait till you see the inside! Archon's Knot consists of several floors and stairs that spiral upwards in a twisted, sideways figure-eight. There's only one way to proceed through the tomb so don't worry about getting lost. Just seek the flit switch on the first floor, then ascend past the spike floors to the Expression Statue on the upper level. Use the Bloodlust Roar expression to satisfy the Expression Statue and follow the caged flit switch upstairs to the next spiked floor. Walk across the spiked panels that the flit switch hovers over to cross the room safely. Continue the ascent and exit the tomb to a ledge in Brightwood.

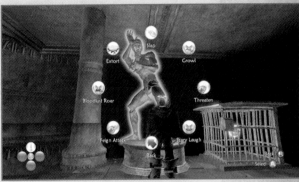

TREASURE OF THE LAND

CHESTS

🗝 CHEST	⚷ SILVER KEYS	LOCATION	CONTENTS
1	-	Ascend to the upper floor of the tomb.	Cursed Warrior Augment

SILVER KEYS

Use the Bloodlust Roar expression to release the flit switch from the cage next to the Expression Statue and follow it across the spiked panels on the upper floor to reach the Silver Key near the gate.

DIVE SPOTS

⚓ DIVE SPOTS	CONTENTS
1	Shiner Dye

DIG SPOTS

🪏 DIG SPOTS	CONTENTS
1	Precious Necklace

GARGOYLES

The Gargoyle is on the wall directly behind you after you make your initial splash-landing in the tomb. Climb out of the water to shoot it.

Bandit Coast
AREA TYPE: COUNTRYSIDE

AREA SYNOPSIS

Known as one of the most dangerous places in all of Albion, the Bandit Coast is the home of ruthless bandits and the even scarier highwaymen. Only those with a significant need to visit Westcliff would ever dare chance traveling this section of road. Not only is this area heavily patrolled by men of a menacing ilk, but it even houses watchtowers and a fortified camp. Sure, there is plenty of treasure to collect along the journey—and a small cave to inspect—but you mustn't let your guard down for a single moment in these parts.

COLLECTIBLES

🗝 CHEST	⛏ DIG SPOTS	⚓ DIVE SPOTS	🗿 GARGOYLES	🔑 SILVER KEYS
8	6	0	2	1

NEIGHBORING REGIONS

NAME	DISTANCE	TIME	DIRECTION
Brightwood	96 miles	21 hours	East
Westcliff	64 miles	14 hours	Northwest

SLUMBER PARTY!

Just because there aren't any buildings to buy in the Bandit Coast doesn't mean you can't get a good night's rest. Get some sleep in the small shed inside the fort once you've defeated all the enemies in the area.

TREASURE OF THE LAND

⬛ CHESTS

🧰 CHEST	🗝 SILVER KEYS	LOCATION	CONTENTS
1	-	Near the columns by the slave cages.	Resurrection Phial and Children's Health Potion x2
2	10	In a patch of woods after the fork.	1000 Gold
3	-	Inside the cave along the cliffs.	Troll Strength Potion
4	-	In the clearing before the bridge.	Emerald
5	-	Inside the fort, to the north.	Cure-All Health Potion
6	-	Atop the tower in the fort.	Watered Down XP Potion
7	-	On the path behind the tower.	Highwayman Coat
8	-	Near the wagons inside the fort.	Light Oak Crossbow

⬛ GARGOYLES

Follow the trail along the cliffs to the small cave entrance at the far end. Approach the chest in the center and turn left to spot the Gargoyle near the rocks.

Climb the tower in the highwayman's fortress and shoot the Gargoyle on the pillar at the top.

△ SILVER KEYS

01

Drop off the ledge to the south of the trail before the hairpin turn near the watchtower.

◭ DIG SPOTS

🕹 DIG SPOTS	CONTENTS
1	Shiny Apple
2	Fumbling Skill Potion
3	Beetle Strength Potion
4	300 Gold
5	500 Gold
6	300 Gold

Bloodstone
AREA TYPE: TOWN

AREA SYNOPSIS

Bloodstone is beyond a doubt the most rough-and-tumble town in Albion. It's a place where pirates and con-men come to live a life of indulgence without the long arm of the law laying its dirty mitts on them. Rumor has it the town's many inhabitants first came to Bloodstone in search of the picturesque seaside views, but then stay for the prostitutes. Bloodstone has nearly everything Bowerstone Market has to offer, minus the upper-class attitudes and prudishness. Make no mistake: Bloodstone is the place to be for the party-going Hero.

COLLECTIBLES

🗝 CHEST	⚒ DIG SPOTS	⚓ DIVE SPOTS	👁 GARGOYLES	🔑 SILVER KEYS
11	9	3	3	1

NEIGHBORING REGIONS

NAME	DISTANCE	TIME	DIRECTION
Hall of the Dead	-	-	-
Reaver's Rear Passage	-	-	-
Sinkhole	-	-	-
Wraithmarsh	60 miles	15 hours	North

JOBS

Bartender at The Leper's Arms

GAMES

Bloodstone at The Leper's Arms

EXPRESSION OF A SARCOPHAGUS

Open the crypt nearest the entrance from Wraithmarsh to find an Expression Statue. Use the Pick Up Line expression to satisfy the Expression Statue inside. This unlocks the door to another crypt slightly farther up the road. Go inside and push aside the lid on the sarcophagus to find a **Silver Key**

TREASURE OF THE LAND

CHESTS

CHEST	SILVER KEYS	LOCATION	CONTENTS
1	15	On the path from Wraithmarsh.	Golden Touch Augment
2	-	Along the path into Bloodstone.	Highwayman Hat
3	-	In a building along the waterfront.	Steel Turret Rifle
4	-	In a building along the waterfront.	1500 Gold
5	-	In a building along the waterfront.	Solid Gold Necklace
6	-	Jump onto the stack of crates.	400 Gold
7	-	On the trail to the Sinkhole cave.	300 Gold
8	-	In the cellar of the large shed.	Live Forever Health Potion
9	-	Inside the Frennick Mansion.	Obsidian Java Potion
10	-	Steal from the second floor.	Troll Strength Potion
11	-	In the attic of Bloodstone Mansion.	Obsidian Java Postion

DIG SPOTS

DIG SPOTS	CONTENTS
1	100 Gold
2	Steel Flintlock Pistol
3	Sleepy Bean Java Potion
4	Beggar's Ring
5	Bits O' Beef Pie
6	500 Gold
7	500 Gold
8	250 Gold
9	500 Gold

SILVER KEYS

01

Attack the blue flit switch on the floor of this cellar with a Flourish attack to raise the gate to the Silver Key. Break through the barrels to reach it.

GARGOYLES

01

Swim out to the tiny beach on the north side of the harbor to get a shot at the Gargoyle on the rocks at the edge of the bay.

02

This particular Gargoyle is on the wooden support tower for the crane on the south side of the docks.

03

Position yourself to the left of the stack of crates (with your back to the sea) and look towards the house on the hill to spot the Gargoyle.

DIVE SPOTS

DIVE SPOTS	CONTENTS
1	Sleepy Bean Java Potion
2	Silver Key
3	Economy Value Necklace

DEMON DOOR

1 WINTER LODGE

Reward: Beyond the Demon Door lies a snow-draped path leading to a picturesque cabin tucked deep into the woods. Enter the cabin and go upstairs to find a chest containing the **Master Longsword**.

The Demon Door on the path leading to Bloodstone from Wraithmarsh is arguably the simplest of all Demon Doors to open. This music-loving demon simply desires to hear someone play the lute for him. Purchase the lute from any number of general goods merchants if you haven't already and return to the Demon Door. Start playing the lute and keep extending the expression until the Demon Door says it's time for the finale, then finish the expression successfully (make sure to stop the needle in the green sweet spot) to gain access to the Winter Lodge.

MERCHANT DIRECTORY

SHOP	WARES	MAX PRODUCT QUALITY
Blood from a Stone	Augments	★★★★★
Bloodsmith	Weapons	★★★★
Bloodstone Fish Stall	Food	★★★
Bloodstone Fruit & Veg Stall	Food	★★
Bloodstone Gift Stall	Gifts	★★★★★
Bloodstone Pie Stall	Food	★★★
Curl Up and Die	Hairstylist	★★★
Fiendish Fashions	Clothing & Dyes	★★★★
The Furniture Graveyard	Furniture	★★★★★
The Leper's Arms	Tavern	★★
Needles of Death	Tattoos	★
Your Health is Low	Potions	★★★★★

Bloodstone is a fantastic place to do your shopping, as it has the perfect blend of high-value items, affordable goods, and appreciative merchants. Many of the merchants will gift you a 25% discount if you complete the *T.O.B.Y.* quest and return to their town. Of particular interest here in Bloodstone is the Curl Up and Die hairstylist shop where you can obtain the dreadlocks hairstyle needed to open the Demon Door in Brightwood. Also worth noting is that The Furniture Graveyard has loads of luxury furniture that will go well in any of your homes and really help you achieve the 2.5 million dollars in real estate value needed for the Achievement.

REAL ESTATE SNAPSHOT

Bloodstone is a bustling place, filled with some pretty wild characters, but the unfortunate truth is that the economy in this town is rather poor on account of the rampant criminal activity. This makes investing in Bloodstone a wise move on account of the super low prices you're bound to find! Although you won't likely be able to sell any shops or houses for a profit until after running the con-man Toby out of town, this is a small price to pay for what stands to be a considerable increase in prices that follow his removal.

SPOTLIGHT HOME

Bloodstone Mansion
Bloodstone Hilltop, Bloodstone

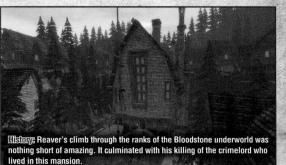

History: Reaver's climb through the ranks of the Bloodstone underworld was nothing short of amazing. It culminated with his killing of the crimelord who lived in this mansion.

Base Value: 88,200 Gold
Owner: Adam the Househusband
Bonuses: Health Regeneration, Speed Boost

Bloodstone Mansion is definitely the house to buy in Bloodstone when you get back from your second trip to The Tattered Spire. Not only is it the only home in Bloodstone of any considerable value, but its furniture is loaded with bags of gold (500 to 750 each), precious jewelry, Obsidian Java Potions, and also pages from Reaver's Diary which you can hear him read aloud. There are five pages in total; search the furniture in the main living space and upstairs bedrooms to collect them all. They're quite funny, so be sure to give them a looking over.

SPOTLIGHT BUSINESS

The Furniture Graveyard
8 Bloodstone Hill, Bloodstone

History: A delightful selection of furniture, with optional torture attachments.

Base Value: 42,000 Gold
Owner: Rebecca the Furniture Seller

There's a good chance that you won't really dig into the task of decorating your many homes until you defeat Lucien and reach the sandbox portion of the game. In that case, consider purchasing The Furniture Graveyard to get an excellent owner's discount on the fine luxury furniture for sale here. Not only will you be able to save money in your future furniture purchases, but by completing the *T.O.B.Y.* quest, Rebecca will have such a high opinion of you that you'll be able to get a great deal on the shop!

Bower Lake
AREA TYPE: COUNTRYSIDE

AREA SYNOPSIS

The Bower Lake region is home to the area's massive namesake lake, surrounded by hills and forest on all sides. A band of gypsies makes their home in the hills to the south of the lake, but much of this region is inhabited only by rabbits, giant beetles, and bandits. A small island in the center of the lake serves as the entrance to the Guild Cave—only those with the Bower Lake Tomb Seal may enter. This isn't the only cave in the area, however. There are three nondescript caves along the southern perimeter of the area that contain chests within—one each. Bower Lake is a unique area in that it contains some semblance of civilized society, thanks to the gypsies, yet the area maintains its rustic charm and wild nature, especially after nightfall...

COLLECTIBLES

🧰 CHEST	🔨 DIG SPOTS	⚓ DIVE SPOTS	🗿 GARGOYLES	🗝 SILVER KEYS
17	8	4	4	3

NEIGHBORING REGIONS

NAME	DISTANCE	TIME	DIRECTION
Bowerstone Market	120 miles	27 hours	West
Brightwood	90 miles	19 hours	East
Guild Cave	-	-	-
Tomb of Heroes	-	-	-

EVAPORATION HAPPENS

The tiny fishing pond on the north end of the area, uphill from the main lake, actually conceals the entrance to the Tomb of Heroes as well as a chest. This pond will dry up at the start of the *Rescuing Charlie* quest.

Bower Lake

CHESTS

🗝 CHEST	🔑 SILVER KEYS	LOCATION	CONTENTS
1	-	Near caravan in gypsy camp.	Rusty Longsword, Light Splintered Crossbow, Placebo Health Potion, Dog Elixir, Collar of Holding, and Spade
2	-	Near the pond to the east.	Economy Value Necklace
3	1	Under the archway.	100 Gold
4	-	On the eastern shore of the lake.	Soylent Dye
5	-	On the western shore of the lake.	Rusty Flintlock Pistol
6	-	Below the pond to the west.	Assassin Coat
7	1	In the hills west of the river.	"Dog Tricks: The Bunny Hop"
8	-	Near the road to Brightwood.	150 Gold
9	-	In a cave near the Bowerstone road.	100 Gold
10	-	In a cave near Thag's bandit camp.	Amethyst
11	-	Inside Thag's cabin.	Thag's Cage Key, Rancid Beef Jerky, and 300 Gold
12	-	On the south shore of the lake.	Children's Health Potion
13	-	On the tower behind the gypsy camp.	2500 Gold
14	10	Next to the tower near the gypsy camp.	Storm Scar Augment
15	-	In a small cave behind the gypsy camp.	Children's Health Potion
16	-	Behind the gypsy camp, off the trail.	Ruby
17	-	Near the entrance to Tomb of Heroes.	750 Gold

SILVER KEYS

This Silver Key is located on the small island in the center of the lake, behind the tomb.

Look behind the tree near the small pond on the eastern side of the area.

Locate the trail behind the gypsy camp after returning from the Tattered Spire and climb the tower atop the cliff to find this Silver Key.

A GYPSY BLOCKADE

Try as you might, you won't be able to explore the clearing to the east of the gypsy camp until you return from the Tattered Spire as an adult. There are a few old ruins and a cave atop this hill that contain some valuable items. Return to the gypsy camp and locate the trail that was created leading from the camp to the old watchtower while you were away.

DIG SPOTS

🪏 DIG SPOTS	CONTENTS
1	Rubber Ball
2	75 Gold
3	"Treasure Hunting, Book 1" and 40 Gold
4	Condom and "Secret of Castle Fairfax, Pt II"
5	"Treasure Hunting, Book 2"
6	Emerald
7	"Treasure Hunting, Book 4"
8	1000 Gold

The 5-Star Treasure Hunter

You'll only be able to advance your dog to a Level 3 treasure hunter during the Early Adulthood phase of the story, but you can quickly get to Level 5 as soon as you return from the Tattered Spire as an adult. Head to the Bowerstone Bookstore in Bowerstone Market and purchase "Treasure Hunting, Book 3" to level-up the dog's treasure-sniffing ability. Now go to Bower Lake and locate the buried book near the bridge over the river to max out his treasure hunting ability.

DIVE SPOTS

🐚 DIVE SPOTS	CONTENTS
1	Potion of Life
2	Rusty Cutlass
3	Amethyst
4	25 Gold

GARGOYLES

Directly above the arch in the ruined wall, on the west side of the structure.

This one is on the east side of that same archway. It's high up on the tower.

Look for the collection of columns and collapsed walls near the beach to find this one.

Use your Zoom ability to shoot this distant Gargoyle on the cliffs above the waterfall.

DEMON DOOR

1 THE ARID SEA

Reward: The area behind this Demon Door is a desolate wind-blown desert with the debris of a shipwreck strewn across the area. Sitting in the middle of that debris is a chest containing the very helpful **Lucky Charm Augment**.

The Demon Door in Bower Lake fancies itself a tremendous tragedian and has written a 7-act play that it would like you to act out. The Demon Door will read the script and it's up to you to perform the expressions that match the action in the play. You'll need each of the following expressions in order to complete the performance:

Bloodlust Roar	Fart	Middle Finger	Worship
Blow Kiss	Growl	Point & Laugh	
Dance	Laugh	Thrust	

MERCHANT DIRECTORY

SHOP	WARES	MAX PRODUCT QUALITY
Gypsy Stone Cutter	Augments	★★★
Gypsy Tattooist	Tattoos	★
Gypsy Trader	General Goods & Clothing	★★★★★

The gypsies don't have a lot of money and, as such, they don't have a high demand for expensive items. No, they pretty much get by with just the basics. The gypsy merchants in the Bower Lake area focus on a small selection of tattoos—tasteful and otherwise—as well as an assortment of augments and general goods. You'll be hard-pressed to find much in these shops that you can't live without.

REAL ESTATE SNAPSHOT

Bower Lake is a remote area that has been all but left to the woodland creatures. The only permanent encampment is the gypsy camp on the south side of the lake. But, being gypsies, they're content living in caravans that not only have little room for living, but even less for furniture. Pickings are equally slim when it comes to businesses. Two of the three shops are run out of caravans while the other is quite a bit larger. Nobody will get rich investing in the gypsy camp, but using your early riches to purchase the Gypsy Trader and a caravan or two could earn you a considerable return over the duration of your time in Albion.

SPOTLIGHT HOME

Gypsy Caravan
1, Gypsy Camp, Bower Lake

History: A delightful caravan that has traveled far across Albion.

Base Value: 800 Gold
Owner: Hero
Bonuses: Animal Magnetism

This is the caravan where you've lived the ten years since that fateful night in Castle Fairfax. Theresa and her fellow gypsies saw fit to make sure you've had a place to call your own, but you no longer have any use for it. Put the caravan up for rent before leaving the camp. You'll receive 7 gold every five minutes for as long as there is a tenant living there. There aren't a whole lot of people running off to live with the gypsies these days, so it may take a few days for a tenant to arrive.

SPOTLIGHT BUSINESS

Gypsy Trader
5, Gypsy Camp, Bower Lake

History: Items gathered from all over Albion can be found here.

Base Value: 4500 Gold
Owner: Neil the Trader

If you're going to buy a business in the Gypsy Camp, it might as well be the one that does the most business, and that's the Gypsy Trader. Not only is this the shop that you'll be most likely to use (and take advantage of discounts), but the other gypsies use it too. You can expect routine payments of 50 gold or more while you own the business. Even lowering your prices isn't likely to attract too much extra business given the low population and seclusion of the gypsy camp.

Bowerstone Cemetery
AREA TYPE: COUNTRYSIDE

AREA SYNOPSIS

Bowerstone Cemetery is a rather peaceful place, once you come to accept the occasional run-in with the hobbes and hollow men that frequent the darker corners of the area. The cemetery has a large central graveyard, a spookier area near a ghoulish camp of sorts, and also a crypt-lined hill that extends far to the south. There are two separate Expression Statues in this area, as well as a secret underground cave, and a much larger tomb known as Shelley Crypt. Nobody has been tacky enough to open a business inside the confines of the cemetery, but you may encounter the occasional traveling merchant.

COLLECTIBLES

✉ CHEST	⚒ DIG SPOTS	⚓ DIVE SPOTS	🕯 GARGOYLES	⚷ SILVER KEYS
5	7	0	4	3

NEIGHBORING REGIONS

NAME	DISTANCE	TIME	DIRECTION
Bowerstone Old Town	2 miles	1 hour	East
Shelley Crypt	-	-	-

A PAIR OF EXPRESSION STATUES

There are two Expression Statues in this area. The one in the center of the main graveyard requires you to perform the Vulgar Thrust expression. Once the statue is satisfied a flit switch will appear and lead you on a lengthy journey up the hillside to the crypt at the very top. Look for the flit switch to stop in trees and even in other crypts. Shoot it each time it stops and continue the chase to find the chest inside the crypt.

The other Expression Statue is in the slightly swampy section of the cemetery, near the stairs leading down to a locked gate. Use the Point & Laugh expression while targeting the statue to open the gate. Follow the path to a secret underground crypt containing another chest.

TREASURE OF THE LAND

CHESTS

🗃 CHEST	🗝 SILVER KEYS	LOCATION	CONTENTS
1	-	Inside the crypt near the entrance.	200 Gold
2	1	In the primary cemetery courtyard.	Mood Ring
3	10	Inside the crypt on the hilly path.	1000 Gold
4	-	In the crypt at the top of the hill.	Noble Lady's Hat, Precious Necklace, and Porcelain Doll
5	-	Accessed through the underground.	"Dead Handy" and "Dog Tricks! Play Dead"

DIG SPOTS

🔨 DIG SPOTS	CONTENTS
1	100 Gold
2	Percolated Java Potion
3	Divine Carrot
4	Leathery Tan Dye
5	1500 Gold
6	Beggar's Ring
7	Resurrection Phial

SILVER KEYS

Follow your dog to the campsite where all of the clocks are located. The Silver Key is in the shed, behind the barrels.

This Silver Key is in front of the three crypts just below the very top of the hilly path.

The Silver Key is located on the second floor of the gravekeeper's mansion at the north end of the cemetery. Gain access to it during the Love Hurts quest.

GARGOYLES

On the right-hand corner of the mausoleum containing the Normanomicon.

On top of the large mausoleum halfway up the hilly path past the Normanomicon.

Enter the garden at the top of the hilly path and turn to the right to find this Gargoyle.

The Gargoyle is hidden behind the tree branches on the wall beyond the gate. Stand back and shoot through the leaves.

DEMON DOOR

1 FORGOTTEN KEEP

Reward: Walk the narrow corridor to the chest straight ahead to find a **balverine Strength Potion**, **Practiced Skill Potion,** and **Infused Will Potion**.

This is one of the easiest Demon Doors to open in all of Albion and also the first you should make a point of opening. The meat-loving Demon Door simply wants you to give it some meat. Fresh meat. Meat so fresh that it's still alive. This may sound like a rather puzzling request until you turn around and notice the chickens running about. Kick a couple chickens at the Demon Door to feed the stony beast. When you see the chicken splatter against the Demon Door, you know you did well!

REAL ESTATE SNAPSHOT

There is only one piece of property for sale in the Bowerstone Cemetery and that is the Gravekeepers Mansion. It's not cheap, but you'll need to purchase it if you're going to ever gain access to Shelley Crypt.

SPOTLIGHT HOME

Bowerstone Cemetery Mansion

Bowerstone Cemetery

History: Though rather extravagant for its purpose, this has traditionally been the home of the Bowerstone gravekeeper, a job passed down from fathers to sons. It was first built by a rather unusual property magnate, who believed rich nobles would fight over a haunted mansion, since spirits and the undead were often spotted walking the cemetery. He was wrong.

Base Value: 100,000 Gold
Owner: Unknown
Bonuses: Health Bonus and Five Minutes of Fame

The beautiful mansion in the cemetery may not be the best place to set as your marital home, but it's a necessary purchase if you're to ever gain access to Shelley Crypt and the treasures locked away inside it. That being said, you can't actually purchase the Bowerstone Cemetery Mansion unless you complete the *Love Hurts* quest. You'll find a few Witchspotter's Notes inside the house, but little else.

Bowerstone Market
AREA TYPE: TOWN

AREA SYNOPSIS

Welcome to Bowerstone Market, the biggest and brightest town in all of Albion. If you can't find it, sell it, or buy it here, well then it probably doesn't exist! Bowerstone Market is loaded with shops and stalls of every variety, as well as several extremely nice houses for those who want to live close to town. Like all bustling town centers, Bowerstone Market is situated on a massive river that not only has a wealth of sunken trinkets at its bottom, but also a trove of treasure rumored to belong to the Gargoyles! Some may say that Bowerstone Market has too strong of a law enforcement presence, but this keeps the bandits at bay. And doesn't your family deserve a chance to live in a place without fear of being attacked?

COLLECTIBLES

🧰 CHEST	🪏 DIG SPOTS	⚓ DIVE SPOTS	👹 GARGOYLES	🗝 SILVER KEYS
13	15	4	4	2

JOBS

Bowerstone Blacksmith
Bartender at the Cow & Corset

GAMES

Keystone at the Cow & Corset

NEIGHBORING REGIONS

NAME	DISTANCE	TIME	DIRECTION
Bower Lake	120 miles	27 hours	East
Bowerstone Old Town	2 miles	1 hour	North
Fairfax Gardens	2 miles	1 hour	West
Gargoyle's Trove	-	-	-

CELLAR RAIDER

Don't forget to explore the three cellars in Bowerstone Market. There is one in the basement of the furniture store, another near the road to Fairfax Gardens, and a third near the houses to the south of the square.

TREASURE OF THE LAND

☐ CHESTS

🎁 CHEST	⚷ SILVER KEYS	LOCATION	CONTENTS
1	-	Lower floor of the coach house.	"Beginner's Guide to Business" and 200 Gold
2	-	Upstairs in the coach house.	Children's Health Potion
3	-	Upstairs in the coach house.	Pretty Necklace
4	-	Use dive spot to enter gated room.	300 Gold
5	-	On the wharf beneath the bridge.	Sleepy Bean Java Potion
6	-	In the cellar of the Cow & Corset.	Sleepy Bean Java Potion
7	5	Along the road to Fairfax Gardens.	Potion of Life
8	-	Inside the cellar by Fairfax Road.	200 Gold
9	-	Inside the Carriage House.	Emerald
10	-	Behind the stylist's shop.	Attenuated Will Potion
11	-	On the second floor of the house.	Amethyst
12	-	In the backyard of "Bit of Skirt".	Emerald
13	-	In the backyard of the house.	100 Gold

◆ DIG SPOTS

⛏ DIG SPOTS	CONTENTS
1	"Murgo's Big Book of Trading" and Amethyst
2	Percolated Java Potion
3	400 Gold
4	"Understanding the Albion Psyche" and Pure Chocolate
5	Emerald
6	Leathery Tan Dye
7	Golden Apple
8	Mood Ring
9	Concentrated XP Potion
10	Ruby
11	Silver Key
12	Obsidian Java Potion
13	2000 Gold
14	Eternal Love Ring
15	Eternal Love Ring

○ DIVE SPOTS

⚓ DIVE SPOTS	CONTENTS
1	Fishtankarous Dye
2	300 Gold
3	Economy Value Necklace
4	Periwinkle Dye

△ SILVER KEYS

01 Dive into the river near the coach house and swim into the dive spot beneath the dock. This will lead you to the gated room near the main entrance.

02 Descend into the basement of the furniture store, then go deeper into the cellar. Shoot the flit switch above the stairs to open the gate to the Silver Key.

○ GARGOYLES

01 You'll hear him mocking you from the town square. Enter the furniture store by the river and go upstairs to find him.

02 Descend the dirt path along the east side of the river bank. The Gargoyle is just north of the bridge.

03 Run along the city wall on the east side of Bowerstone Market to find this Gargoyle on the wooden tower at the far end.

04 The Gargoyle is on the wall inside the carriage house's garage. It's possible to shoot around the side of the carriage to hit it, but you may also just wait until you return from the Tattered Spire when the carriage won't necessarily be blocking the entrance.

MERCHANT DIRECTORY

SHOP	WARES	MAX PRODUCT QUALITY
The Beautification Factory	Hairstylist	★★★★★
Bit of Skirt	Women's Clothing	★★★★★
Bower Stones	Augments	★★★
Bowerstone Drinks Stall	Drinks	★★★
Bowerstone Fish Stall	Fish	★★★
Bowerstone Fruit & Veg Stall	Food	★★★
Bowerstone Jewelry Store	Jewelry, Books, & Gifts	★★★★★
Bowerstone Meat Stall	Meat	★★★
Bowerstone Pie Stall	Food	★★★
Bowerstone's Big Pile of Stuff	General Goods	★★★
The Cow & Corset	Drinks	★★★
Fiction Burns	Books	★★★★★
Pants!	Men's Clothing & Dyes	★★★★★
Potion in Motion	Potions	★★★★★
Up in Arms	Weapons	★★★
World of Chairs	Furniture & Books	★★★★★

As its name implies, Bowerstone Market is the place to do your shopping in Albion. There isn't a single type of item you can't buy here, but perhaps none more important than the books at the Fiction Burns shop. You can really expand your arsenal of expressions and learned dog tricks with the books for sale in this shop. Heroes looking to maintain a slender figure will indeed want to frequent the Bowerstone Fruit & Veg Stall for their abundant celery selection. Take your time wandering the shops here and be sure to return often as the inventory changes, particularly as your shopping helps to elevate the town's economy.

REAL ESTATE SNAPSHOT

Bowerstone Market serves as the downtown area for all of Bowerstone and although it has several helpful shops and appealing homes, the prices are actually quite affordable. The stalls on the bridge provide the perfect starter investment for young Heroes and those with a bit more gold in the bank can look to purchasing the more established businesses and even some of the homes along the road to Fairfax Gardens.

SPOTLIGHT HOME

The Silk Moon
4 Market Square, Bowerstone Market

History: This was not only the house of one of the finest seamstresses in Albion, it is also the place where she created many of her most beautiful fashion designs. There is still an air of stylishness permeating the very walls.

Base Value: 3600 Gold
Owner: Faye the Jeweler
Bonuses: Animal Magnetism

This is a great home to purchase early on as it's already well-furnished and, thanks to its proximity to the jewelry stall, the owner will immediately rent the house from you (provided you don't jack the rent up too high). Of course, you don't have to rent it out. Who can blame you for wanting to move in to a house right next to the Cow & Corset? Sure, it might be loud at night, but you'd never have to worry about drinking & carriaging again!

SPOTLIGHT BUSINESS

Fiction Burns
3 Market Square, Bowerstone Market

History: Improve your mind, your soul and owner's pockets. Buy a book!

Base Value: 16,000 Gold
Owner: Robert the Shopkeeper

There are a lot of shops to purchase in Bowerstone Market and it could be said that owning the Cow & Corset would bring the most bang for your buck. We don't disagree, but the Fiction Burns shop is the only special property in Bowerstone Market and owning it provides certain tangible benefits. For starters, you can gain a significant discount on all of the books in the shop. This can come in handy when looking to acquire the seedier expression manuals. More importantly, owning Fiction Burns allows you to raid the bookshelves in the attic and acquire the **Book of Worship**, a one-of-a-kind book needed to gain the Completionist Achievement.

Bowerstone Old Town
AREA TYPE: TOWN

AREA SYNOPSIS

Regardless of your choice as a child, you'll barely recognize Bowerstone Old Town when you return to it after your years at the gypsy camp. Those who decided to give the search warrants to Derek as a child will find their old stomping grounds to be a welcoming, if somewhat snobby, neighborhood filled with manicured lawns, picture-perfect homes, and a satisfying selection of street vendors. You will find none of this if you gave the search warrants to Arfur. Instead you'll find a town not only overrun with criminal activity, but one that is falling apart before your very eyes. Although you will be able to gain a few "Assassination Society" jobs in Old Town if you give the search warrants to Arfur as a child, this pales in comparison to what you stand to gain if you do the right thing and give them to Derek.

COLLECTIBLES

CHEST	DIG SPOTS	DIVE SPOTS	GARGOYLES	SILVER KEYS
7	13	0	2	3

NEIGHBORING REGIONS

NAME	DISTANCE	TIME	DIRECTION
Bowerstone Cemetery	2 miles	1 hour	West
Bowerstone Market	2 miles	1 hour	South
Rookridge	85 miles	15 hours	North

A TALE OF TWO CITIES

The slums version of Old Town lies in stark contrast to the neighboring Bowerstone Market. Everything is dilapidated, there are no guards keeping the peace, and beggars and prostitutes roam the streets while assassins stalk the alleys. A Hero seeking a life of purity will be far from comfortable in this place, but an immoral and corrupt Hero will find it to be a veritable playground. Someone can do a lot of damage when there aren't any guards around to stop them...

TREASURE OF THE LAND

CHESTS

CHEST	SILVER KEYS	LOCATION	CONTENTS
1	-	In a cellar along the main road.	Civil Ring
2	-	In a cellar in the eastern alley.	250 Gold
3	5	Along the road to Rookridge.	500 Gold
4	-	On the balcony at the House of Might.	Attenuated Will Potion
5	-	Upstairs at The Dark Mark house.	Watered Down XP Potion
6	-	Upstairs at The Bennett House.	Attenuated Will Potion
7	-	Upstairs at The Helping Hand house.	Hobbe Strength Potion

DIG SPOTS

DIG SPOTS	CONTENTS
1	Jet
2	300 Gold
3	Fumbling Skill Potion
4	Emerald
5	300 Gold
6	Epiphanic Blueberry Pie
7	The Yellow Fairy
8	Instant Java Potion
9	Kangarouge Dye
10	1500 Gold
11	Solid Gold Necklace
12	Concentrated Will Potion
13	1000 Gold

GARGOYLES

01

On the wooden tower next to the warehouse. Shoot it from in front of the exit to Rookridge.

02

You'll hear it outside, but it's actually in the stairwell of The Felling Residence.

◭ SILVER KEYS

01 Loop around the buildings east of the main road into Old Town and venture into the cellar near the stalls to find this Silver Key.

02 Enter the warehouse on the edge of town and look behind the crates under the stairs to find this Silver Key.

03 Enter the Invisible Hand house across from the town exit to Rookridge and head out onto the second floor balcony to find this Silver Key. You will likely have to break the doors unless you buy the house outright.

MERCHANT DIRECTORY

SHOP	WARES	MAX PRODUCT QUALITY
Human Museum (Slums)	Tattoos	★
Old Town Alchemists	Potions	★★★★
Old Town Clothing Stall	Clothing	★★★★★
Old Town Food Stall	Food & Drink	★★★★
Old Town General Store (Slums)	General Goods	★★
Old Town Gift Stall	Gifts	★★★★★
Old Town Miscellany Stall	General Goods	★★★
Old Town Weapons	Weapons	★★★★

Those who gave the warrants to Arfur as a child will find precious little shopping opportunities in the slums that decision has led to. On the other hand, Bowerstone Old Town is the perfect place to come shopping if you received Derek's special 50% discount. The numerous stalls in the beautified version of Old Town have myriad useful items, many of which can go a long way towards keeping you fit, healthy, and attractive. There are huge savings to be made here, so return frequently.

REAL ESTATE SNAPSHOT

Whether Bowerstone Old Town was transformed into a trendy upscale neighborhood or plummeted into lawless slums only matters as far as the business opportunities are concerned. All the same homes are available—with the same exact base values—regardless the choice you made as a child. The houses are naturally in far better shape and the tenants less likely to shoot you for trespassing in the nicer version of Old Town, but the home values are identical. On the other hand, there is only one shop in the slums and it's a tattoo stand that is quite frankly not worth buying.

SPOTLIGHT HOME

House of Hard Knocks
5 Lookout Way, Bowerstone Old Town

History: Some of the toughest men and women in Albion have lived under this roof. Not all of them were criminals, but the house a acquired a reputation for being a dangerous place to visit.

Base Value: 8400 Gold
Owner: Gareth the Househusband
Bonuses: Tough as Nails

This is a fantastic house with a great view and right near a small park, but the real reason to buy this home out of all the houses in Bowerstone Old Town is for the sleeping bonus. Many of the houses in this neck of the woods have some pretty disfiguring side-effects when they sleep in the bed, but the Tough as Nails bonus simply makes you tougher. Whether you want to play moral and pure or as evil as possible, it always helps to wake up feeling a bit tougher in the morning. Plus, this house is right next to the shack you and Rose lived in as children.

SPOTLIGHT BUSINESS

Old Town Weapons
1c Market Walk, Bowerstone Old Town

History: Come here for all your weapon needs.

Base Value: 6500 Gold
Owner: Peter the Stall Vendor

There really isn't much point in owning any of the "good" stalls in Bowerstone Old Town since they don't exist if not for your good deeds early on which therefore has gained you an unbelievable 50% discount. That said, if you are going to buy a business in this beautiful little neighborhood, it may as well be the weapons stall. They have a great selection (that only gets better with time) and you'll generate a fair bit of money as the owner over time.

Brightwood
AREA TYPE: COUNTRYSIDE

AREA SYNOPSIS

Brightwood is a heavily forested area filled with rolling hills, a long winding river, numerous ponds, and even a few remote properties. bandits, hobbes, and highwaymen patrol the area seeking to terrorize anyone who dares explore this corner of Albion and chief among their targets is Farmer Giles's family and their farm in the northwest corner of the area. There are several secluded areas that can be accessed from Brightwood, namely the Forsaken Fortress and Archon's Knot. Legend also has it that there are secrets hidden in the Farm Cellar too. The maze of trails and undulating topography make Brightwood a difficult place to get your bearings, so consult the map frequently. You're going to need it.

COLLECTIBLES

CHEST	DIG SPOTS	DIVE SPOTS	GARGOYLES	SILVER KEYS
12	12	4	3	3

NEIGHBORING REGIONS

NAME	DISTANCE	TIME	DIRECTION
Archon's Knot	-	-	-
Bandit Coast	96 miles	21 hours	South
Bower Lake	90 miles	19 hours	West
Farm Cellar	-	-	-
Forsaken Fortress	-	-	-
Nightmare Hollow	-	-	-

TREASURE OF THE LAND

DIVE SPOTS

DIVE SPOTS	CONTENTS
1	Amethyst
2	Ranger Trousers and Diver's Dye
3	300 Gold
4	40 Gold

DIG SPOTS

DIG SPOTS	CONTENTS
1	Economy Value Necklace
2	Civil Ring
3	Concentrated XP Potion
4	Shiny Apple
5	100 Gold
6	Hobbe Strength Potion
7	Ruby
8	Mansfield Green Dye
9	Jet
10	Quality Banana Juice
11	Resurrection Phial
12	500 Gold

CHESTS

CHEST	SILVER KEYS	LOCATION	CONTENTS
1	-	Inside Brightwood Tower.	Standard Health Potion, Resurrection Phial, and Dog Treat
2	-	Follow the dive spot to the dungeon.	Practiced Skill Potion
3	-	In the hills east of Bower Road.	Iron Clockwork Rifle
4	-	Near the ruins in the south end.	Amethyst
5	-	In the windmill during Adulthood.	Obsidian Java Potion
6	15	On the terraces behind the tower.	Discipline Augment
7	-	Along the north edge of Brightwood.	100 Gold
8	5	Atop the tower east of the river.	Slash & Burn Augment
9	-	On the river bank, opposite the tower.	Ranger Coat and Red Letter Dye
10	-	Near the river to the northwest.	1000 Gold
11	-	South of the bandit camp area.	500 Gold
12	-	Near the exit from Archon's Knot.	The Daichi

△ SILVER KEYS

Atop the cliffs directly adjacent the road from Bower Lake. It's near the giant statue.

02

On the broken bridge near the Demon Door. Head up onto the collapsed bridge after returning from the Tattered Spire.

03

This Silver Key is in a narrow valley near the bandit camp. It's just over the hill from the southeastern lake.

◯ GARGOYLES

This Gargoyle is on the ruins near the puddles of water south of the Demon Door.

Swim out to the large island at the southern end of the river and locate the Gargoyle on the side of the tomb.

Shoot through the window at the very top of Brightwood Tower (presumably after purchasing it) to hit the Gargoyle outside.

DEMON DOOR

1 THE SEPULCHRE

Reward: Enter the large mausoleum in the center of the area to find a chest containing a **Merchant's Cap, Knotted Shirt,** and **Harlequin Trousers.**

At first glance, this seems like an easy Demon Door to satisfy. His initial request is to simply bring him some cheese (any cheese will do), but then he tells you about the special appearance cheese carriers are supposed to have. You must show up with dreadlocks or a mullet and mutton chops or a handlebar moustache. When you return with these styles, he then tells you about the outfit you need to wear. You'll now need to wear a Yokel Hat or Bandit Bandana, Tart Skirt or Noble Trousers, and a Noble Gent's Shirt or Corset. Apparently the Demon Door likes his cheese from hairy, cross-dressing types. Assemble the outfit by purchasing the necessary items in Bowerstone Market and in Bloodstone, then stand around in front of the Demon Door patiently as you wait for him to finally open up. The Door is finicky and smart. If you show up wearing any of these items, then it will ask for the item(s) you are not wearing.

REAL ESTATE SNAPSHOT

There are only two pieces of property for sale in Brightwood and, truthfully, you should buy both of them. Giles Farm is far cheaper than Brightwood Tower and contains access to the Farm Cellar which contains the legendary shotgun, the Enforcer. Brightwood Tower is necessary to reach Nightmare Hollow. Save up and buy them both, but don't spend any time looking for shops or stalls to acquire in this neck of the woods as there aren't any. You'll occasionally see a traveling merchant walking along the main road in Brightwood, but that's about it.

SPOTLIGHT HOME

Brightwood Tower
Brightwood

History: Built by Stella Malgrave, a Will user of tremendous power, who spent her life researching spells rather than using them. After she perished in the civilian destruction of the Heroes Guild, the tower remained empty thanks to the many magical defense measures she had implemented. Only a Will user of equal abilities would ever be able to make it their home. That person was to be Garth.

Base Value: 250,000 Gold
Owner: Unknown
Bonuses: Health Bonus, Health Regeneration, and Five Minutes of Fame

Both the Giles Farm and Brightwood Tower are important to purchase if you want to truly see everything Albion has to offer, but we recommend Brightwood Tower as the better investment. Sure, this spacious home costs a quarter of a million gold, but not only do you get to access Nightmare Hollow by owning it, taking over Brightwood Tower also eliminates the risk of future invasions by the Spire guards. You won't be able to rent out Brightwood Tower, but its tremendous value will go a long way towards helping you earn the "Ruler of Albion" Achievement.

Echo Mine
AREA TYPE: CAVE

AREA SYNOPSIS

Echo Mine is a small hobbe-filled cave in the south end of Oakfield. The cave is roughly circular in shape, but it does slope upwards in the northern end and leads to a bridge that crosses back over the main chamber. This cave is off limits until accepting the "Hobbe Squatters" quest during the Adulthood phase of the story.

COLLECTIBLES

🗝 CHEST	⛏ DIG SPOTS	⚓ DIVE SPOTS	👁 GARGOYLES	🗝 SILVER KEYS
1	3	0	0	1

NEIGHBORING REGIONS

NAME	DISTANCE	TIME	DIRECTION
Oakfield	-	-	-

TREASURE OF THE LAND

CHESTS

🗝 CHEST	🗝 SILVER KEYS	LOCATION	CONTENTS
1	-	Across the wooden bridge.	Children's Health Potion

DIG SPOTS

⛏ DIG SPOTS	CONTENTS
1	Civil Ring
2	Sleepy Bean Java Potion
3	Ruby

SILVER KEYS

The Silver Key is in the first large cavern you come to, behind the stalagmites on the right-hand side, just beyond the overhead bridge.

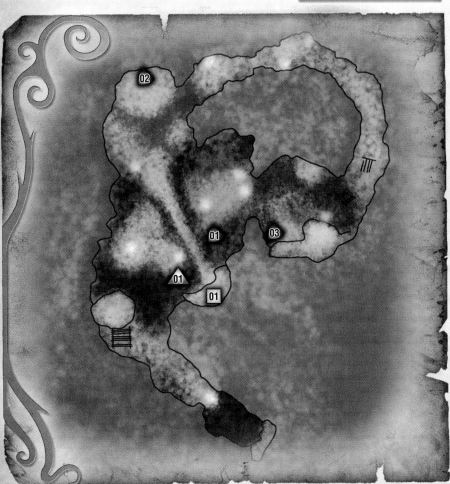

Fairfax Gardens
AREA TYPE: TOWN

AREA SYNOPSIS

Fairfax Gardens is the most luxurious spot in all of Albion. The area—not to mention much of the skyline in Bowerstone—is dominated by the massive Castle Fairfax where you had gone to visit Lord Lucien so long ago. The castle has been empty since that night, but that doesn't keep the Bowerstone elite from strolling the gardens outside the castle. The sidewalks and lawns of Fairfax Gardens are abuzz with social activity all through the day and you can make a lot of fans here. Numerous traveling merchants make the rounds through this tiny area too, but don't think about attacking them! If there's one thing Fairfax Gardens has more of than powdered wigs, it's security! No place in Albion is more heavily guarded than the pretty pathways located here.

COLLECTIBLES

CHEST	DIG SPOTS	DIVE SPOTS	GARGOYLES	SILVER KEYS
3	8	0	2	1

NEIGHBORING REGIONS

NAME	DISTANCE	TIME	DIRECTION
Bowerstone Market	2 miles	1 hour	East
Fairfax Tomb	-	-	-
Lady Grey's Tomb	-	-	-

TREASURE OF THE LAND

CHESTS

CHEST	SILVER KEYS	LOCATION	CONTENTS
1	-	Outside Lady Grey's Tomb.	Economy Value Necklace
2	-	In the tomb of the archaeological dig.	The Archon's Dream
3	50	Inside the throne room of the castle.	50,000 Gold

GARGOYLES

The Gargoyle is located in a window high off the ground on the front of Castle Fairfax. Stand back and shoot it with a long-range weapon and the Zoom ability.

Purchase Castle Fairfax and make your way down the hall to the left of the throne room to enter the octagonal library. The Gargoyle is high above the floor on the book shelves.

SILVER KEYS

The Silver Key is in the tunnel under the main stairs leading up to Castle Fairfax. You can get it without buying the castle.

DIG SPOTS

DIG SPOTS	CONTENTS
1	300 Gold
2	Collar of Regality and "Dog Tricks! The Wave"
3	Jet
4	Burning Orange Dye
5	Autograph Card x3
6	Rusty Necklace
7	Solid Gold Necklace
8	300 Gold

DEMON DOOR

1 FOREST SANCTUM

Reward: The tranquil beauty of Forest Sanctum contains two items worth acquiring. The first is a book titled **Marcus's Poems** and it's near the waterfall. More importantly, however, is the chest down the right-hand path; in it you'll find **50,000 Gold**.

You don't need to own Castle Fairfax in order to access the Demon Door in its basement—just use the tunnel under the main stairs outside the castle. The Demon Door here doesn't require you to perform any tricks or run and fetch it anything. All it wants is the satisfaction of being the last Demon Door standing. Open the other eight Demon Doors (it will help remind you which you have yet to open) then return to this one. It will bemoan its lonely situation and eventually open up for you.

REAL ESTATE SNAPSHOT

Fairfax Gardens has but one single piece of property that can be bought, and even that can't be yours until you've defeated Lucien and returned from your second trip to the Tattered Spire. You might balk at the 7-figure asking price for Castle Fairfax, but you'll be missing out on one of the most unique opportunities in the game if you don't make the purchase. Not to mention you can earn the right to be called "Mayor" for free if you purchase the castle.

SPOTLIGHT HOME

Castle Fairfax
Fairfax Gardens

History: Built by the legendary alchemist Leo Head, the castle was subsequently bought by the Fairfax family, whose kindness and nobility brought forth an era of prosperity for Bowerstone. Its last occupant was the unfortunate Lord Lucien Fairfax, who disappeared some years ago.

Base Value: 1,000,000 Gold
Owner: Unknown
Bonuses: Health Bonus, Health Regeneration, and Animal Magnetism

Castle Fairfax is an incredible purchase, despite its high asking price, thanks to the many treasures that lurk within it. For starters, the 50th and final Gargoyle is inside the castle library and the chest rewarding your collection of 50 Silver Keys is inside the throne room. Perhaps more importantly is that you won't be able to complete the Castle Fairfax quest, will never see Fairfax Tomb, and won't have a chance at obtaining the one and only sample of the Potion of Transmogrification!

Fairfax Tomb
AREA TYPE: TOMB

AREA SYNOPSIS

Fairfax Tomb can only be entered through a secret passage within Castle Fairfax and only during the "Castle Fairfax" quest. Of course, the first step in that quest is spending 1,000,000 Gold to buy the castle. From the entrance in the library, the tomb dives deep under the castle to a water-filled corridor that leads to one of the rarest substances in all of Albion, and believed to have been the life's work of Leo Head—the Potion of Transmogrification! In other words, the sex-change potion!

COLLECTIBLES

🗃 CHEST	⛏ DIG SPOTS	⚓ DIVE SPOTS	⚱ GARGOYLES	🔑 SILVER KEYS
9	5	1	0	0

NEIGHBORING REGIONS

NAME	DISTANCE	TIME	DIRECTION
Bowerstone Cemetery	-	-	-
Fairfax Gardens	-	-	-

FLIT SWITCH EXTRAORDINAIRE

Fairfax Tomb has what is certainly the most difficult flit switch puzzle to complete. Proceed through the tomb to the room with rubble and locate the flit switch on the right. Quickly hit it with a magic spell, then switch to your ranged weapon and shoot it three times as it relocated around the room. You'll have to shoot from the hip as you move across the room, since the flit switch will return to its initial position with any hesitation on your part. It will move much closer to your position after you shoot it a third time. Quickly slash at it with your sword then shoot it again to complete the puzzle.

TREASURE OF THE LAND

DIVE SPOTS

DIVE SPOTS	CONTENTS
1	Civil Ring

DIG SPOTS

DIG SPOTS	CONTENTS
1	Troll Strength Potion
2	Pretty Necklace
3	Mustela Java Potion
4	Mustela Java Potion
5	Hobbe Strength Potion

CHESTS

CHEST	SILVER KEYS	LOCATION	CONTENTS
1	-	Behind the first gate on the right.	Amethyst
2	-	Atop the spiraling staircase.	Standard Health Potion
3	-	Below the last flight of stairs.	Emerald
4	-	Just beyond the water-filled corridor.	Pretty Necklace
5	-	Right before the room of caskets.	Fumbling Skill Potion
6	-	In the final room with the altar.	Sleepy Bean Java Potion
7	-	In the final room with the altar.	Emerald
8	-	In the final room with the altar.	300 Gold
9	-	In the final room with the altar.	300 Gold

Farm Cellar

AREA TYPE: TOMB

AREA SYNOPSIS

This well-hidden underground lair is accessed through the door inside the barn on the Giles family farm in Brightwood. The Farm Cellar is divided into two separate portions: a standard basement-like area, and a much darker and foreboding tomb section. You'll need the portcullis key in order to reach the second area, but the effort is worth it since farmer Giles had quite a secret hidden deep within his cellar. The area is crawling with hollow men, but the legendary blunderbuss is well worth the battle!

COLLECTIBLES

🗝 CHEST	🪏 DIG SPOTS	⚓ DIVE SPOTS	🗿 GARGOYLES	🔑 SILVER KEYS
1	1	0	0	1

NEIGHBORING REGIONS

NAME	DISTANCE	TIME	DIRECTION
Brightwood	-	-	-

COMPETING INTERESTS

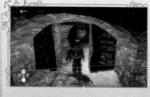

Depending on the quests you decide to participate in, you may find yourself instructed to visit the Farm Cellar on two different occasions. The first instance would be during *Cold Comfort Farmer*, but you'll only be able to access the storage area of the cellar at that time. You'll need Giles's Portcullis Key obtained from the dresser in the house in order to unlock the gate leading to the tomb-like portion of the cellar. You can only get this key once the Giles family puts the farm up for sale. However, in *Red Harvest*, the Porticullis Key is found at a dig site on Giles's grave.

TREASURE OF THE LAND

⬜ CHESTS

🗝 CHEST	🔑 SILVER KEYS	LOCATION	CONTENTS
1	-	In a chest in the cellar entrance.	Giles's Manuscript

🪏 DIG SPOTS

🪏 DIG SPOTS	CONTENTS
1	The Enforcer

🔺 SILVER KEYS

The Silver Key is located in the main chamber of the tomb, but you'll need to use the three switch plates in order to reach it. The key is on the opposite side of the room as the altar.

Forsaken Fortress
AREA TYPE: TOMB

AREA SYNOPSIS

The Forsaken Fortress is a small castle ruins on the outskirts of Brightwood, not far from Brightwood Tower, that contains a wealth of treasure, both above ground and below. The Forsaken Fortress has several winding ramparts that section off the ruins into a number of small areas. Be sure to follow your dog and scour the area fully to gain the many valuable potions in the area. Travel to Forsaken Fortress can't be accomplished on your initial visit to Brightwood; the only quest that will take you to these parts is "The Hit."

COLLECTIBLES

🗝 CHEST	🗡 DIG SPOTS	⚓ DIVE SPOTS	👹 GARGOYLES	🔑 SILVER KEYS
5	6	0	1	0

NEIGHBORING REGIONS

NAME	DISTANCE	TIME	DIRECTION
Brightwood	-	-	-

TREASURE OF THE LAND

DIG SPOTS

🗡 DIG SPOTS	CONTENTS
1	Beggar's Ring
2	Mood Ring
3	150 Gold
4	Emerald
5	2000 Gold
6	Resurrection Phial

GARGOYLES

Follow the stairs on the eastern side halfway to their end and look out onto the ruins to the right to spot the Gargoyle.

CHESTS

🗝 CHEST	🔑 SILVER KEYS	LOCATION	CONTENTS
1	-	Near the trees, right of the trail.	Live Forever Health Potion
2	-	Between the columns on the left.	Expert Skill Potion
3	-	Behind the wall on the right.	Adept Skill Potion
4	-	Atop the stairs at the north end.	Live Forever Health Potion
5	-	At the top of the eastern stairs.	Mustela Java Potion

Gargoyle's Trove
AREA TYPE: TOMB

AREA SYNOPSIS

The secretive Gargoyle's Trove is accessed via a dive spot under the main bridge in Bowerstone Market, but finding it is the easy part! The treasures within this legendary tomb only become available to those who shoot the 50 Gargoyle statues scattered across Albion. This scavenger hunt begins once you obtain the Aimed Range Attack and the Gargoyle statues begin to call out to you in mocking tones. Let their snarky comments be your guide and shoot them to pieces. For every ten Gargoyle statues you destroy, another gate inside the Gargoyle's Trove will open. Shoot all fifty for the grand prize!

COLLECTIBLES

CHEST	DIG SPOTS	DIVE SPOTS	GARGOYLES	SILVER KEYS
6	0	0	0	0

NEIGHBORING REGIONS

NAME	DISTANCE	TIME	DIRECTION
Bowerstone Market	-	-	-

A Bridge to Somewhere

Don't just take what's in the chest behind each gate! You have to stand on the switch plate near each of the chests to gradually piece together the light bridge leading across the void to the super-duper bonus chest at the far end. Shooting all 50 Gargoyles has to be worth something special, right?

TREASURE OF THE LAND

CHESTS

CHEST	SILVER KEYS	LOCATION	CONTENTS
1	-	Behind the first gate on the right.	"Dog Tricks! The Growl"
2	-	Behind the first gate on the left.	Potion of Life
3	-	Behind the second gate on the right.	Emerald x3
4	-	Behind the second gate on the left.	10,000 Gold
5	-	Behind the third gate on the right.	Ghoul Augment
6	-	At the far end of the light bridge.	A joke prize from the gargoyles
7	-	Through the breakable wall behind Chest 6.	It's a secret…

Gemstone Grotto
AREA TYPE: CAVE

AREA SYNOPSIS

Gemstone Grotto is a tiny off-the-beaten-path cave in the Rookridge region. Thorough explorers will likely encounter it on their first trip to Rookridge. Swim past the beach with the entrance to Hobbe Cave to find a second beach and follow it around to the entrance to this crystalline cavern. Gemstone Grotto is essentially circular in shape with two large semi-circles connected by narrow tunnels. There's no real way to get lost inside this tiny area, but it is possible to miss the chest atop the ledge near the entrance. When in doubt, go up the steps!

COLLECTIBLES

📦 CHEST	⛏ DIG SPOTS	⚓ DIVE SPOTS	👹 GARGOYLES	🔑 SILVER KEYS
1	0	0	0	1

NEIGHBORING REGIONS

NAME	DISTANCE	TIME	DIRECTION
Rookridge	-	-	-

BEETLES & CRYSTALS

The narrow pathways and shimmering crystals can make navigating this tiny cave a bit challenging, but the giant beetles will let you know that you're still headed in the right direction. These critters don't repopulate once you've cleared them out so keep moving forward in search of bugs to squash and you'll know you're on the right path.

TREASURE OF THE LAND

CHESTS

📦 CHEST	🔑 SILVER KEYS	LOCATION	CONTENTS
1	-	On the upper ledge near the entrance.	200 Gold

🔺 SILVER KEYS

Inside the Gemstone Grotto in the northwest corner of the map. Follow the path inside the cave to find the Silver Key.

Guild Cave
AREA TYPE: CAVE

AREA SYNOPSIS

The Guild Cave is a cavernous underground area that was once home to a special academy of Heroes, but is now sealed away beneath an island in the center of Bower Lake. Theresa has a special seal that will grant you access to the Old Tomb on the island, which is the gateway to the cave below. The Guild Cave isn't a large cave, but it does have its share of giant beetles, water-filled caverns, and rickety bridges. You'll need to use both ranged and melee attacks to advance past the flit switches as you proceed to the Chamber of Fate. Once navigated, you can return to the Guild Cave's far entrance via the Cullis Gate on the hilltop in Bower Lake.

COLLECTIBLES

🗝 CHEST	⚒ DIG SPOTS	🌊 DIVE SPOTS	👹 GARGOYLES	🗝 SILVER KEYS
5	5	1	1	1

NEIGHBORING REGIONS

NAME	DISTANCE	TIME	DIRECTION
Bower Lake	-	-	-

TREASURE OF THE LAND

CHESTS

CHEST	SILVER KEYS	LOCATION	CONTENTS
1	-	Beyond the first gate in the cave.	150 Gold
2	-	Under the stone arch.	Rusty Mace
3	-	In the room with the books.	Amethyst
4	-	In the room with the books.	150 Gold
5	-	A special in the Chamber of Fate.	Visit www.fable2.com

DEAD MEN TELL NO LIES

You must collect the three letters from the skeletons in this cave if you want to get the **Bewitching Augment** from the dive spot. The dive spot will not appear if you don't first search the three skeletons.

DIG SPOTS

DIG SPOTS	CONTENTS
1	300 Gold
2	Amethyst
3	250 Gold
4	Economy Value Necklace
5	Mood Ring

DIVE SPOTS

DIVE SPOTS	CONTENTS
1	Bewitching Augment

GARGOYLES

Look behind the boulders on the left side of the first large room inside the cave.

SILVER KEYS

The Gargoyle is on the ceiling of the cavern with the water. It's directly above the ledge you drop off of upon entering the room.

Hall of the Dead
AREA TYPE: TOMB

AREA SYNOPSIS

Hall of the Dead is an exclusive dungeon available only to those who purchased the "Fable II: Limited Collector's Edition". Enter your purchase code and downloading bonus content from Xbox LIVE, then head to the town of Bloodstone and go for a swim. You'll see a new dive spot location just off the central pier. The Hall of the Dead is a combination of rocky cave and sophisticated tomb and it's crawling with hollow men. Fight through the throngs of high-level hollow men and complete each flit switch sequence to come away with the second-best weapon in Albion!

COLLECTIBLES

CHEST	DIG SPOTS	DIVE SPOTS	GARGOYLES	SILVER KEYS
2	0	0	0	0

NEIGHBORING REGIONS

NAME	DISTANCE	TIME	DIRECTION
Bloodstone	-	-	-

TREASURE OF THE LAND

UNDERWATER PASSAGEWAYS

There are two dive spots in the Hall of the Dead, but neither of them lead you sunken treasure. Instead, they simply provide a link between two different areas within the tomb. You'll have to use the dive spot to follow after the first flit switch.

Prepare for Battle

Don't even think about coming to the Hall of the Dead until you have a sizeable health bar and some pretty powerful magic and weaponry! We
recommend using a Level 3 or higher Raise Dead spell to distract the enemies, then finish them off with a legendary weapon. Try using a Time Control spell to slip behind the enemy and blast him with The Enforcer.

CHESTS

CHEST	SILVER KEYS	LOCATION	CONTENTS
1	-	On the ledge in the cave portion.	Standard Health Potion, Cure-All Health Potion and Percolated Java Potion
2	-	Locked away at the top of the tomb.	The Wreckager

Hobbe Cave
AREA TYPE: CAVE

AREA SYNOPSIS

This lengthy winding cave provides an essential link between Bowerstone and Oakfield, so long as the bridge is out. You'll be forced to dive off the bridge and swim to the sandy beach where the entrance to Hobbe Cave is on your initial visit to the area. Make your way up through the spiraling network of tunnels and walkways to the exit, just downhill from the road to Oakfield, on the far side of the canyon in Rookridge. The cave gets its name from the hobbes that dwell inside. Rumor has it they kidnap little kids and turn them into more hobbes. Be on the lookout!

COLLECTIBLES

🗝 CHEST	⛏ DIG SPOTS	⚓ DIVE SPOTS	💡 GARGOYLES	🗝 SILVER KEYS
3	5	1	1	0

NEIGHBORING REGIONS

NAME	DISTANCE	TIME	DIRECTION
Rookridge	-	-	-

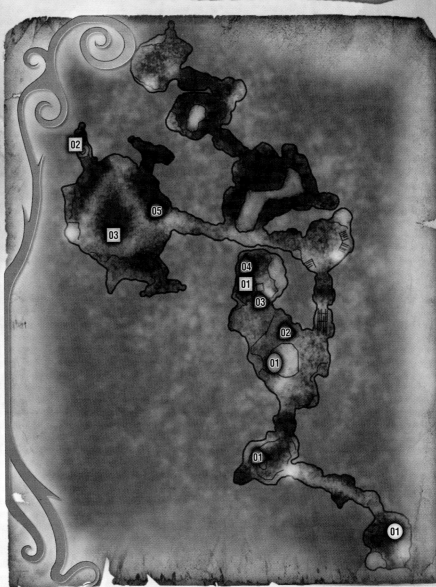

Well-Hidden Treasure

Don't let the sniveling commentary from the Gargoyle distract you as you climb the spiraling wooden walkway. There is a secret area off to the side of this walkway that you need to leap down into in order to find one of the chests and dig spots. Keep your eyes peeled for areas like this wherever you go—not every chest will be sitting out in the open.

TREASURE OF THE LAND

CHESTS

CHEST	SILVER KEYS	LOCATION	CONTENTS
1	-	Leap off the spiraling walkway.	Attenuated Will Potion
2	-	In the side tunnel near the exit.	Standard Health Potion
3	-	On a ledge below the cave exit.	Watered Down XP Potion

DIG SPOTS

DIG SPOTS	CONTENTS
1	Practiced Skill Potion
2	300 Gold
3	Jet
4	Silver Key
5	200 Gold

DIVE SPOTS

DIVE SPOTS	CONTENTS
1	Amethyst

GARGOYLES

This one is on a beam in the center of the spiraling walkway. Shoot it from the top.

Howling Halls
AREA TYPE: TOMB

AREA SYNOPSIS

The Howling Halls get their name from the pack of vicious balverines that live in these parts. The balverines, led by a massive white balverine, rely on a large spiked pit to prevent intruders from escaping their grasp. Those who manage to defeat the balverines and cross the pit of spikes will find their journey through the rest of the Howling Halls and onward to Westcliff Camp to be much more relaxed. Howling Halls provides a necessary connection between the northern and southern halves of Westcliff during the Adolescence phase of the game. Those Heroes who choose to help Barnum develop Westcliff will find a new bridge constructed across the gorge when they return from the Tattered Spire, thereby making a second trip through Howling Halls unnecessary.

COLLECTIBLES

🗝 CHEST	🪓 DIG SPOTS	⚓ DIVE SPOTS	👹 GARGOYLES	🗝 SILVER KEYS
2	0	0	1	1

NEIGHBORING REGIONS

NAME	DISTANCE	TIME	DIRECTION
Westcliff	-	-	-

CROSSING THE SPIKES

You won't be able to get across the spiked floor without Hammerin' Hannah's help. But don't let her excitement hurry you out the door on the other side before you can open the chest and shoot the Gargoyle.

TREASURE OF THE LAND

△ SILVER KEYS

On the second floor of the circular room, opposite the exit.

◯ GARGOYLES

In the upper right-hand corner of the main room, across the spike-filled pit.

CHESTS

🗝 CHEST	🗝 SILVER KEYS	LOCATION	CONTENTS
1	-	Across the spiked pit, on the left.	Precious Necklace
2	-	In the center of the ruined room.	400 Gold

DIG SPOTS

🪓 DIG SPOTS	CONTENTS
1	150 Gold

Lady Grey's Tomb
AREA TYPE: TOMB

AREA SYNOPSIS

You might be wondering why anyone in their right mind would want to enter Lady Grey's Tomb, but there is one twisted soul who will ask you to do just that during the "Love Hurts" quest. Lady Grey's tomb is sealed off by gates in the Fairfax Gardens area of Bowerstone until this quest is initiated. The tomb is an eerily dark place filled with sand, but it is small and all but impossible to get lost in. However, to even get into the cave you'll be required to open the portcullis and enter the tomb. There may be something even more disturbing to find once you're inside. Enter the tomb through the mausoleum on the left-hand side of Fairfax Gardens (as viewed while facing Castle Fairfax) and exit on the right.

COLLECTIBLES

🗝 CHEST	🔨 DIG SPOTS	⚓ DIVE SPOTS	⚱ GARGOYLES	🔑 SILVER KEYS
2	0	0	1	1

NEIGHBORING REGIONS

NAME	DISTANCE	TIME	DIRECTION
Fairfax Gardens	-	-	-

TREASURE OF THE LAND

CHESTS

🗝 CHEST	🔑 SILVER KEYS	LOCATION	CONTENTS
1	-	In a corner of the dark sandy room.	Diamond
2	-	In a corner of the dark sandy room.	Cure-All Health Potion

⚱ GARGOYLES

The Gargoyle is in the upper section of the tomb, near the entrance. Shoot it before dropping down the hole.

△ SILVER KEYS

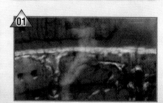

This Silver Key is located in the darkened corner of the tomb, near the stairs leading up to the exit. Your dog will help you find it.

Lion's Head Isle
AREA TYPE: COUNTRYSIDE

AREA SYNOPSIS

Lion's Head Isle is the secret location of Captain Dread's treasure and is only reachable by commandeering the pirate ghost's ship during the "Treasure Island of Doom" quest. The island itself contains a small sandy beach with a shipwreck and a larger interior oasis, complete with waterfalls and a small pond. Head up the path from the beach and leap from ledge to ledge on the cliffs to collect the treasure.

COLLECTIBLES

🗝 CHEST	⛏ DIG SPOTS	⚓ DIVE SPOTS	⚱ GARGOYLES	🗝 SILVER KEYS
8	1	1	1	1

NEIGHBORING REGIONS

NAME	DISTANCE	TIME	DIRECTION
Bloodstone	-	-	-
Sinkhole	-	-	-

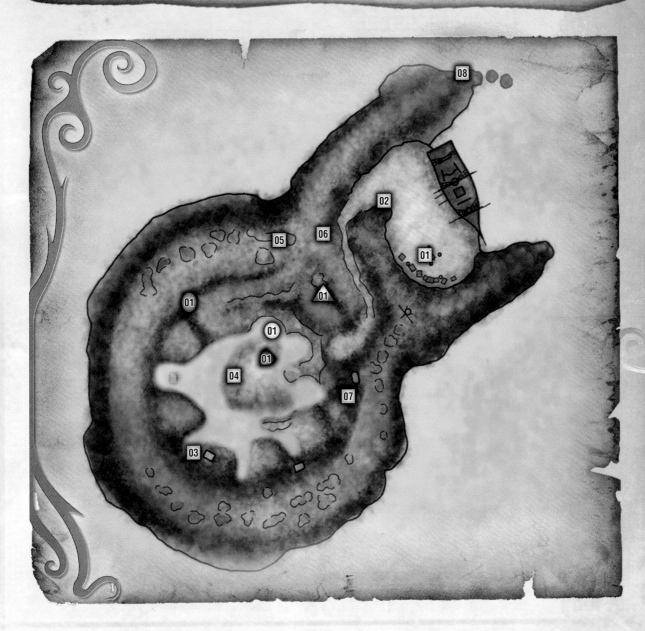

CHESTS

🧳 CHEST	⚷ SILVER KEYS	LOCATION	CONTENTS
1	-	On the deck of the beached ship.	1500 Gold
2	-	In the hull of the beached ship.	1500 Gold
3	-	Behind the tree on the island.	1500 Gold
4	-	Behind the widest waterfall.	1500 Gold
5	-	Along the path near the cliffs.	1500 Gold
6	-	Behind the boards in the tunnel.	1500 Gold
7	-	On an upper ledge on the cliffs.	1500 Gold
8	-	On the rocky point near the water.	1500 Gold

DIG SPOTS

🪏 DIG SPOTS	CONTENTS
1	1500 Gold

DIVE SPOTS

⚓ DIVE SPOTS	CONTENTS
1	1500 Gold

CHESTS AND MORE

Captain Dread didn't just leave his treasure lying out in the open in chests, he also buried some too! Two of the 10 treasures found at Lion's Head Isle are hidden beneath dig and dive spots.

GARGOYLES   ## SILVER KEYS

On a ledge outside the tunnel in the cliffs. Follow the tunnel through to the other end and jump down to the cliff below.

Climb out of the water onto the path near the cliffs and approach the waterfall on the left. The Gargoyle is near the tree on the ledge near the waterfall.

Nightmare Hollow
AREA TYPE: COUNTRYSIDE

AREA SYNOPSIS

Nightmare Hollow is a place nobody ever wants to visit, yet few can resist. If you'd like to see this dreamscape for yourself, all you have to do is purchase Brightwood Tower and sleep in the bed in the attic. Doing so will return you to your childhood and drop you in a mystical forest filled with enemies of all kinds. A treasure chest claiming to be your friend will unleash wave after wave of enemies after you and only by defeating them all will you receive the valuable contents inside. This is all a part of the "Brightwood Tower" quest.

COLLECTIBLES

📦 CHEST	🪏 DIG SPOTS	⚓ DIVE SPOTS	👤 GARGOYLES	🗝 SILVER KEYS
2	0	0	0	0

NEIGHBORING REGIONS

NAME	DISTANCE	TIME	DIRECTION
Brightwood	-	-	-

TREASURE OF THE LAND

CHESTS

📦 CHEST	🗝 SILVER KEYS	LOCATION	CONTENTS
1	-	Defeat the fifth wave of enemies.	100,000 Gold and Diamond of Sorrow
2	-	Use the Expression Statue to access.	Emerald

RETURN VISIT

Although you'll be able to use all of the magic and weaponry you amassed over the course of your life thus far at Nightmare Hollow, your childhood version won't be able to use any expressions. This means you'll have to return to Nightmare Hollow a second time (this time as an adult) to perform the Chicken expression in front of the Expression Statue. Do so to access the chest in the small house near the farm.

Oakfield
AREA TYPE: TOWN

AREA SYNOPSIS

Oakfield is a tranquil farming community set between the picturesque seashore and forested hills to the east. The villagers are friendly, outgoing, and hard-working. Although there are a few giant beetles in the woods, and a gang of hobbes near the entrance to Echo Mine, Oakfield is a peaceful place. Oakfield is known throughout Albion for its spectacular trees and Harvest Festival. The monks at the Temple of Light attribute the region's fertile ground to a single golden acorn that they raise into a towering oak tree every hundred years.

COLLECTIBLES

📦 CHEST	🪏 DIG SPOTS	🤿 DIVE SPOTS	👹 GARGOYLES	🗝 SILVER KEYS
8	6	1	3	4

NEIGHBORING REGIONS

NAME	DISTANCE	TIME	DIRECTION
Echo Mine	-	-	-
Rookridge	70 miles	13 hours	South
Wellspring Cave	-	-	-

JOBS

Bartender at The Sandgoose
Oakfield Farm Woodcutter
Oakfield Windmill Woodcutter

GAMES

Spinnerbox at The Sandgoose

THE FATE OF OAKFIELD

Your actions in the latter stages of your quest for the Hero of Will—before going to the Tattered Spire—will greatly impact this peace-loving town. Those who side with the Temple of Light and protect it from attackers will return to find the Temple expanded (and for sale). Those who ignore the Temple's pleas for help or, worse still, help the Temple of Shadows massacre the people of Oakfield, will return to a place far less inviting. Which path will you choose?

TREASURE OF THE LAND

CHESTS

📦 CHEST	🗝 SILVER KEYS	LOCATION	CONTENTS
1	-	Near the Oakfield Windmill.	Sleepy Bean Java Potion
2	-	In the cemetery past the Demon Door.	Percolated Java Potion
3	10	Inside the small cemetery.	Slash & Burn Augment
4	-	In the hills east of Temple of Light.	Standard Health Potion
5	-	In the field near Echo Mine entrance.	500 Gold
6	-	Behind the sculptor's barn.	"Wedding Bells", Freshly Picked Flowers, and Civil Ring
7	-	On the ledge after Wellspring Cave.	Economy Value Necklace
8	-	On the hills near Wellspring Cave.	Dog Treat x3

DIG SPOTS

🪏 DIG SPOTS	CONTENTS
1	Sunshine Yellow Dye
2	400 Gold
3	200 Gold
4	Attenuated Will Potion
5	750 Gold
6	Solid Gold Necklace

DIVE SPOTS

🤿 DIVE SPOTS	CONTENTS
1	Rusty Turret Pistol

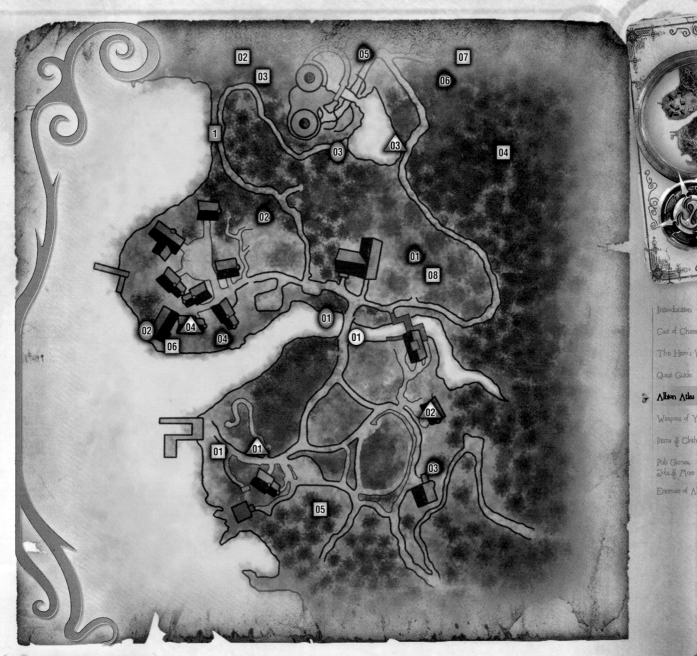

△ SILVER KEYS

01 This Silver Key is sitting out in the open near the bales of hay in front of the farmhouse.

02 Inside Manure Manor, the house nearest the barn with the waterwheel.

03 Follow the path along the waterfall ponds to the Temple of Light to find this Silver Key.

04 Inside the farmhouse next to the Sculptor's barn. The Silver Key is on the second floor.

◯ GARGOYLES

01 This Gargoyle is mounted on the stone bridge over the river in the center of the village, on the downstream side.

02 Go around the back of the barn where the sculptor is to find this next Gargoyle.

03 Swim through the pond near the waterfall and follow the path uphill towards the columns on the rocks.

DEMON DOOR

1 HOMESTEAD

Reward: Serenity Farm, a small two-story house in the country valued at 32000 Gold. The nightstand upstairs contains the **"Come Hither, Dear"** expression manual and there is a chest in the barn containing the very valuable **Hammerthyst**.

This particular Demon Door is a romantic through and through and wants nothing more than to see a marriage proposal happen before his eyes. Bring someone who's in love with you to Oakfield and have them follow you to the Demon Door near the water. Get the Demon Door's attention, then gift that special someone a ring to propose. The Demon Door will open and you'll gain access to the Homestead area, a small picturesque home in the country. This is the perfect place to set a marital residence, especially for those who want to have multiple families and ensure they don't run into one another.

MERCHANT DIRECTORY

SHOP	WARES	MAX PRODUCT QUALITY
Oakfield Clothing Stall	Miscellaneous & Clothes	★★★
Oakfield Fruit & Veg Stall	Food	★★★
Oakfield Weapon Stall	Weapons	★★★
The Sandgoose	Drinks	★★★★★

People living in small country towns like Oakfield tend to get by on the bare essentials, and that's what you're going to have to do. Oakfield merchants carry the basic clothes, produce, and weapons that you come to expect but you won't find any bookstores, furniture shops, or potion dealers here. Nor will you find any stylists or tattoo parlors. While you might not be able to get those big-city items here, you will be able to sit down for a nice foamy pint at The Sandgoose. However, while most of these businesses are just stalls, the coach house outside can be quite lucrative.

REAL ESTATE SNAPSHOT

Would-be property magnates have more buildings to choose from in Oakfield than in many other areas, but the selection is still rather limited. The majority of the country homes in this area are cursed with the Troll Face sleeping bonus which will only appeal to those wishing to scare everyone they meet. The businesses, aside from the Temple of Light and The Sandgoose, are just simple stalls. They provide a nice early-stage investment, but you won't get rich owning them. If profits are your desire, then focus on The Sandgoose, otherwise take your riches to another town or buy up a few of the homes here while they're cheap and rent them out.

SPOTLIGHT HOME

Luminous Cottage
2 Oakfield Way

History: When Albert the Luminous, founder of the Temple of Light, planted the first Golden Oak, bringing hope and plenty to Oakfield, the residents gave him this house in gratitude. Here he lived till the end of his days. The nearby windmill is part of the property.

Base Value: 4800 Gold
Owner: Eli the Farmer
Bonuses: Purification

Luminous Cottage provides a nice investment, particularly if you buy it early before it gets redecorated. This is a good place to set as a marital home for those looking to achieve full purity since the sleeping bonus will ensure you gain purity with every snooze. The house is conveniently located—straight down the path from the tavern—and you can often find work as a woodcutter right behind the house. The view of the windmill, the setting moon, and the Tattered Spire make this one of the most picturesque homes in Albion.

SPOTLIGHT BUSINESS

Temple of Light
Oakfield

History: Founded by Albert the Luminous, whose desperate pilgrimage into the nearby caves led him to a moment of epiphany. It was there that the Light spoke to him, and there that he discovered the Golden Oak.

Base Value: 100,000 Gold
Owner: Matthew the Monk

A hundred large may sound like too much money for a business (actually a Temple) but you'll soon see that's only because you're not thinking big enough! For there are many more bonuses to owning the Temple of Light aside from the 925 gold profit you'll be making. Assuming you saved the Temple of Light from falling to the Shadow-worshippers, you'll be able to buy this Temple and significantly pad your real estate holdings, while simultaneously earning some morality and the right to be called the Chosen One. Not only that, but you'll earn gold as well!

Old Tin Mine
AREA TYPE: CAVE

AREA SYNOPSIS

Old Tin Mine is a small Y-shaped cave. You'll find the entrance on the cliff face opposite the entrance to Howling Halls in Westcliff. Dive from the cliffs and swim upstream to the entrance. The main passage through the cave quickly rounds a corner then forks. The right-hand path simply leads to a dead-end, so head left through the narrow opening. This leads to a large, mist-filled cavern where an old mining operation has long since been abandoned. Slaughter the bandits and highwaymen and collect the valuable potion in the center.

COLLECTIBLES

CHEST	DIG SPOTS	DIVE SPOTS	GARGOYLES	SILVER KEYS
1	0	0	0	0

NEIGHBORING REGIONS

NAME	DISTANCE	TIME	DIRECTION
Westcliff	-	-	-

Taking a Swim

Old Tin Mine is one of the more challenging caves to discover on account of the limited access to the river on which it sits. To reach the cave, you must follow the standard route towards the entrance to the Howling Halls. Cross the bridge and turn left towards Howling Halls. Now veer off the trail to the right and look for a small place alongside the cliff where you can safely jump into the river below.

TREASURE OF THE LAND

Proceed With Caution

Enter the main chamber slowly so as to not rush into the gang of highwaymen and bandits that lie in wait for you! Ready up your Time Control, take out the few nearest your position, then cast Raise Dead to battle the rest.

CHESTS

CHEST	SILVER KEYS	LOCATION	CONTENTS
1	-	Atop the stone ramp in the main cave.	Thunder's Strength Potion

Reaver's Rear Passage
AREA TYPE: CAVE

AREA SYNOPSIS

Guys like Reaver don't get to their place in the world without having a backup plan for everything they do, so it should come as no surprise that there is a secret passageway leading out of his mansion in Bloodstone. You'll know when the time comes to visit this secret place so we won't go into any details about that matter here. Instead, we will tell you to take the time to explore the cavern after each wave of Spire guards is defeated. Check the walkways and the tunnels off to the side for treasure—you just might need it!

COLLECTIBLES

🗰 CHEST	⚑ DIG SPOTS	⚓ DIVE SPOTS	⚐ GARGOYLES	⚷ SILVER KEYS
4	1	0	0	0

NEIGHBORING REGIONS

NAME	DISTANCE	TIME	DIRECTION
Bloodstone	-	-	-

TREASURE OF THE LAND

⬦ DIG SPOTS

⚑ DIG SPOTS	CONTENTS
1	Bad XP Potion

☐ CHESTS

🗰 CHEST	⚷ SILVER KEYS	LOCATION	CONTENTS
1	-	In the underground study area.	500 Gold
2	-	Atop the walkway in the first cave.	Live Forever Health Potion
3	-	In a side-tunnel in the first cave.	Live Forever Health Potion
4	-	Just beyond the railcar tracks.	Obsidian Java Potion

WHERE ARE WE GOING?

If you've read this far, you already know too much. Reaver has instructed us that the whereabouts of the cave's northern terminus is on a need to know basis and you, dear Hero, do not yet need to know. Follow the man with the gun and enjoy the trip.

Rookridge
AREA TYPE: COUNTRYSIDE

AREA SYNOPSIS

Rookridge will be one of the areas you visit most frequently as you travel back and forth across Albion. Situated between Bowerstone Old Town and Oakfield, Rookridge serves as a refuge for those who would rather live outside the reach of law's arm than enjoy the benefits of city life. The area features a long river canyon that, until a bridge is built, prohibits travel from town to town. The mountains near the waterfalls are home to an old mining camp—now overrun by bandits—and the beaches along the river are home to not one, but two separate caves. Last but not least, Rookridge is home to the Temple of Shadows; Fridays are poker night.

COLLECTIBLES

🗄 CHEST	⛏ DIG SPOTS	🤿 DIVE SPOTS	👹 GARGOYLES	🗝 SILVER KEYS
11	4	0	3	3

NEIGHBORING REGIONS

NAME	DISTANCE	TIME	DIRECTION
Bowerstone Old Town	85 miles	15 hours	South
Gemstone Grotto	-	-	-
Hobbe Cave	-	-	-
Oakfield	70 miles	13 hours	North
The Temple of Shadows	-	-	-
The Wellspring	-	-	-

JOBS

Bartender at The Lucky Heather

GAMES

Spinnerbox at The Lucky Heather

TREASURE OF THE LAND

△ SILVER KEYS

The first of the Silver Keys in this area is on the promenade near the statue warning of a ghost. Cross the bridge to get it.

Exit Hobbe's Cave and run around to the back of the cabin where you emerge. The Silver Key is on the deck behind the house.

This Silver Key is on the end of the mine car bridge, east of the abandoned Rookridge Inn.

○ GARGOYLES

This Gargoyle is on the cliffs to the right of the entrance to Hobbe Cave. It may well be the first Gargoyle you shoot.

Come back to Rookridge after returning from the Tattered Spire and climb the path to the mineshaft at the end of the rail track.

Gain access to the Temple of Shadows and cross the entrance courtyard to the far right-hand corner to find this Gargoyle on the wall.

DIG SPOTS

DIG SPOTS	CONTENTS
1	200 Gold
2	Apple Pie Pocket
3	Bits O' Beef Pie

CHESTS

CHEST	SILVER KEYS	LOCATION	CONTENTS
1	5	Along the main path from Bowerstone.	Ruby
2	–	On the rocky ledge above the trail.	Standard Health Potion
3	–	On the main path, south of the river.	"The Dogs of War, Book 1"
4	–	In the clearing, near the Demon Door.	"Dog Tricks! Hide Snout"
5	–	Behind the gate at Temple of Shadows.	200 Gold
6	–	Near the road to Oakfield.	Sleepy Bean Java Potion
7	–	Inside the Rookridge Inn.	Pretty Necklace
8	–	At the mine camp east of the inn.	Standard Health Potion and Dog Treat x2
9	–	South of the mine car bridge.	Standard Health Potion
10	–	Near the stone monument atop the hill.	100 Gold, Bandit Bandana, Bandit Shirt, and Bandit Trousers
11	15	North of the mine car bridge.	5000 Gold

DEMON DOOR

1 MEMORY LANE

Reward: This timeless trip into the past contains several subtle reminders of your Childhood. Perhaps more importantly, there is also a chest containing a Potion of Life.

The Demon Door in Rookridge has seen all sorts of human tomfoolery and now wants to see your furry companion do a number of tricks. Have your dog perform at least five unique tricks in front of the Demon Door in order to convince it to open. The Demon Door has an extremely good memory so don't waste its time by having the dog perform the same the trick more than once. Each of the Dog Tricks your dog has learned feed off your own expressions. Consult the list of tricks in 'The Hero's Way' chapter for a reminder of which expressions trigger which dog tricks (you still must get the book to teach the dog the trick). As for the area behind the Demon Door, there isn't much there besides some old-timey reminders of your youth and a chest with a Potion of Life.

REAL ESTATE SNAPSHOT

There are only two buildings for sale in Rookridge and they couldn't be more different. The first is the poorly-visited Lucky Heather tavern near the waterfall. The Lucky Heather may have been a hub of activity when the mines were still active, but it's struggling to turn a profit these days. On the other hand, there's the Temple of Shadows. Only those who make a point of joining their ranks and bringing the town of Oakfield to its knees will have the luxury of buying this foreboding place.

SPOTLIGHT BUSINESS

Temple of Shadows
Rookridge

History: ???

Base Value: ???
Owner: Cornelius Grim

Those who chose the path of darkness and corruption will have the opportunity to own the Temple of Shadows after returning from the Tattered Spire. The Temple of Shadows can generate tremendous income for you over time and also adds significantly to your real-estate empire. And if that wasn't enough of a reason for you to own this damp, dreary place, you will also gain the rights to be called the Shadow Fiend. Head to the nearest Town Crier and lay claim to your new title!

Shadow Court
AREA TYPE: TOMB

AREA SYNOPSIS

This massive tomb in the Wraithmarsh area will only open to those who seek to return the Dark Seal. The Shadow Court is crawling with shadows of hobbes, men, and balverines, and is not a place for the faint of heart. Bring high-powered magic and plenty of health potions because you're bound to need them. The path through the area isn't entirely visible at first glance; expect to break through a couple of cracked walls. A hefty decision awaits those who manage to come face to face with the judges of this strange place.

COLLECTIBLES

CHEST	DIG SPOTS	DIVE SPOTS	GARGOYLES	SILVER KEYS
4	0	0	1	1

NEIGHBORING REGIONS

NAME	DISTANCE	TIME	DIRECTION
Wraithmarsh	-	-	-

TREASURE OF THE LAND

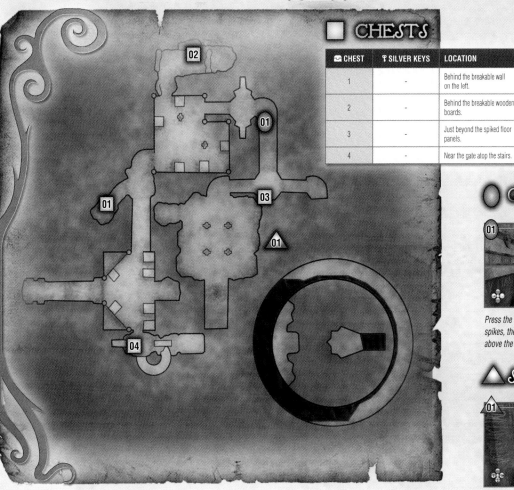

CHESTS

CHEST	SILVER KEYS	LOCATION	CONTENTS
1	-	Behind the breakable wall on the left.	Live Forever Health Potion
2	-	Behind the breakable wooden boards.	Thunder's Strength Potion
3	-	Just beyond the spiked floor panels.	Thunder's Strength Potion
4	-	Near the gate atop the stairs.	Undiluted Will Potion

GARGOYLES

Press the switch to turn off the first set of spikes, then turn around to locate the Gargoyle above the door you just came through.

SILVER KEYS

Smash through the cracked wall on the left-hand side of the room following the first spiked floor.

161

Shelley Crypt
AREA TYPE: CAVE

AREA SYNOPSIS

As you might suspect by its name, Shelley Crypt is located in Bowerstone Cemetery. This winding puzzle-filled cave can only be accessed after purchasing the Bowerstone Cemetery Mansion which in turn can only be accomplished after completing the "Love Hurts" quest. Shelley Crypt is roughly circular in shape, but it has several small secret passages jutting off the main route, but you'll have to smash through cracked walls to find them. The dominant feature in Shelley Crypt is a light bridge that you'll need to activate while crossing a seemingly bottomless room.

COLLECTIBLES

📦 CHEST	⛏ DIG SPOTS	⚓ DIVE SPOTS	🗿 GARGOYLES	🗝 SILVER KEYS
3	1	0	1	1

NEIGHBORING REGIONS

NAME	DISTANCE	TIME	DIRECTION
Bowerstone Cemetery	-	-	-

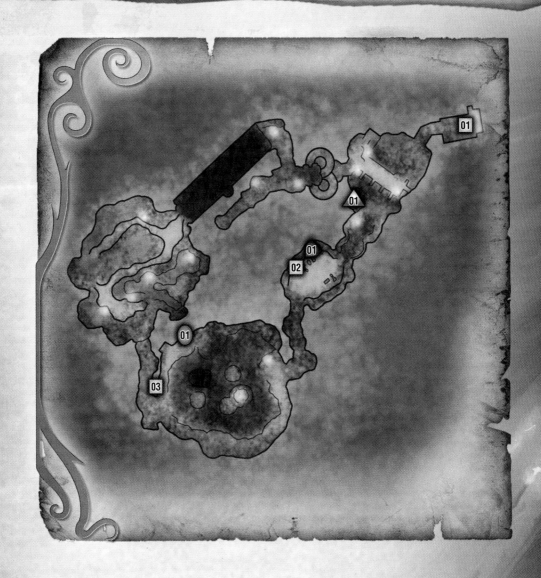

Bridge Building 101

The main large room at the south end of the crypt contains a series of pedestals that can only be reached by activating a number of light bridge segments. You can only accomplish this by first slashing the flit switch on the near-side of the void, then quickly using your ranged weapon to shoot it when it relocates. Rush across the bridge that appears, strike the flit switch, and repeat the process again with your ranged weapon.

TREASURE OF THE LAND

CHESTS

CHEST	SILVER KEYS	LOCATION	CONTENTS
1	-	In the hall north of the crypt.	The Stone of Myr'Bregothil
2	-	On the floor beside the cage.	Obsidian Java Potion
3	-	Across the cavern with the pedestals.	Obsidian Java Potion

DIG SPOTS

DIG SPOTS	CONTENTS
1	Jet

SILVER KEYS

01

Smash through the cracked wall in the room with the sarcophagi to find the Silver Key at the bottom of a secret staircase.

GARGOYLES

01

Cross the room with the light bridges then walk to the right along the rocky ledge near the torches to spot this Gargoyle on the cavern's roof.

163

Sinkhole
AREA TYPE: CAVE

AREA SYNOPSIS

The Sinkhole is a small cave located off the southern edge of Bloodstone, but you won't be able to explore its true secrets until the "Treasure Island of Doom" quest. There is a lever hidden in the cave can be used to flood the cavern and float the currently landlocked pirate ship. Although the Silver Key near the entrance is an important discovery, your main goal here is to put Captain Dread's ship to use and sail to Lion's Head Isle.

COLLECTIBLES

📦 CHEST	🔱 DIG SPOTS	⚓ DIVE SPOTS	🗿 GARGOYLES	🗝 SILVER KEYS
1	0	0	0	1

NEIGHBORING REGIONS

NAME	DISTANCE	TIME	DIRECTION
Bloodstone	-	-	-
Lion's Head Isle	-	-	-

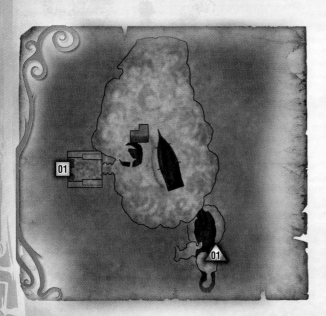

Mess Hall Massacre

Nobody likes their meal interrupted, not even the ghosts of pirates past. Expect a huge fight in the galley of this secret ghost pirate fortress. Use level 1 and 3 Time Control spells to buy yourself time to cast a level 4 or 5 Shock or Inferno spell, then quickly cast Raise Dead to help you in taking out the remaining forces.

TREASURE OF THE LAND

△ SILVER KEYS

Return to the cave after flooding the cavern and swim across the hole in the opening to get the Silver Key from the ledge across from the entrance.

☐ CHESTS

📦 CHEST	🗝 SILVER KEYS	LOCATION	CONTENTS
1	-	In Captain Dread's bedroom.	Lever

KEYFINDER

You won't be able to open the chest without doing a thorough search of the room. Try the nightstand...

The Tattered Spire
AREA TYPE: MYSTERY

AREA SYNOPSIS

Your quest to find the Hero of Skill will take you to The Tattered Spire, but not as a conquering Hero but something much slyer. Your time at The Tattered Spire is strictly governed by the Commandant and you will therefore see little of this massive structure. You will be given orders and expected to follow them, forever biding your time and waiting to make your move.

COLLECTIBLES

🗃 CHEST	🔨 DIG SPOTS	⚓ DIVE SPOTS	👹 GARGOYLES	🔑 SILVER KEYS
2	0	0	0	0

NEIGHBORING REGIONS

NAME	DISTANCE	TIME	DIRECTION
Westcliff	-	-	-

FINDING TREASURE IN THE SPIRE

Lord Lucien isn't recruiting Westcliff's dumbest and strongest just so they can raid his precious of spire for treasure. The only bits of loot present here are two chests in the barracks area. The first is on the level where you begin, the second is in a room directly above the first. Ignore the glowing path and take the stairs on the left when first summoned to meet with the Commandant.

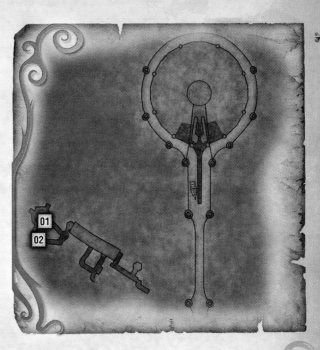

TREASURE OF THE LAND

🗃 CHESTS

🗃 CHEST	🔑 SILVER KEYS	LOCATION	CONTENTS
1	-	Guard's quarters, first floor.	Cure-All Health Potion
2	-	Guard's quarters, second floor.	Ruby

The Temple of Shadows
AREA TYPE: TOMB

AREA SYNOPSIS

Unlike the Temple of Light in Oakfield, the Temple of Shadows is its own separate entity and one that you have to be initiated into, at least at first. There are two ways to go about gaining access to the Temple of Shadows. One way is to complete the initiation ritual of eating five Crunchy Chicks during the Adolescence phase of life. The other option is to return during Adulthood and walk right in. You may think this is the morally right path to walk, but that all depends on whether or not you allowed the Shadow-worshippers to slaughter the monks at the Wellspring Cave. Either way, those looking to pledge their allegiance to the Temple of Shadows should start early. Cornelius Grim has several diabolical tasks in store for those with the stomach to take them on.

COLLECTIBLES

🎁 CHEST	⛏ DIG SPOTS	🌊 DIVE SPOTS	👹 GARGOYLES	🗝 SILVER KEYS
2	1	0	1	1

NEIGHBORING REGIONS

NAME	DISTANCE	TIME	DIRECTION
Rookridge	-	-	-

UNHOLY MISFORTUNE

Could there be anything crueler than befriending people only to sacrifice them for your own twisted enjoyment at the Wheel of Unholy Misfortune? Why, yes, there is! Sacrifice your spouse! The Temple of Shadows offers Loyalty Points for repeat visitors and you can accumulate points faster by making sacrifices at night and by sacrificing monks and family members. Maximize your sacrificing points tally by sacrificing a spouse and three monks at midnight!

TREASURE OF THE LAND

CHESTS

🎁 CHEST	🗝 SILVER KEYS	LOCATION	CONTENTS
1	-	Next to the Wheel of Misfortune.	Shadow-Worshipper Robes and Shadow-Worshipper Mask
2	-	In the cave to the east.	150 Gold

DIG SPOTS

⛏ DIG SPOTS	CONTENTS
1	"Treasure Hunting, Book 1"

SILVER KEYS

01

Atop the altar in the fire-lit ceremony room, down the hall to the left of the Wheel of Unholy Misfortune.

GARGOYLES

01

On the wall above the entrance to the ceremony room. Head down the hall to the left of the Wheel of Misfortune.

Tomb of Heroes
AREA TYPE: TOMB

AREA SYNOPSIS

The Tomb of Heroes will remain forever out of reach until you talk to Granny Miggins during the "Rescue Charlie" quest. Only then will the pond dry up and the entrance to this secret underground tomb be revealed. As for the tomb, it consists of just three rooms, the last of which contains a sarcophagus that you'll need to help Charlie open. There are a couple of switch plates in the floor that control gates and a number of hollow men, but these should be nothing for an experienced Hero like yourself.

COLLECTIBLES

📦 CHEST	⛏ DIG SPOTS	⚓ DIVE SPOTS	👹 GARGOYLES	🔑 SILVER KEYS
3	0	0	1	1

NEIGHBORING REGIONS

NAME	DISTANCE	TIME	DIRECTION
Bower Lake	-	-	-

TREASURE OF THE LAND

🔺 SILVER KEYS

The lone Silver Key in this area is behind a column near the sarcophagus that Charlie is trying to open.

⬭ GARGOYLES

The Gargoyle is over the doorway you'll walk through on your way to find Charlie near the sarcophagus. You'll hear it call out as you walk underneath.

⬛ CHESTS

📦 CHEST	🔑 SILVER KEYS	LOCATION	CONTENTS
1	-	In the large room with the stairs.	Cure-All Health Potion
2	-	Behind a column in a dark corner.	Solid Gold Necklace
3	-	Near the switch plate on the floor.	Troll Strength Potion

Twinblade's Tomb
AREA TYPE: TOMB

AREA SYNOPSIS

The "Love Hurts" quest will take you to this otherwise locked tomb in the northern end of Wraithmarsh. Twinblade's Tomb has numerous hollow men in it, as well as several sophisticated puzzles and traps designed to keep tomb-raiders, like you, out. Look for switch plates and flit switches to disable the spiked floors and do your best Chicken expression to satisfy the Expression Statue in the middle of the tomb. There is only one path through the tomb so don't worry about getting lost. Just seek out the switch plates and shoot the flit switches to get through.

COLLECTIBLES

🗄 CHEST	⚒ DIG SPOTS	⚓ DIVE SPOTS	⛨ GARGOYLES	⚷ SILVER KEYS
1	0	0	1	1

NEIGHBORING REGIONS

NAME	DISTANCE	TIME	DIRECTION
Wraithmarsh	-	-	-

THE OTHER WHITE MEAT

The Expression Statue in the locked room isn't hard to figure out, it's clearly asking for the Chicken expression, but what might be tricky to decipher is exactly how to continue. Complete the expression then head up the stairway in the left-hand corner to the ledge above the next room. Stand on this ledge and use your ranged weapon to shoot the flit switch in the recess high on the opposite wall. This unlocks the lower door and provides a way to continue.

TREASURE OF THE LAND

🗄 CHESTS

🗄 CHEST	⚷ SILVER KEYS	LOCATION	CONTENTS
1	-	In the corner of the final room.	750 Gold

△ SILVER KEYS   ● GARGOYLES

You can't help but find this Silver Key during the Love Hurts quest, as it's right next to the body part you're seeking.

Stand on the dais between the flames in the final room of the tomb and face the door you entered through to spot the Gargoyle.

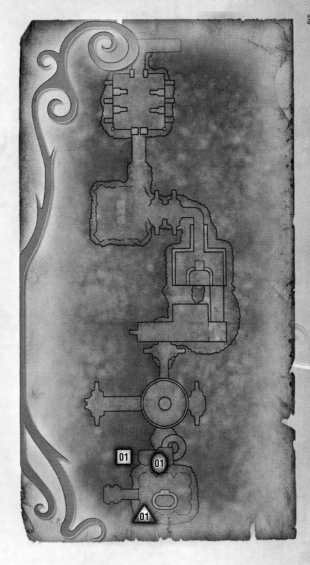

The Well
AREA TYPE: CAVE

AREA SYNOPSIS

The Well is the tiniest of the caves in Albion and contains but two chests and no other pieces of treasure. This cavern is located at the base of the well in Wraithmarsh and is accessible during the "Evil in Wraithmarsh" quest after speaking to Mrs. Spade in Bowerstone Market. Do you dare get involved with Sam & Max again? If so, make a wish and climb in...

COLLECTIBLES

🗃 CHEST	⛏ DIG SPOTS	⚓ DIVE SPOTS	👤 GARGOYLES	🗝 SILVER KEYS
2	0	0	0	0

NEIGHBORING REGIONS

NAME	DISTANCE	TIME	DIRECTION
Wraithmarsh	-	-	-

TREASURE OF THE LAND

CHESTS

🗃 CHEST	🗝 SILVER KEYS	LOCATION	CONTENTS
1	-	In the hall north of the crypt.	Cure-All Health Potion
2	-	Across the cavern with the pedestals.	Mustela Java Potion

The Wellspring
AREA TYPE: CAVE

AREA SYNOPSIS

The Wellspring, not to be confused with Wellspring Cave, is a small hollow on the north side of Rookridge, not far from the waterfall. The cave is one of the smallest in Albion, but one that serves as a refuge for many of the area's most feared bandits. The main path spirals down to a water-filled cave bottom where several valuable items can be found. You can visit this cave at any time or wait until directed there during the "Something Rotten" quest.

COLLECTIBLES

🗃 CHEST	🪏 DIG SPOTS	⚓ DIVE SPOTS	👹 GARGOYLES	🔑 SILVER KEYS
2	4	0	0	0

NEIGHBORING REGIONS

NAME	DISTANCE	TIME	DIRECTION
Rookridge	-	-	-

The Nose Knows

Give your dog plenty of treats and praise when searching this cave. There are four dig spots located in the main chamber of the cave and it's easy to miss one if he's not thoroughly interested in sniffing them out for you. Be sure to reward him after every second or third treasure identification.

TREASURE OF THE LAND

CHESTS

🗃 CHEST	🔑 SILVER KEYS	LOCATION	CONTENTS
1	-	On the left of the main entryway.	Infused Will Potion
2	-	In the bottom of the cave.	Emerald

DIG SPOTS

🪏 DIG SPOTS	CONTENTS
1	Epiphanic Blueberry Pie
2	Bits O' Beef Pie
3	100 Gold
4	Clumsy Skill Potion

Wellspring Cave
AREA TYPE: CAVE

AREA SYNOPSIS

Wellspring Cave is a place held sacred to the order of monks at the Temple of Light. It is believed that the water flowing through the springs and fountains in this cave hold mystical properties and are the only water of a high enough quality to be fed to the Golden Oak. You'll make the journey into this cave as part of an escort assignment during "The Ritual" quest. There is only one piece of treasure in this cave–a Silver Key–and you can get it during your initial visit.

COLLECTIBLES

🗃 CHEST	⚒ DIG SPOTS	⚓ DIVE SPOTS	🗿 GARGOYLES	🔑 SILVER KEYS
0	0	0	0	1

NEIGHBORING REGIONS

NAME	DISTANCE	TIME	DIRECTION
Oakfield	-	-	-

TREASURE OF THE LAND

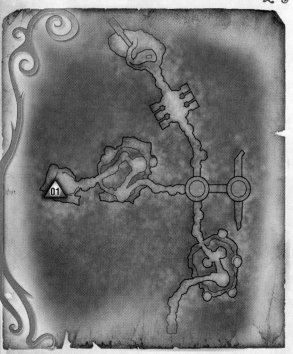

△ SILVER KEYS

The one and only piece of treasure in this cave is the Silver Key located in the left-hand fountain room.

RETURN VISIT?

Whether you choose to return to Wellspring Cave during the shadow-worshipper's assault is up to you, but do know that failure to heed the call will result in a very different place when you return from the Tattered Spire. Wellspring Cave is an extension of the Temple of Light and those seeking a life of morality will want to protect it.

Westcliff
AREA TYPE: COUNTRYSIDE & TOWN

AREA SYNOPSIS

The Westcliff region is one of the most diverse in Albion and its unique regional disparities only exaggerate with time. The area south of the river and closest to the Bandit Coast is a wild, inhospitable land and home to many balverines. Across the river, however, near the ocean to the north lies Westcliff Camp, lies a small settlement of bandits with a few shops and games, as well as the infamous Crucible arena. Those who lend 5000 Gold to Barnum before leaving for the Tattered Spire will return to find Westcliff a bustling tourist town with major improvements throughout the area—even a new bridge across the river canyon!

COLLECTIBLES

🎁 CHEST	⛏ DIG SPOTS	🤿 DIVE SPOTS	🗝 GARGOYLES	🗝 SILVER KEYS
17	0	3	4	3

NEIGHBORING REGIONS

NAME	DISTANCE	TIME	DIRECTION
The Bandit Coast	64 miles	14 hours	Southeast
Bloodstone	-	7 hours (ship)	Southeast
Howling Halls	-	-	-
Old Tin Mine	-	-	-
The Tattered Spire	-	-	-

JOBS

Bartender at The Foaming Jugs

GAMES

Westcliff Shooting Range
Fortune's Tower at The Foaming Jugs
The Crucible

Introduction
Cast of Characters
The Hero's Way
Quest Guide
➢ Albion Atlas
Weapons of Yore
Items & Clothing
Pub Games, Jobs & More
Enemies of Albion

NOT THAT THERE'S ANYTHING WRONG WITH THAT...

Those wishing to embark on a same-sex tryst or even find that special someone to enter into a gay or lesbian marriage with can probably find him or her in Westcliff. Not only are there a number of bisexual whores hanging around The Foaming Jugs tavern, but you can find several gay men here as well.

TREASURE OF THE LAND

🗹 CHESTS

🎁 CHEST	🗝 SILVER KEYS	LOCATION	CONTENTS
1	-	Along the path near the entrance.	Steel Cutlass and Resurrection Phial x2
2	-	Near the stone monuments.	Wizard Hat and Moonless Midnight Dye
3	-	Behind the small wooden house.	Infused Will Potion
4	-	Atop the stone tower near the lady.	Standard Health Potion
5	-	On the ledge beneath the tower.	Will User Robe and Autograph Card
6	20	Just past the wooden bridge.	10,000 Gold
7	-	Before the entrance to Howling Halls.	400 Gold
8	-	Near the entrance to Howling Halls.	Forever Ring
9	-	Inside a caravan at Westcliff Camp.	Cure-All Health Potion

🎁 CHEST	🗝 SILVER KEYS	LOCATION	CONTENTS
10	5	Up the path from the statue plinth.	Bewitching Augment and Diamond
11*	-	Inside the Foaming Jugs bar & brothel.	Adept Skill Potion
12*	-	Inside the Foaming Jugs bar & brothel.	Adept Skill Potion
13*	-	Inside the Foaming Jugs bar & brothel.	Diamond
14*	-	Inside the Foaming Jugs bar & brothel.	Mustela Java Potion
*15	-	In the cabin across the new bridge.	2000 Gold
16	-	Near the entrance to Old Tin Mine.	Ruby
17	-	Inside the cave near the waterfall.	Resurrection Phial

* Requires a 5000 gold investment with Barnum.

Westcliff

02
04
14
11
13
12
09
03
10
01
16
07
08
03
02
02
04
01
05
06
01
15
03
17
01
03
02
1

GARGOYLES

01

02

03

04

Grab the contents from the second chest then turn around to spot this heckling Gargoyle on the stone monument you walked under.

The Gargoyle is on the rocky ledge near the tower. Shoot it from the stairs of the tower.

Approach the entrance to the Howling Halls and turn to the right to find a Gargoyle high on the wall, in the corner.

Descend the path towards the beach after returning from the Tattered Spire to find this Gargoyle on the cliff above the trail.

SILVER KEYS

01

02

03

Cross the bridge after meeting the lady and look in the wooden shed on the left-hand side of the trail.

Follow the path down to the beach near Westcliff Camp to find a Silver Key behind the crates.

Jump down into the water before Howling Halls and swim upstream to find this Silver Key on the riverbank.

DIVE SPOTS

DIVE SPOTS	CONTENTS
1	Golden Apple
2	Sleepy Bean Java Potion
3	300 Gold

DEMON DOOR

1 THE VAULT

Reward: The Vault is one of the smallest Demon Door areas and in it is just a single chest containing the **Calavera**, the legendary mace! This is one of the easiest Demon Doors to unlock and one you should definitely aim to do prior to going to The Crucible.

This particular Demon Door is located in the southern section of Westcliff. You'll likely pass it on your way to the Howling Halls. This Demon Door is a fan of all things hedonistic and it only opens to those who have showed to travel a path of self-indulgence. Embark on a life of corrupt behavior and tilt the purity needle at least halfway in favor of corruption to satisfy this Demon Door's requirement. Don't worry; there's still plenty of time to regain your purity.

BARNUM'S DREAM

Westcliff looks drastically different depending entirely on your decisions earlier in the game. If you decide to invest in Barnum's scheme to turn Westcliff into a family-friendly destination, more chests, business, and buildings will be available when you return from the Spire quest. However, if you choose not to invest, nothing changes and Westcliff remains the same.

MERCHANT DIRECTORY

SHOP	WARES	MAX PRODUCT QUALITY
The Foaming Jugs	Drinks & Food	★★★★
Westcliff Alchemist Stall	Potions	★★★★
Westcliff Blacksmith	Weapons	★★★★
Westcliff Clothes Stall	Clothes	★★★★★
Westcliff Food Stall	Food	★★★
Westcliff General Store	General Goods	★★★★
Westcliff Miscellany Stall	Gifts & Items	★★★★★
Westcliff Tattooist	Tattoos	★
Westcliff Weapon Stall	Weapons	★★★★

All the shopping in Westcliff is confined to a short merchant street in Westcliff Camp, outside The Crucible. Although you'll be able to buy a few essential items during your first trip to Westcliff, it's not until you return from the Tattered Spire when the town really starts to grow. The 5000 gold you leant Barnum (you *did* lend it to him, right?) has helped transform the town's economy and now full-scale operations like the Westcliff General Store and The Foaming Jugs are thriving.

REAL ESTATE SNAPSHOT

Unlike other towns with a number of established businesses to purchase, Westcliff is lacking in suitable home sites. There are a number of caravans (after the *Westcliff Development* quest) grouped together outside the business section of Westcliff Camp, but that is all. In contrast, the numerous merchant stalls, blacksmith shop, Westcliff General Store, and The Foaming Jugs tavern offer plenty of investment options for Heroes with varying amounts of gold.

SPOTLIGHT HOME

Westcliff Caravan

2 Barnum Road, Westcliff

History: Whatever Barnum paid to have these caravans built, it was well worth it: they really add to the ambiance.

Base Value: 1000 Gold
Owner: Glen the Househusband
Bonuses: -

There are plenty of choices for home buying in Westcliff. You can buy *this* caravan or you can have *that* caravan. Or perhaps you prefer *that other* caravan. They're all the same: same looks, same costs, and the same lack of a sleeping bonus. If you're going to purchase any of these, try to do it right after coming back from the Tattered Spire so that you can at least maximize the amount of time you'll be pulling in that seven gold coins in rent.

SPOTLIGHT BUSINESS

The Foaming Jugs

1 Crucible Walk, Westcliff

History: Visitors to Westcliff can stop here for some refreshments before taking in a Crucible show.

Base Value: 36,000 Gold
Owner: Martin the Barman

Aside from the blacksmith's shop and the Westcliff General Store, The Foaming Jugs is the only place in Westcliff of any significant value and is definitely the tavern to invest in Albion. The people in Westcliff are a mixture of rough-and-tumble types as well as some of the more well-heeled travelers from fancier parts. The one thing they have in common is that they're here to party—and the spacious brothel located upstairs doesn't hurt either!

Wraithmarsh
AREA TYPE: COUNTRYSIDE

AREA SYNOPSIS

Wraithmarsh is the undeniable epicenter of all things spooky in Albion. This swampland isn't just crawling with hollow men and banshees, but it also contains some of the largest tombs in the region–tombs filled with ghosts and yet even more hollow men. Despite the onslaught of banshee attacks and even the presence of a troll, no part of Wraithmarsh can frighten like a trip through the old Oakvale neighborhood. Oakvale has a special, if not infamous, place in the history of Albion and seeing the mist-shrouded swamp consume it is sobering. As is the evidence of what one man's greed could do to a village.

COLLECTIBLES

CHEST	DIG SPOTS	DIVE SPOTS	GARGOYLES	SILVER KEYS
9	8	0	4	4

NEIGHBORING REGIONS

NAME	DISTANCE	TIME	DIRECTION
Bloodstone	60 miles	15 hours	East
Shadow Court	-	-	-
Twinblade's Tomb	-	-	-
The Well	-	-	-

TREASURE OF THE LAND

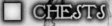

DIG SPOTS

DIG SPOTS	CONTENTS
1	Sleepy Bean Java Potion
2	Pretty Necklace
3	Instant Java Potion
4	1500 Gold
5	Amethyst
6	300 Gold
7	Rusty Necklace
8	Precious Necklace

CHESTS

CHEST	SILVER KEYS	LOCATION	CONTENTS
1	-	Below the bridge near the start.	Mustela Java Potion
2	-	In a valley southeast of farm.	Obsidian Java Potion
3	-	Right of the path along the hill.	750 Gold
4	-	Near the ruins on the right.	750 Gold
5	-	In the east-most corner of the marsh.	Cure-All Health Potion
6	-	In a cabin to the east of the troll.	Pure Experience Extract
7	20	On the bridge during return visit.	Devastation Augment
8	-	In the river below the bridge.	Ruby
9	-	Near marshes on south end of area.	750 Gold

◭ SILVER KEYS

01 Proceed to the drowned farm and head inside the first house on the left. The Silver Key is on the second floor.

02 This Silver Key is in the crypt on the left-hand side as you descend down into the circle of tombs.

03 Leave the circle of tombs and loop around to the northeast to find this Silver Key in a corner near some gravestones.

04 You'll all but walk right into this Silver Key as you exit Twinblade's Tomb during the Love Hurts quest.

◯ GARGOYLES

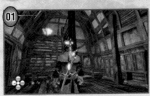

01 Search inside the barn near the cage where you first appear in the area.

02 This Gargoyle is on the outside of the large house north of the drowned farm.

03 Look behind the ruins on the right-hand side of the path as you make your way up the slope away from the ruins of Oakvale.

04 Start down the hill from the circle of tombs, then turn around when you hear the Gargoyle. It's on the ruin on the right.

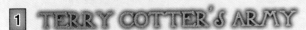

DEMON DOOR

1 TERRY COTTER'S ARMY

Reward: Travel through the Demon Door to the home of a scared little boy who built hundreds of statues to protect him while he slept. Go to the cave behind the house and slash your way through the rows of statues to find **The Perforator**, another legendary weapon!

The Demon Door in the northeast corner of Wraithmarsh is yet another fan of theatre, only this one wants to be the actor. He is tired of performing for small, undeserving crowds and wants you to assemble a large crowd of intelligent, upper class (or at least middle class) people to listen to his reading. You'll need to have achieved enough renown in order to have increased number of followers at once. We recommend heading to Fairfax Gardens or the Cow & Corset in Bowerstone Market and gathering up ten followers. This way you'll be sure to have at least the number of intellectuals he's looking for. Now stand and listen to his drivel and remember that there's an impressive weapon in it for you. Just grin and bear it.

Weapons of Yore

Albion is no stranger to war. As the centuries pass and leaders rise and fall, the one constant in this land is the need for improved weaponry. There was a time when a Hero could travel the countryside with nothing but a short sword and bow, but those days have long since been relegated to the history books. Time has marched on since then. Progress has been made and inventions discovered, and in the era of our current Hero, the need for firearms is great. This is not to say gunpowder and bullets have completely replaced the cold steel of a finely-crafted blade, but their importance cannot be understated in this age. Nevertheless, the Hero most likely to win widespread renown from coast to coast is the one who best combines the use of melee and ranged weaponry.

Melee Weapons

Melee weapons come in different shapes and sizes, but all serve the same purpose: bashing and slashing enemies an arm's length away. Although melee weapons are useless against distant foes, they are extremely handy when standing face-to-ugly-face with an enemy. Weapons of this type come in different shapes and sizes. Generally, the larger the melee weapon is, the more damage it will inflict but the slower it can be swung. These larger, more cumbersome weapons (axes, hammers, and maces) are perfect for use against isolated, large enemies. On the other hand, the smaller blades (cutlasses and katanas) can be swung blazingly quick and are perfect for swarms of low-level enemies. Naturally, there are also several all-purpose melee weapons that blend power with attack speed.

MELEE WEAPON EXPLANATION

(1) **NAME:** This is the name of the weapon. Most weapons have a descriptive name that indicates their quality (Rusty < Iron < Steel < Master), but special weapons have unique names.

(2) **STARS:** Every item has a star value. This is your guide to the relative rarity and value of a particular weapon or item. The more stars, the more valuable it is.

(3) **IMAGE:** This shows you what the weapon looks like so you can imagine it hanging off your Hero's back. Weapons as accessories, who knew?

(4) **DAMAGE:** The amount of health a single attack from this weapon will inflict before modifiers are applied.

(5) **TYPE:** Some weapons inflict cutting damage while others inflict blunt damage. Both hurt a great deal; one is just messier than the other.

(6) **ATTACK SPEED:** This tells you how fast you can swing a weapon repeatedly. Heavy weapons are slower than smaller, lighter weapons.

(7) **BASE VALUE:** The fair market amount (in gold) that the weapon is worth with zero augment slots. The weapon will be bought or sold for a different value depending on various economics of the merchant, as well as how many augment slots it has. Weapons with augment slots may cost significantly more.

(8) **AUGMENT SLOTS:** Each of the standard weapons comes in a form with a different number of augment slots ranging from zero to four. Weapons with customizable augment slots only range from zero to two. Augments are special stones that can be applied to a weapon to infuse it with special powers. See the full assortment of augments in the "Items and Collectibles" chapter.

(9) **DESCRIPTION:** Every weapon has a brief description that reveals a bit about its craftsmanship, its history, or even how useful it is.

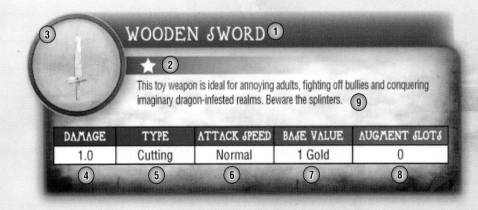

WOODEN SWORD (1)

★ (2)

This toy weapon is ideal for annoying adults, fighting off bullies and conquering imaginary dragon-infested realms. Beware the splinters. (9)

DAMAGE	TYPE	ATTACK SPEED	BASE VALUE	AUGMENT SLOTS
1.0 (4)	Cutting (5)	Normal (6)	1 Gold (7)	0 (8)

CHILDREN'S SERIES

WOODEN SWORD
★

This toy weapon is ideal for annoying adults, fighting off bullies and conquering imaginary dragon-infested realms. Beware the splinters.

DAMAGE	TYPE	ATTACK SPEED	BASE VALUE	AUGMENT SLOTS
1.0	Cutting	Normal	1 Gold	0

LONGSWORDS

RUSTY LONGSWORD
★

A rudimentary weapon that is more commonly wielded by poor farmers desperate to protect their harvest from hobbes than it is by warriors.

DAMAGE	TYPE	ATTACK SPEED	BASE VALUE	AUGMENT SLOTS
18.0	Cutting	Normal	250 Gold	0-4

IRON LONGSWORD
★★

An effective weapon in the right hands, this is considered a beginner's sword, more practical for training purposes than real battle.

DAMAGE	TYPE	ATTACK SPEED	BASE VALUE	AUGMENT SLOTS
30.0	Cutting	Normal	1000 Gold	0-4

STEEL LONGSWORD
★★★

A fine piece of steel, designed to skewer your enemy in the most elegant manner possible.

DAMAGE	TYPE	ATTACK SPEED	BASE VALUE	AUGMENT SLOTS
53.0	Cutting	Normal	4000 Gold	0-4

MASTER LONGSWORD
★★★★

This is a sword kings would be proud to wield in battle. It has perfect balance, and serrated edges that will slash through enemies as if they were made of paper.

DAMAGE	TYPE	ATTACK SPEED	BASE VALUE	AUGMENT SLOTS
79.0	Cutting	Normal	16,000 Gold	0-4

CUTLASSES

RUSTY CUTLASS
★

Only the most pathetic of pirates, or one who had spent a great deal of time on the bottom of the sea, would be seen holding a sword like this.

DAMAGE	TYPE	ATTACK SPEED	BASE VALUE	AUGMENT SLOTS
20.0	Cutting	Normal	250 Gold	0-4

IRON CUTLASS
★★

It may be cheap, but many a head has been sliced at seas with an iron cutlass.

DAMAGE	TYPE	ATTACK SPEED	BASE VALUE	AUGMENT SLOTS
28.5	Cutting	Normal	1000 Gold	0-4

STEEL CUTLASS
★★★

Favored by the more professional pirates sailing the ocean, these fine swords are designed to intimidate sailors, passengers, and captains alike.

DAMAGE	TYPE	ATTACK SPEED	BASE VALUE	AUGMENT SLOTS
50.0	Cutting	Normal	4000 Gold	0-4

MASTER CUTLASS
★★★★

The pirate captain's weapon of choice. It's perfectly balanced, and able to strike down a mutiny in a moment.

DAMAGE	TYPE	ATTACK SPEED	BASE VALUE	AUGMENT SLOTS
75.0	Cutting	Normal	16,000 Gold	0-4

KATANA

RUSTY KATANA
★

Real katana originated in the Eastern regions of Samarkand, and this appears to be nothing more than a cheap imitation.

DAMAGE	TYPE	ATTACK SPEED	BASE VALUE	AUGMENT SLOTS
19.0	Cutting	Fast	275 Gold	0-4

IRON KATANA
★★

Not one of the finer examples of the sword that originates from Eastern Samarkand. Most likely this is an Albion blacksmith's attempt to recreate that fine steel.

DAMAGE	TYPE	ATTACK SPEED	BASE VALUE	AUGMENT SLOTS
27.0	Cutting	Fast	1100 Gold	0-4

STEEL KATANA
★★★

These remarkable swords are imported from the hills of Eastern Samarkand, where they are forged by warrior monks. Few weapons are as deadly.

DAMAGE	TYPE	ATTACK SPEED	BASE VALUE	AUGMENT SLOTS
48.0	Cutting	Fast	4400 Gold	0-4

MASTER KATANA
★★★★

The warrior monks of the hills in Eastern Samarkand not only forge these exceptional blades, they do not hesitate to use them on invaders or dangerous creatures. There is no finer steel, nor sword more finely crafted.

DAMAGE	TYPE	ATTACK SPEED	BASE VALUE	AUGMENT SLOTS
71.0	Cutting	Fast	17,600 Gold	0-4

CLEAVERS

RUSTY CLEAVER
★

Cleavers are swift and cause light damage. And while this one is more likely to cause death through disease than the effective rendering of flesh, there is nonetheless something rather brutal and nasty about it.

DAMAGE	TYPE	ATTACK SPEED	BASE VALUE	AUGMENT SLOTS
21.0	Cutting	Normal	300 Gold	0-4

IRON CLEAVER
★★

Primarily an instrument for butchers, the trusty iron cleaver gained something of a reputation 200 years ago when a serial killer, wearing a mask he'd fashioned to resemble that of Jack of Blades, used it to murder and quarter 27 victims.

DAMAGE	TYPE	ATTACK SPEED	BASE VALUE	AUGMENT SLOTS
31.5	Cutting	Normal	1200 Gold	0-4

STEEL CLEAVER
★★★

A light but effective weapon, able to gash and tear the flesh of enemies with great speed, steel cleavers are a fearsome weapon in close-combat.

DAMAGE	TYPE	ATTACK SPEED	BASE VALUE	AUGMENT SLOTS
55.0	Cutting	Normal	4800 Gold	0-4

MASTER CLEAVER
★★★★

Though popular among well-to-do Fairfax citizens who use them as decorative items and to carve unicorn meat, there are few weapons as likely to tear a ribbon to shreds than these magnificent cleavers.

DAMAGE	TYPE	ATTACK SPEED	BASE VALUE	AUGMENT SLOTS
83.0	Cutting	Normal	19,200 Gold	0-4

AXES

RUSTY AXE
★

This rudimentary weapon only just qualifies as an axe. Probably cobbled together by hobbes using a piece of wood and a filed-down piece of machinery, it may be slow, but its jagged edges will leave some ugly wounds behind.

DAMAGE	TYPE	ATTACK SPEED	BASE VALUE	AUGMENT SLOTS
25.0	Cutting	Slow	300 Gold	0-4

IRON AXE
★★

Here's a basic, but sturdy weapon. It was traditionally the weapon of choice of the wild warriors of ancient Brightwood. It may be slow, but it can deliver a hefty bit of damage.

DAMAGE	TYPE	ATTACK SPEED	BASE VALUE	AUGMENT SLOTS
37.5	Cutting	Slow	1200 Gold	0-4

STEEL AXE
★★★

A beautifully crafted battleaxe. Don't be fooled by the patterns engraved into the steel. It specializes in dismemberments, decapitations and other slight injuries.

DAMAGE	TYPE	ATTACK SPEED	BASE VALUE	AUGMENT SLOTS
66.0	Cutting	Slow	4800 Gold	0-4

MASTER AXE
★★★★

This devastating battle axe was the favored weapon of the elite guard of Lord Onish, ruler of northern Samarkand a thousand years ago. Despite their age, they are as sharp an effective as any axe forged by a modern master blacksmith.

DAMAGE	TYPE	ATTACK SPEED	BASE VALUE	AUGMENT SLOTS
99.0	Cutting	Slow	19,200 Gold	0-4

MACES

RUSTY MACE
★

As crude and ugly as it is effective, one can imagine this mace being wielded by the very first men to walk upon this world.

DAMAGE	TYPE	ATTACK SPEED	BASE VALUE	AUGMENT SLOTS
23.0	Blunt	Slow	325 Gold	0-4

IRON MACE
★★

There is no better instrument for bludgeoning enemies than a trusty iron mace.

DAMAGE	TYPE	ATTACK SPEED	BASE VALUE	AUGMENT SLOTS
34.0	Blunt	Slow	1300 Gold	0-4

STEEL MACE
★★★

The bones of your enemies will not only be broken by a swing of this mace, they will be pulverized.

DAMAGE	TYPE	ATTACK SPEED	BASE VALUE	AUGMENT SLOTS
61.0	Blunt	Slow	5200 Gold	0-4

MASTER MACE
★★★★

A truly vicious weapon, used by the elite order of guards established after the fall of the Heroes Guild to deal with the chaos that followed, these maces have since fallen into disuse by all but the most ferocious warriors.

DAMAGE	TYPE	ATTACK SPEED	BASE VALUE	AUGMENT SLOTS
91.0	Blunt	Slow	20,800 Gold	0-4

HAMMERS

RUSTY HAMMER
★

As primitive a weapon as one is likely to find in Albion, it still serves its purpose. If the purpose is to cave someone's head in.

DAMAGE	TYPE	ATTACK SPEED	BASE VALUE	AUGMENT SLOTS
27.0	Blunt	Slow	350 Gold	0-4

IRON HAMMER
★★

You can try to put pictures up on the wall with the aid of this hammer, but it would be wiser to put dents in your enemies' skulls instead.

DAMAGE	TYPE	ATTACK SPEED	BASE VALUE	AUGMENT SLOTS
40.5	Blunt	Slow	1400 Gold	0-4

STEEL HAMMER
★★★

This powerful and rather heavy warhammer might be slow, but when it connects with its target it can do untold damage.

DAMAGE	TYPE	ATTACK SPEED	BASE VALUE	AUGMENT SLOTS
71.0	Blunt	Slow	5600 Gold	0-4

MASTER HAMMER
★★★★

An exquisite example of a warhammer, wielded in countless battles by the ancient warriors of the Northern Wastes.

DAMAGE	TYPE	ATTACK SPEED	BASE VALUE	AUGMENT SLOTS
107.0	Blunt	Slow	22,400 Gold	0-4

LEGENDARY WEAPONS

THE CALAVERA

★★★★★

The augment in this weapon allows you to inflict fire damage on your enemies. It was first wielded by Vipress, a half-warrior, half-witch, whose beauty was equaled only by her strength and her wrath. Men worshipped her, and she led many of them into some of the most savage battles Albion has ever witnessed.

DAMAGE	TYPE	ATTACK SPEED	BASE VALUE	AUGMENT SLOTS
67.0	Blunt	Slow	4385 Gold	Flame

THE CHOPPER

★★★★★

The augments in this weapon make you resistant to scarring, and allow you to earn more experience in combat. This axe belonged to the legendary Crucible fighter Mad-dog "The Strangler" McGraw, who set the standard by which all other competitors would be judged. The day he retired, he promised to hand over his beloved weapon to anyone who could break his records, never believing such a day would come.

DAMAGE	TYPE	ATTACK SPEED	BASE VALUE	AUGMENT SLOTS
86.0	Cutting	Slow	16,200 Gold	Discipline & Stoneskin

THE DAICHI

★★★★★

The augments in this weapon allow you to inflict greater damage on your enemies, with additional electric damage. It will also make you appear more attractive. This exceptional sword once belonged to the legendary Zuna Daichi, a female warrior monk whose exploits in Eastern Samarkand have become part of popular myth. There are stories that she may have visited Albion once, while on a quest. Perhaps it was in this land that she died, and here that she left her katana.

DAMAGE	TYPE	ATTACK SPEED	BASE VALUE	AUGMENT SLOTS
96.0	Cutting	Fast	59,400 Gold	Devastation, Bewitching & Killerwatt

HAL'S SWORD (UNLOCKED CONTENT)

★

Long ago, when Albion was still under rule of the Old Kingdom, a rift in space opened a portal between dimensions. Through the rift stepped a warrior of immense power, clad in armor and carrying a striking crystal sword. Though he never revealed his real name, he was known to all as Hal. Made out of a strange material resembling glass, this sword once emitted a powerful energy when wielded by Hal.

DAMAGE	TYPE	ATTACK SPEED	BASE VALUE	AUGMENT SLOTS
22.0	Cutting	Fast	3375 Gold	3

THE HAMMERTHYST

★★★★★

The augment in this weapon makes you more resistant to damage, but less resistant to scarring. The origins of this gorgeous gem-headed warhammer are shrouded in mystery. It has resurfaced many times in history, and served many masters, all of which were said to become invincible when wielding it. According to popular myth, it is the hammer that finds and chooses its next master.

DAMAGE	TYPE	ATTACK SPEED	BASE VALUE	AUGMENT SLOTS
78.0	Blunt	Slow	4725 Gold	Barkskin

THE MAELSTROM

★★★★★

The augment in this weapon causes it to inflict greater damage on lawful beings, such as guards and citizens. This longsword has been forged by the First Shadows themselves, beings far purer in their evil and their power than the ordinary shadows that haunt Albion. When the founders of the Temple of Shadows tried to summon one of these beings, they were unable to control it. Before it disappeared into its own dimension, it slaughtered every one of them for their insolence, and left its instrument of punishment behind as a warning to others.

DAMAGE	TYPE	ATTACK SPEED	BASE VALUE	AUGMENT SLOTS
58.0	Cutting	Normal	3375 Gold	Scourge

THE RISING SUN

★★★★★

The augment in this weapon causes it to inflict greater damage on truly evil beings, such as banshees and shadows. This magnificent cleaver belonged to Roamer, the greatest Hero from a long-extinct Southern Samarkand tribe for whom dawns were sacred. His combat style involved whirling among his enemies, shredding anyone who came in contact with the Rising Sun.

DAMAGE	TYPE	ATTACK SPEED	BASE VALUE	AUGMENT SLOTS
61.0	Cutting	Normal	4050 Gold	Righteous Violence

THE WRECKAGER

★★★★★

The augments in this weapon make you resistant to scarring, earn you gold for every kill and cause all citizens who see it to cower in terror. Legend has it that this cutlass once belonged to Captain Dread himself, the most feared pirate in all the world's

DAMAGE	TYPE	ATTACK SPEED	BASE VALUE	AUGMENT SLOTS
65.0	Cutting	Normal	54,000 Gold	Fear Itself, Golden Touch, & Stoneskin

Ranged Weapons

There are many types of ranged weaponry, but every last one of them can be used to damage an enemy standing too far away to hit with a melee weapon. Ranged weapons are great for taking down enemies flying out of reach of your sword, or for those positioned on a cliff or across a broken bridge. The different types of ranged weapons each have their own unique pros and cons, namely how fast they can be reloaded, their ammo capacity, the damage they inflict, and their effective range. As you might expect, the weapons that can inflict the most damage at the farthest range also typically have the slowest reload times and carry the least ammo. Other weapons have faster reload times, but inflict less damage or carry less ammunition. Which you choose to use depends as much on your own personal preference as it will the augments with which you equip the weapon.

RANGED WEAPON EXPLANATION

(1) **NAME:** This is the name of the weapon. Most weapons have a descriptive name that indicates their quality (Rusty < Iron < Steel < Master), but special weapons have unique names. Crossbows have a different set of descriptors, but are just as easy to decipher (Splintered < Yew < Oak < Master).

(2) **STARS:** Every item has a star value. This is your guide to the relative rarity and value of a particular weapon or item. The more stars, the more valuable it is.

(3) **IMAGE:** This shows you what the weapon looks like so you can image it hanging off your Hero's back.

(4) **DAMAGE:** The amount of health a single attack from this weapon will inflict before modifiers.

(5) **TYPE:** This is the type of projectile the weapon fires. Most of these weapons are firearms that shoot bullets, but the crossbows shoot bolts.

(6) **ATTACK SPEED:** This tells you how fast the weapon can be fired. This rating really only applies to those weapons with an ammo capacity greater than 1 since all other weapons must be reloaded after being fired.

(7) **AMMO CAPACITY:** How many arrows or bullets the weapon can hold at once. Weapons with increased ammo capacity can be fired repeatedly between reloads.

(8) **RELOAD TIME:** How long it takes to reload the weapon. Weapons with higher ammo capacities generally take longer. Times of 1 second or less are favorable.

(9) **RANGE:** How far the weapon's projectile travels. The greater this number, the farther away you can be from your target and still fire the weapon effectively.

(10) **BASE VALUE:** The fair market amount (in gold) that the weapon is worth with zero augment slots. The weapon will be bought or sold for a different value depending on various economics of the merchant, as well as how many augment slots it has. Weapons with augment slots may cost significantly more.

(11) **AUGMENT SLOTS:** Each of the standard weapons comes in a form with a different number of augment slots ranging from zero to four. Weapons with customizable augment slots only range from zero to two. Augments are special stones that can be applied to a weapon to infuse it with special powers. See the full assortment of augments in the "Items and Collectibles" chapter.

(12) **DESCRIPTION:** Every weapon has a brief description that reveals a bit about its craftsmanship, its history, or even how useful it is.

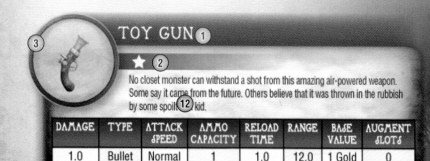

TOY GUN (1)

★ (2)

No closet monster can withstand a shot from this amazing air-powered weapon. Some say it came from the future. Others believe that it was thrown in the rubbish by some spoiled (12) kid.

DAMAGE	TYPE	ATTACK SPEED	AMMO CAPACITY	RELOAD TIME	RANGE	BASE VALUE	AUGMENT SLOTS
1.0	Bullet	Normal	1	1.0	12.0	1 Gold	0
(4)	(5)	(6)	(7)	(8)	(9)	(10)	(11)

CHILDREN'S SERIES

TOY GUN

★

No closet monster can withstand a shot from this amazing air-powered weapon. Some say it came from the future. Others believe that it was thrown in the rubbish by some spoilt rich kid.

DAMAGE	TYPE	ATTACK SPEED	AMMO CAPACITY	RELOAD TIME	RANGE	BASE VALUE	AUGMENT SLOTS
1.0	Bullet	Normal	1	1.0	12.0	1 Gold	0

LIGHT CROSSBOWS

LIGHT SPLINTERED CROSSBOW

★

It's not the best constructed crossbow ever made, and it's slow and clunky compared to modern firearms, but it's still better than a spitball shooter.

DAMAGE	TYPE	ATTACK SPEED	AMMO CAPACITY	RELOAD TIME	RANGE	BASE VALUE	AUGMENT SLOTS
20.0	Arrow	Normal	1	0.65	40.0	150 Gold	0-4

LIGHT YEW CROSSBOW

★★

Tough, lacking in style, and liable to fall apart in your hands, this can still be very useful when you don't want to get too close to an enemy.

DAMAGE	TYPE	ATTACK SPEED	AMMO CAPACITY	RELOAD TIME	RANGE	BASE VALUE	AUGMENT SLOTS
30.0	Arrow	Normal	1	0.65	40.0	600 Gold	0-4

LIGHT OAK CROSSBOW

★★★

This light but powerful crossbow will destroy an enemy's head from quite a distance.

DAMAGE	TYPE	ATTACK SPEED	AMMO CAPACITY	RELOAD TIME	RANGE	BASE VALUE	AUGMENT SLOTS
53.0	Arrow	Normal	1	0.65	40.0	2400 Gold	0-4

LIGHT MASTER CROSSBOW

★★★★

These stylish crossbows were favored by the Archers of the White Order, mercenaries once hired by armies to turn the tide of wars.

DAMAGE	TYPE	ATTACK SPEED	AMMO CAPACITY	RELOAD TIME	RANGE	BASE VALUE	AUGMENT SLOTS
68.0	Arrow	Normal	1	0.65	40.0	9600 Gold	0-4

HEAVY CROSSBOWS

HEAVY SPLINTERED CROSSBOW

★

As its name implies, this is a heavy, slow weapon, unwieldy even in the best of circumstances. It will still hurt your enemies; just make sure they're not close enough to strike you while you reload it.

DAMAGE	TYPE	ATTACK SPEED	AMMO CAPACITY	RELOAD TIME	RANGE	BASE VALUE	AUGMENT SLOTS
23.0	Arrow	Normal	1	0.9	45.0	200 Gold	0-4

HEAVY YEW CROSSBOW

★★

Slow and awkward, this crossbow still packs a mean punch if you can control it.

DAMAGE	TYPE	ATTACK SPEED	AMMO CAPACITY	RELOAD TIME	RANGE	BASE VALUE	AUGMENT SLOTS
34.5	Arrow	Normal	1	0.9	45.0	800 Gold	0-4

HEAVY OAK CROSSBOW

★★★

A solid and well-crafted crossbow, it causes panic among the ranks of your enemies if you can wield it properly.

DAMAGE	TYPE	ATTACK SPEED	AMMO CAPACITY	RELOAD TIME	RANGE	BASE VALUE	AUGMENT SLOTS
61.0	Arrow	Normal	1	0.9	45.0	3200 Gold	0-4

HEAVY MASTER CROSSBOW

★★★★

There is no more finely crafted heavy crossbow than this. Devastating from a distance, and more maneuverable than its name might imply, it is no wonder generations of royal archers have defended castles all over the world using one.

DAMAGE	TYPE	ATTACK SPEED	AMMO CAPACITY	RELOAD TIME	RANGE	BASE VALUE	AUGMENT SLOTS
91.0	Arrow	Normal	1	0.9	45.0	12,800 Gold	0-4

REPEATER CROSSBOWS

SPLINTERED REPEATER CROSSBOW

★

It won't win any beauty contests, and it may end up shooting an arrow in your eye, but without the need to constantly reload, this crossbow still has its uses.

DAMAGE	TYPE	ATTACK SPEED	AMMO CAPACITY	RELOAD TIME	RANGE	BASE VALUE	AUGMENT SLOTS
17.0	Arrow	Normal	3	1.0	35.0	250 Gold	0-4

YEW REPEATER CROSSBOW

★★

Deliver a volley of arrows without having to reload. Though not as solid or powerful as its oak counterpart, this crossbow still comes in useful in the heat of battle.

DAMAGE	TYPE	ATTACK SPEED	AMMO CAPACITY	RELOAD TIME	RANGE	BASE VALUE	AUGMENT SLOTS
25.5	Arrow	Normal	4	1.0	35.0	1000 Gold	0-4

OAK REPEATER CROSSBOW

★★★

Even amateur archers are bound to hit their target with this high quality repeater crossbow.

DAMAGE	TYPE	ATTACK SPEED	AMMO CAPACITY	RELOAD TIME	RANGE	BASE VALUE	AUGMENT SLOTS
45.0	Arrow	Normal	5	1.0	35.0	4000 Gold	0-4

MASTER REPEATER CROSSBOW

★★★★

Perhaps the most beautiful and most sophisticated series of crossbows ever constructed, the Master Repeaters bear the signature of Earl Mason, the only craftsman with the skill to put these marvels together.

DAMAGE	TYPE	ATTACK SPEED	AMMO CAPACITY	RELOAD TIME	RANGE	BASE VALUE	AUGMENT SLOTS
68.0	Arrow	Normal	6	1.0	35.0	16,000 Gold	0-4

FLINTLOCK PISTOLS

RUSTY FLINTLOCK PISTOL

★

It's possible this was once a perfectly good pistol, but time has dulled its power and reliability. Like all pistols, it has a faster reload speed than its rifle counterpart, though it has a much shorter range and does less damage.

DAMAGE	TYPE	ATTACK SPEED	AMMO CAPACITY	RELOAD TIME	RANGE	BASE VALUE	AUGMENT SLOTS
22.0	Bullet	Normal	1	0.65	40.0	250 Gold	0-4

IRON FLINTLOCK PISTOL

★★

The flintlock mechanism was once hailed as the second greatest invention in Albion's history of warfare—gunpowder having been discovered in Samarkand—though it has been superseded by the clockwork firearm design. This is a cheap but effective weapon which, like all pistols, has a fast reload speed, though it has a much shorter range than rifles and does less damage.

DAMAGE	TYPE	ATTACK SPEED	AMMO CAPACITY	RELOAD TIME	RANGE	BASE VALUE	AUGMENT SLOTS
33.0	Bullet	Normal	1	0.65	40.0	1000 Gold	0-4

STEEL FLINTLOCK PISTOL

★★★

The flintlock mechanism has been hailed as the second greatest invention in the history of warfare—gunpowder having been discovered in Samarkand. You won't find many firearms as finely constructed as this pistol. Perfect for making holes in your enemies' heads.

DAMAGE	TYPE	ATTACK SPEED	AMMO CAPACITY	RELOAD TIME	RANGE	BASE VALUE	AUGMENT SLOTS
58.0	Bullet	Normal	1	0.65	40.0	4000 Gold	0-4

MASTER FLINTLOCK PISTOL

★★★★

As stylish a firearm as you could hope to carry, those who die from one of its shots should count themselves lucky. It may lack the range and power of a rifle, but its faster reload times more than make up for that.

DAMAGE	TYPE	ATTACK SPEED	AMMO CAPACITY	RELOAD TIME	RANGE	BASE VALUE	AUGMENT SLOTS
87.0	Bullet	Normal	1	0.65	40.0	16,000 Gold	0-4

TURRET PISTOLS

RUSTY TURRET PISTOL

★

The invention of the turret firearm revolutionized warfare in Albion. Multibarrel technology obviated the need for continuous reloads, and gave its users a marked advantage in the battlefield. This pistol's best days are long behind it, but will still be appreciated by those too lazy or too much in a hurry to reload after every shot.

DAMAGE	TYPE	ATTACK SPEED	AMMO CAPACITY	RELOAD TIME	RANGE	BASE VALUE	AUGMENT SLOTS
16.0	Bullet	Normal	3	1.0	35.0	300 Gold	0-4

IRON TURRET PISTOL

★★

The invention of the turret firearm revolutionized warfare in Albion. Multibarrel technology obviated the need for continuous reloads, and gave its users a marked advantage in the battlefield. This pistol is a rather poor example, but it will still prove more useful than any other pistol of a similar level.

DAMAGE	TYPE	ATTACK SPEED	AMMO CAPACITY	RELOAD TIME	RANGE	BASE VALUE	AUGMENT SLOTS
24.0	Bullet	Normal	4	1.0	35.0	1200 Gold	0-4

STEEL TURRET PISTOL
★★★

The invention of the turret firearm revolutionized warfare in Albion. Multibarrel technology obviated the need for continuous reloads, and gave its users a marked advantage in the battlefield. This pistol is a rather fine example of the technology, capable of bringing down a small army.

DAMAGE	TYPE	ATTACK SPEED	AMMO CAPACITY	RELOAD TIME	RANGE	BASE VALUE	AUGMENT SLOTS
42.0	Bullet	Normal	5	1.0	35.0	4800 Gold	0-4

MASTER TURRET PISTOL
★★★★

The invention of the turret firearm revolutionized warfare in Albion. Multibarrel technology obviated the need for continuous reloads, and gave its users a marked advantage in the battlefield. This is an exceptional and rather rare example of the mechanism. One would be foolish to get too close to a shooter brandishing such a pistol.

DAMAGE	TYPE	ATTACK SPEED	AMMO CAPACITY	RELOAD TIME	RANGE	BASE VALUE	AUGMENT SLOTS
63.0	Bullet	Normal	6	1.0	35.0	19,200 Gold	0-4

CLOCKWORK PISTOLS

RUSTY CLOCKWORK PISTOL
★

You wouldn't rely on a cheap rusty clock to you places on time, and you would be foolish to rely on this pistol to keep you alive in a serious gunfight.

DAMAGE	TYPE	ATTACK SPEED	AMMO CAPACITY	RELOAD TIME	RANGE	BASE VALUE	AUGMENT SLOTS
12.0	Bullet	Normal	3	1.25	35.0	350 Gold	0-4

IRON CLOCKWORK PISTOL
★★

Clockwork firearms were invented by a master clockmaker dissatisfied with the speed of flintlock mechanisms. This pistol is a cheap imitation of his design, but at least it works.

DAMAGE	TYPE	ATTACK SPEED	AMMO CAPACITY	RELOAD TIME	RANGE	BASE VALUE	AUGMENT SLOTS
18.0	Bullet	Normal	4	1.25	35.0	1400 Gold	0-4

STEEL CLOCKWORK PISTOL
★★★

Guaranteed to almost never misfire, the clockwork mechanism on this pistol is a top-of-the-range example of firearm technology.

DAMAGE	TYPE	ATTACK SPEED	AMMO CAPACITY	RELOAD TIME	RANGE	BASE VALUE	AUGMENT SLOTS
31.0	Bullet	Normal	5	1.25	35.0	5600 Gold	0-4

MASTER CLOCKWORK PISTOL
★★★★

This rare and expensive pistol was created by Horatio Peel himself, the inventor of the clockwork firearm mechanism. Popular among nobles who once used it in duels, before realizing they were too powerful for such activity. Cleaning up after a duel has become much less messy since then.

DAMAGE	TYPE	ATTACK SPEED	AMMO CAPACITY	RELOAD TIME	RANGE	BASE VALUE	AUGMENT SLOTS
47.0	Bullet	Normal	6	1.25	35.0	22,400 Gold	0-4

FLINTLOCK RIFLES

RUSTY FLINTLOCK RIFLE
★

It's possible this was once a perfectly good rifle, but time has dulled its power and reliability. Like all rifles it has a great range and does much more damage than a pistol, though it is also much slower to reload.

DAMAGE	TYPE	ATTACK SPEED	AMMO CAPACITY	RELOAD TIME	RANGE	BASE VALUE	AUGMENT SLOTS
26.0	Bullet	Normal	1	0.75	60.0	275 Gold	0-4

IRON FLINTLOCK RIFLE
★★

The flintlock mechanism was once hailed as the second greatest invention in Albion's history of warfare—gunpowder having been discovered in Samarkand—though it has been superseded by the clockwork firearm design. This is a cheap but effective weapon which, like all rifles, has great range and does much more damage than a pistol, though it is also much slower to reload.

DAMAGE	TYPE	ATTACK SPEED	AMMO CAPACITY	RELOAD TIME	RANGE	BASE VALUE	AUGMENT SLOTS
39.0	Bullet	Normal	1	0.9	60.0	1100 Gold	0-4

STEEL FLINTLOCK RIFLE
★★★

The flintlock mechanism has been hailed as the second greatest invention in the history of warfare—gunpowder having been discovered in Samarkand. You won't find many firearms as finely constructed as this rifle. Perfect for picking off your enemies at a great distance.

DAMAGE	TYPE	ATTACK SPEED	AMMO CAPACITY	RELOAD TIME	RANGE	BASE VALUE	AUGMENT SLOTS
68.0	Bullet	Normal	1	1.0	60.0	4400 Gold	0-4

MASTER FLINTLOCK RIFLE
★★★★

As stylish a firearm as you could hope to carry. Those who die from one of its shots should count themselves lucky.

DAMAGE	TYPE	ATTACK SPEED	AMMO CAPACITY	RELOAD TIME	RANGE	BASE VALUE	AUGMENT SLOTS
102.0	Bullet	Normal	1	0.9	60.0	17,600 Gold	0-4

TURRET RIFLES

RUSTY TURRET RIFLE

★

The invention of the turret firearm revolutionized warfare in Albion. Multibarrel technology obviated the need for continuous reloads, and gave its users a marked advantage in the battlefield. This rifle's best days are long behind it, but will still be appreciated by those too lazy or too much in a hurry to reload after every shot.

DAMAGE	TYPE	ATTACK SPEED	AMMO CAPACITY	RELOAD TIME	RANGE	BASE VALUE	AUGMENT SLOTS
19.0	Bullet	Normal	3	1.1	50.0	300 Gold	0-4

IRON TURRET RIFLE

★★

The invention of the turret firearm revolutionized warfare in Albion. Multibarrel technology obviated the need for continuous reloads, and gave its users a marked advantage in the battlefield. This rifle is a rather poor example, but it will still prove more useful than any other rifle of a similar level.

DAMAGE	TYPE	ATTACK SPEED	AMMO CAPACITY	RELOAD TIME	RANGE	BASE VALUE	AUGMENT SLOTS
28.5	Bullet	Normal	4	1.1	50.0	1200 Gold	0-4

STEEL TURRET RIFLE

★★★

The invention of the turret firearm revolutionized warfare in Albion. Multibarrel technology obviated the need for continuous reloads, and gave its users a marked advantage in the battlefield. This rifle is a rather fine example of the technology, capable of bringing down a small army.

DAMAGE	TYPE	ATTACK SPEED	AMMO CAPACITY	RELOAD TIME	RANGE	BASE VALUE	AUGMENT SLOTS
50.0	Bullet	Normal	5	1.1	50.0	4800 Gold	0-4

MASTER TURRET RIFLE

★★★★

The invention of the turret firearm revolutionized warfare in Albion. Multibarrel technology obviated the need for continuous reloads, and gave its users a marked advantage in the battlefield. This is an exceptional and rather rare example of the mechanism. Had any army been equipped with but a dozen of these rifles, nobody would have been able to stop them.

DAMAGE	TYPE	ATTACK SPEED	AMMO CAPACITY	RELOAD TIME	RANGE	BASE VALUE	AUGMENT SLOTS
75.0	Bullet	Normal	6	1.1	50.0	19,200 Gold	0-4

CLOCKWORK RIFLES

RUSTY CLOCKWORK RIFLE

★

You wouldn't rely on a cheap rusty clock to you places on time, and you would be foolish to rely on this rifle to keep you alive in a serious gunfight.

DAMAGE	TYPE	ATTACK SPEED	AMMO CAPACITY	RELOAD TIME	RANGE	BASE VALUE	AUGMENT SLOTS
15.0	Bullet	Normal	3	1.35	50.0	350 Gold	0-4

IRON CLOCKWORK RIFLE

★★

Clockwork firearms were invented by a master clockmaker dissatisfied with the speed of flintlock mechanisms. This rifle is a cheap imitation of his design, but at least it works.

DAMAGE	TYPE	ATTACK SPEED	AMMO CAPACITY	RELOAD TIME	RANGE	BASE VALUE	AUGMENT SLOTS
22.5	Bullet	Normal	4	1.35	50.0	1400 Gold	0-4

STEEL CLOCKWORK RIFLE

★★★

Guaranteed to almost never misfire, the clockwork mechanism on this rifle is a top-of-the-range example of firearm technology, allowing its user to reload much faster than a flintlock rifle would.

DAMAGE	TYPE	ATTACK SPEED	AMMO CAPACITY	RELOAD TIME	RANGE	BASE VALUE	AUGMENT SLOTS
39.0	Bullet	Normal	5	1.35	50.0	5600 Gold	0-4

MASTER CLOCKWORK RIFLE

★★★★

This rare and expensive rifle was created by Horatio Peel himself, the inventor of the clockwork firearm mechanism. Only the richest armies can afford to equip their soldiers with such a fine weapon.

DAMAGE	TYPE	ATTACK SPEED	AMMO CAPACITY	RELOAD TIME	RANGE	BASE VALUE	AUGMENT SLOTS
59.0	Bullet	Normal	6	1.35	50.0	22,400 Gold	0-4

BLUNDERBUSSES

RUSTY BLUNDERBUSS

★

There is no more powerful, or messier, class of firearm than the blunderbuss. Though only useful at short range, it spreads in a wide radius. Nothing is safe when one of these goes off. In the case of this rusty example, not even the user is safe.

DAMAGE	TYPE	ATTACK SPEED	AMMO CAPACITY	RELOAD TIME	RANGE	BASE VALUE	AUGMENT SLOTS
35.0	Bullet	Normal	1	1.25	25.0	325 Gold	0-4

IRON BLUNDERBUSS

★★

There is no more powerful, or messier, class of firearm than the blunderbuss. Though only useful at short range, it spreads in a wide radius. Nothing is safe when one of these goes off. This isn't the best example of the weapon, but it will still bring down a number of enemies if they're in close proximity.

DAMAGE	TYPE	ATTACK SPEED	AMMO CAPACITY	RELOAD TIME	RANGE	BASE VALUE	AUGMENT SLOTS
52.0	Bullet	Normal	1	1.25	25.0	1300 Gold	0-4

STEEL BLUNDERBUSS

★★★

There is no more powerful, or messier, class of firearm than the blunderbuss. Though only useful at short range, it spreads in a wide radius. Nothing is safe when one of these goes off. This is a particularly fine example of the weapon, often used by guards in an extreme riot situation.

DAMAGE	TYPE	ATTACK SPEED	AMMO CAPACITY	RELOAD TIME	RANGE	BASE VALUE	AUGMENT SLOTS
91.0	Bullet	Normal	1	1.25	25.0	5200 Gold	0-4

MASTER BLUNDERBUSS

★★★★

There is no more powerful, or messier, class of firearm than the blunderbuss. Though only useful at short range, it spreads in a wide radius. Nothing is safe when one of these goes off. And there can be no better example than this exquisitely crafted weapon. Able to spit death in all directions, it is akin to wielding a dragon's mouth in battle.

DAMAGE	TYPE	ATTACK SPEED	AMMO CAPACITY	RELOAD TIME	RANGE	BASE VALUE	AUGMENT SLOTS
136.0	Bullet	Normal	1	1.25	25.0	20,800 Gold	0-4

LEGENDARY WEAPONS

THE ENFORCER

★★★★★

The augments in this weapon allow you to inflict more damage. You will take less yourself, but will be more prone to scarring. This is perhaps the most powerful blunderbuss ever assembled, built by a guard by the name of Giles. Before retiring to work on a family and raise a farm, Giles was the terror of all outlaws, and was famous for his commitment and single-mindedness, even in the face of insurmountable odds.

DAMAGE	TYPE	ATTACK SPEED	AMMO CAPACITY	RELOAD TIME	RANGE	BASE VALUE	AUGMENTS
177.0	Bullet	Normal	1	1.0	20.0	17,550 Gold	Barkskin & Lucky Charm

THE PERFORATOR

★★★★★

The augments in this weapon will instill fear in any citizen who sees you wielding it, allow you to earn more experience than usual from combat, but also make you prone to scarring. The most powerful turret rifle ever constructed, The Perforator first belonged to Maniac Mary, a bandit queen who lived around 150 years ago, and who managed to unite hundreds of bandit gangs under her banner. Inevitably, such a gathering of villains resulted in a violent uprising as her lieutenants attempted to take the rifle, and the leadership, from her. After her fall, the weapon passed through the hands of dozens of bandits, until it was lost, seemingly forever.

DAMAGE	TYPE	ATTACK SPEED	AMMO CAPACITY	RELOAD TIME	RANGE	BASE VALUE	AUGMENTS
81.0	Bullet	Normal	6	0.75	60.0	59,400 Gold	Fear Itself, Discipline, & Barkskin

THE RAMMER

★★★★★

The augments in this weapon inflict fire damage on your enemies and allow you to drain the life of the targets you hit. This extraordinarily powerful crossbow belonged to the heroic farmer Sabre, who protected his lands from bandits and invaders using the weapon he had constructed himself. It was said that a shot from The Rammer was like a stampede of animals crushing its target.

DAMAGE	TYPE	ATTACK SPEED	AMMO CAPACITY	RELOAD TIME	RANGE	BASE VALUE	AUGMENTS
119.0	Arrow	Normal	1	0.75	45.0	54,000 Gold	Ghoul, Flame, & Bewitching

THE RED DRAGON

★★★★★

The augments in this weapon allow you to cause more damage to your enemies while taking less yourself. This unique and exotic pistol once belonged to Wicker, the finest shot Albion had ever seen. Until Reaver appeared. Wicker visited Reaver and challenged him to an honorable duel to decide who had the greatest skill. Reaver's reply was to shoot him in the head.

DAMAGE	TYPE	ATTACK SPEED	AMMO CAPACITY	RELOAD TIME	RANGE	BASE VALUE	AUGMENTS
41.0	Bullet	Normal	6	0.75	35.0	13,500 Gold	Devastation & Lucky Charm

Items and Collectibles

Time has brought many innovations to Albion, not just in the form of weaponry, but also in the style of books, potions, furniture, and numerous other creature comforts. This chapter details the hundreds of items this great world contains including the food and clothing your Hero will come to rely on. Here you'll find the stats for every item, their star rating, and their base value as well. The descriptions for many of the items (particularly the food) are quite funny and we've reprinted many of them here for your enjoyment.

Tools for Hero and Dog

The majority of these items are obtained throughout the main set of story quests. This section contains a number of different items, not least of which are those essential to the Hero's health (Condoms) and that of your dog (Dog Treats).

FOR THE HERO...

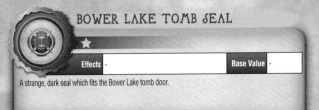

BOWER LAKE TOMB SEAL

★

| Effects | - | Base Value | - |

A strange, dark seal which fits the Bower Lake tomb door.

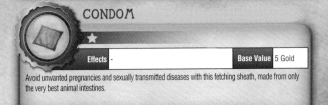

CONDOM

★

| Effects | - | Base Value | 5 Gold |

Avoid unwanted pregnancies and sexually transmitted diseases with this fetching sheath, made from only the very best animal intestines.

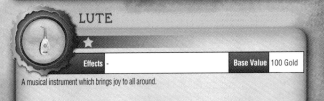

LUTE

★

| Effects | - | Base Value | 100 Gold |

A musical instrument which brings joy to all around.

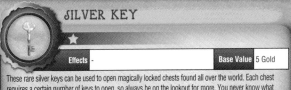

SILVER KEY

★

| Effects | - | Base Value | 5 Gold |

These rare silver keys can be used to open magically locked chests found all over the world. Each chest requires a certain number of keys to open, so always be on the lookout for more. You never know what you'll find inside a silver key chest!

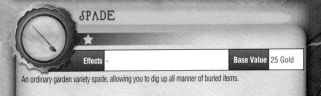

SPADE

★

| Effects | - | Base Value | 25 Gold |

An ordinary garden variety spade, allowing you to dig up all manner of buried items.

FOR THE DOG...

COLLAR OF BROODING

⭐

| Effects | - | Base Value | 50 Gold |

Don't worry, it's just a phase. Use the collar in your inventory to put it on your dog. This also allows you to rename him any time you want.

COLLAR OF FIBROUS UTILITY

⭐

| Effects | - | Base Value | 50 Gold |

Your dog is a fantastic place to keep some spare rope. Use the collar in your inventory to put it on your dog. This also allows you to rename him any time you want.

COLLAR OF HOLDING

⭐

| Effects | - | Base Value | 50 Gold |

Effectively binds your dog to, well, the collar itself using ancient magic. Use the collar in your inventory to put it on your dog. This also allows you to rename him any time you want.

COLLAR OF HOLY SKY

⭐

| Effects | - | Base Value | 50 Gold |

Bestows upon sorcerer dogs an impressively potent boost to Will. No effects on non-magic using dogs. Use the collar in your inventory to put it on your dog. This also allows you to rename him any time you want.

COLLAR OF RADIANT EYE

⭐

| Effects | - | Base Value | 50 Gold |

Dramatically increases Skill in ranged weaponry, especially crossbows. No effects on non-marksman dogs. Use the collar in your inventory to put it on your dog. This also allows you to rename him any time you want.

COLLAR OF REGALITY

⭐

| Effects | - | Base Value | 50 Gold |

You can tell a lot about a person by their dog's collar. For instance, that they have no taste and don't know how to handle money. Use the collar in your inventory to put it on your dog. This also allows you to rename him any time you want.

DOG ELIXIR

⭐

| Effects | - | Base Value | 20 Gold |

This pungent potion will cure all your dog's wounds. It also keeps his coat shiny, his nose cool, and his breath smelling like daisies.

DOG TREAT

⭐

| Effects | - | Base Value | 30 Gold |

These tender, juicy morsels contain rare seasonings with taste frequencies too high for human tongues.

RUBBER BALL

| Effects | - | Base Value | 5 Gold |

As all dogs know, humans are ignorant as to the true value of these precious items, which they discard seemingly at random. According to ancient pet lore, the dog deity Cainine killed his brother Fabel to gain possession of his rubber ball.

Books & Documents

There are a significant number of texts contained in the world of Albion, but only the Expression Manuals and the books on dog training are of any real significance to the Hero's development. These items are often found contained within chests, inside dig spots, and elsewhere. Many of the other books and documents can be found by snooping around people's homes or by purchasing them from stores. Some of these may prove valuable to people in other towns; a skilled trader may make a few gold coins from selling them. Do note that there are many other texts of interest that relate to the story.

NOVELS, DIARIES, & MORE

TITLE	STARS	BASE VALUE	COMMENT
Avo is Dead	★	40	A controversial book about the downfall of the god Avo.
Barnum's Thesaurus	★★★★	320	A hand-written book of synonyms guaranteed to help you talk like an idiot.
Becoming a Parent	★	40	Contains information on having and raising children.
A Beginner's Guide to Business	★	40	Contains valuable business and real-estate tips.
Bowerstone Old Town	★	40	A traveler's guide to the old neighborhood in Bowerstone.
Bowerstone Real Crime!	★	40	Real life accounts of Old Town's super-sheriff, Derek!
Cold Lips	★	40	An erotic novel about the maid of a wealthy household.
The Crucible	★	40	A history of that great arena in Westcliff.
The End is Almost Nigh	★	40	A collection of predictions and doom-mongerings.
The Fall of the Guild	★	40	Passages from the circulating stories about the fall of the Hero's Guild.
The Hero of Oakvale	★★	80	For those who didn't play Fable.
Introduction to Navigation	★	40	A beginner's guide for the modern Albion seafarer.
Living Forever: The Immortalists	★★	80	A philosophical book exploring the possibilities of eternal beings.
Lord Lucien: A Biography	★	40	An authorized biography on Lord Lucien's upbringing.
Lucien the Lunatic	★★★★★	640	The far more scandalous unauthorized biography of Lord Lucien.
Marriage and How to Survive It	★	40	Contains helpful tips for maintaining a happy marriage.
Megafowl	★	40	A horror/adventure novel about chickens.

TITLE	STARS	BASE VALUE	COMMENT
Megafowl 2: Revenge of the Hen	★★★★	320	A sequel to the smash hit "Megafowl".
Murgo's Big Book of Trading	★	40	Contains tips for successful trading, swindling, and scamming.
Norm and Aggie	★	40	A love story about two retired schoolteachers.
Objection! Overruled!	★	40	Court room drama about Albio's most important legal matters.
ORBS and Multiworlds	★	40	Ancient theories about online play.
A Perilous Adventure, Bronze Ed.	★	40	A torn page from a Pick Your Own Destiny game book.
A Perilous Adventure, Gold Ed.	★★★★	320	A torn page from a Pick Your Own Destiny game book.
A Perilous Adventure, Silver Ed.	★★	80	A torn page from a Pick Your Own Destiny game book.
Phantoms from the Beyond	★	40	A popular horror story about monsters and portals.
Pretty on the Inside	★	40	Discusses the importance of furniture.
The Secret of Castle Fairfax, Pt I	★★	80	A history of the impressive Castle Fairfax.
The Secret of Castle Fairfax, Pt II	★★★★	320	The continuation of the history of Castle Fairfax.
The Tattered Spire	★★★	160	An old book devoted to the fall of the Old Kingdom and what caused it.
The Temple of Light	★	40	The history of the Temple of Light and its importance in Albion.
The Temple of Shadows	★	40	A brief history about the rise of the Temple of Shadows.
Understanding the Albion Psyche	★	40	An opinionated guide to understanding the people of Albion.
Wedding Bells	★	40	Contains tips for finding a spouse.

EXPRESSION MANUALS

TITLE	STARS	BASE VALUE	COMMENT
The Art of Seduction	★★★	400	Use this book to learn the Seduce expression.
Belching for Beginners	★★★	400	Use this book to learn the Belch expression.
Book of Worship	★★★★	600	Use this book to learn the Worship expression.
Come Hither, Dear	★★★★★	800	Use this book to learn the Come Back to My Place expression.
The Counterfeit Warrior	★★★★	600	Use this book to learn the Feign Attack expression.
Dead Handy	★★★	400	Use this book to learn the Play Dead expression.
The Finger	★★★★	600	Use this book to learn the Insult expression.
The Perv's Handbook	★★	200	Use this book to learn the Vulgar Thrust expression.
Sock it to 'Em	★★★★★	800	Use this book to learn the Sock Puppet expression.

DOG TRAINING

TITLE	STARS	BASE VALUE	COMMENT
Dog Tricks! Begging	★★★	200	Teaches your dog to beg. Use a pick-up line, ask someone back to your place, or do a spot of begging yourself to get him to do this.
Dog Tricks! Hide Snout	★★★	200	Teaches your dog to hide his snout with his paws. To see him do this, either belch or fart.
Dog Tricks! Play Dead	★★★	200	Teaches your dog how to play dead. To see him do this, you can either play dead yourself or accuse someone else of being a chicken.
Dog Tricks! Roll Over	★★★	200	Teaches your dog to roll over. To see him do this, seduce, worship or apologize to someone.
Dog Tricks! Tail Chase	★★★	200	Teaches your dog to chase his tail. Perform a vulgar thrust, victory arm pump, or put on a hand puppet show to make your dog chase his own tail.
Dog Tricks! Targeted Urination	★★★	200	Teaches your dog how to relieve himself on those you want to mock and infuriate. To see him do this, point and laugh at someone, insult them, or tell them to kiss your arse.
Dog Tricks! The Backflip	★★★	200	Teaches your dog to do backflips. See him perform this tricky by showing off a trophy or playing a game of Hat, Headband, Moustache.
Dog Tricks! The Bunny Hop	★★★	200	Teaches your dog how to hop like a bunny. To see him do this, dance, laugh, whistle, play the lute, or strike a heroic pose.
Dog Tricks! The Growl	★★★	200	Teaches your dog how to growl at people you don't like. To see him do this, perform any scary expression.
Dog Tricks! The Wave	★★★	200	Teaches your dog how to wave. To see him do this, blow a kiss, give a present, make someone follow or wait for you, or give them a thumbs up or down.
The Dogs of War, Book 1	★★	200	Use this to train your dog in the art of fighting, increasing the damage he can do in battle.
The Dogs of War, Book 2	★★★	400	Use this to train your dog in the art of fighting, increasing the damage he can do in battle.
The Dogs of War, Book 3	★★★★	800	Use this to train your dog in the art of fighting, increasing the damage he can do in battle.
The Dogs of War, Book 4	★★★★★	1600	Use this to train your dog in the art of fighting, increasing the damage he can do in battle.
Treasure Hunting, Book 1	★★	200	Use this book to train your dog to sniff out level 2 dig spots.
Treasure Hunting, Book 2	★★★	400	Use this book to train your dog to sniff out level 3 dig spots.
Treasure Hunting, Book 3	★★★★	800	Use this book to train your dog to sniff out level 4 dig spots.
Treasure Hunting, Book 4	★★★★★	1600	Use this book to train your dog to sniff out level 5 dig spots.

Food

As great as Heroes are portrayed, they aren't really all that different from normal folk. They bleed when cut, they tire after long journeys, and they get fat if they drink too much beer. Food and drink plays a big role in Fable II, particularly after battles. Heroes can consume various meals and beverages to regain health, to increase their experience, and to even affect their attractiveness. All food isn't created equal however. Greasy, fattening foods of low quality not only offer little nutritional benefit, but they also decrease the Hero's purity rating which can adversely affect their appearance. On the other hand, maintaining a diet of vegetables, fruit, non-alcoholic drinks, and tofu will not only keep you slender, but can even provide a boost to the Hero's morality and purity ratings.

1 Name: This is the name of the food or beverage. These names often provide a pretty clear indication to the quality of the food.

2 Stars: Every item has a star value. This is your guide to the relative rarity and value of a particular food or drink. The more stars the food has, the more likely it is to be healthy for you.

3 Image: This shows you what the food looks like so you can better imagine having to eat it yourself.

4 Healing Pts: The amount of health consuming this food or drink will replenish.

5 Morality: The Hero who eats tofu will enjoy an increase in morality. At least they'll enjoy something...

6 Purity: The food you eat and the drinks you imbibe say a lot about you as a Hero. Eat foods high in purity if you care at all about the way others view you.

7 Fatness: The unfortunate reality in Albion is that eating healthily doesn't come cheaply. The cheaper foods often replenish little health and come with a high fatness rating. Stay clear of the fatty foods (desserts and beer, specifically) if you're watching your waistline.

8 Base Value: This is your guide to the value of the food you're about to consume. The base value ignores economic variables and serves as a general guide to the price of the item.

9 Experience: Several food types not only heal, but also offer increases in general experience, Skill Experience, Strength Experience, or Will Experience. Quickly collect the experience orbs that appear after you eat the items.

10 Description: The oft-hilarious descriptions of the food and drinks, reprinted here for your enjoyment.

POISONBERRY BREW

It is said that the feet of those treading poisonberries to make this wine are apt to turn green and fall off. On the other hand, if you don't mind a bit of rotgut and blindness, it will get you drunk fast.

HEALING PTS	MORALITY	PURITY	FATNESS	BASE VALUE
10	-	-20.0	5.0%	4 Gold

EXPERIENCE	SKILL EXPERIENCE	STRENGTH EXPERIENCE	WILL EXPERIENCE
-	-	-	-

DRINKS (ALCOHOLIC)

ANY PORT IN A STORM
★★★★

Surprise, it's port.

HEALING PTS	MORALITY	PURITY	FATNESS	BASE VALUE
80	-	-5.0	1.0%	46 Gold
EXPERIENCE	SKILL EXPERIENCE	STRENGTH EXPERIENCE	WILL EXPERIENCE	
-	125	-	-	

BALVERINE'S SPLEEN BEER
★

It's not just a sassily lowbrow beer name. It's also the ingredient list.

HEALING PTS	MORALITY	PURITY	FATNESS	BASE VALUE
10	-	-20.0	10.0%	4 Gold
EXPERIENCE	SKILL EXPERIENCE	STRENGTH EXPERIENCE	WILL EXPERIENCE	
-	-	-	-	

BOWERSTONE BROWN BEER
★★★

This brew has been getting the population of Albion drunk for centuries.

HEALING PTS	MORALITY	PURITY	FATNESS	BASE VALUE
40	-	-10.0	10.0%	18 Gold
EXPERIENCE	SKILL EXPERIENCE	STRENGTH EXPERIENCE	WILL EXPERIENCE	
-	-	25	-	

BOX WINE
★★

Evenly proportioned, almost hedonistic Voignier. Opens with pork rind, hairspray, and hints of anise.

HEALING PTS	MORALITY	PURITY	FATNESS	BASE VALUE
20	-	-15.0	5.0%	8 Gold
EXPERIENCE	SKILL EXPERIENCE	STRENGTH EXPERIENCE	WILL EXPERIENCE	
-	-	-	5	

CLASSY CLARET
★★★★

One would be able to detect hints of raspberry, honeydew, and marmoset with one's nose, if one was a pompous ass.

HEALING PTS	MORALITY	PURITY	FATNESS	BASE VALUE
80	-	-5.0	1.0%	46 Gold
EXPERIENCE	SKILL EXPERIENCE	STRENGTH EXPERIENCE	WILL EXPERIENCE	
-	-	-	125	

GUTTER BEER
★★

This low-quality beer will coat your mouth with a bitter sheen of sadness. Best imbibed only after following several other drinks or a swift blow to the head.

HEALING PTS	MORALITY	PURITY	FATNESS	BASE VALUE
20	-	-15.0	10.0%	8 Gold
EXPERIENCE	SKILL EXPERIENCE	STRENGTH EXPERIENCE	WILL EXPERIENCE	
-	-	5	-	

HOBBE'S WATER
★★★

Despite its unappetizing name, this liquor has become immensely popular thanks to its affordability and the relatively few cases of blindness it has been known to cause.

HEALING PTS	MORALITY	PURITY	FATNESS	BASE VALUE
40	-	-10.0	5.0%	18 Gold
EXPERIENCE	SKILL EXPERIENCE	STRENGTH EXPERIENCE	WILL EXPERIENCE	
-	25	-	-	

HOPTIMUS PRIME
★★★★★

This is as good as beer gets. Transform yourself into a drunken pillar of health and strength with this superhuman brew.

HEALING PTS	MORALITY	PURITY	FATNESS	BASE VALUE
145	-	-1.0	5.0%	145 Gold
EXPERIENCE	SKILL EXPERIENCE	STRENGTH EXPERIENCE	WILL EXPERIENCE	
-	-	625	-	

OAKFIELD SOUR
★

Cocktail of tabasco sauce, salt, and possibly paint thinner.

HEALING PTS	MORALITY	PURITY	FATNESS	BASE VALUE
10	-	-20.0	5.0%	4 Gold
EXPERIENCE	SKILL EXPERIENCE	STRENGTH EXPERIENCE	WILL EXPERIENCE	
-	-	-	-	

POISONBERRY BREW

It is said that the feet of those treading poisonberries to make this wine are apt to turn green and fall off. On the other hand, if you don't mind a bit of rotgut and blindness, it will get you drunk fast.

HEALING PTS	MORALITY	PURITY	FATNESS	BASE VALUE
10	-	-20.0	5.0%	4 Gold
EXPERIENCE	SKILL EXPERIENCE	STRENGTH EXPERIENCE	WILL EXPERIENCE	
-	-	-	-	

PORTENTOUS STOUT
★★★★

Make yourself drunk. Make others drunk. What's not to like?

HEALING PTS	MORALITY	PURITY	FATNESS	BASE VALUE
80	-	-5.0	10.0%	46 Gold
EXPERIENCE	SKILL EXPERIENCE	STRENGTH EXPERIENCE	WILL EXPERIENCE	
-	-	125	-	

SANDGOOSE RUM
★★

Developed long ago by enterprising sailors who found that they could not drink sea water, the effects of this combination of rum and water are not unlike those of a burly boatswain punching you in the face.

HEALING PTS	MORALITY	PURITY	FATNESS	BASE VALUE
20	-	-15.0	5.0%	8 Gold
EXPERIENCE	SKILL EXPERIENCE	STRENGTH EXPERIENCE	WILL EXPERIENCE	
-	5	-	-	

TABLE WINE
★★★

Hints of vanilla, touches of oak and whispers of fruity jam are purely imaginary in this bog-standard claret.

HEALING PTS	MORALITY	PURITY	FATNESS	BASE VALUE
40	-	-10.0	5.0%	18 Gold
EXPERIENCE	SKILL EXPERIENCE	STRENGTH EXPERIENCE	WILL EXPERIENCE	
-	-	-	25	

THE TENEBROUS
★★★★★

Also known in some circles as the Tenebrous Vintage of Exsanguinated Shadows. An extremely rare and ancient wine made by the first order of monks from the Temple of Shadows. Once used in ritual sacrifices, now sniffed, sipped, and expectorated by the obscenely wealthy.

HEALING PTS	MORALITY	PURITY	FATNESS	BASE VALUE
160	-	-1.0	-	145 Gold
EXPERIENCE	SKILL EXPERIENCE	STRENGTH EXPERIENCE	WILL EXPERIENCE	
-	-	-	625	

THE YELLOW FAIRY
★★★★★

Thusly named because you'll be turning yellow from the resulting liver damage. 250 proof, tastes like marshmallows.

HEALING PTS	MORALITY	PURITY	FATNESS	BASE VALUE
160	-	-1.0	-	145 Gold
EXPERIENCE	SKILL EXPERIENCE	STRENGTH EXPERIENCE	WILL EXPERIENCE	
-	125	-	-	

DRINKS
(NON-ALCOHOLIC)

CONCENTRATED APPLE JUICE
★★★

Once a semi-frozen cylinder, now a passable imitation of the real thing.

HEALING PTS	MORALITY	PURITY	FATNESS	BASE VALUE
80	-	5.0	0.1%	25 Gold
EXPERIENCE	SKILL EXPERIENCE	STRENGTH EXPERIENCE	WILL EXPERIENCE	
25	-	-	-	

DILUTED TOMATO JUICE
★★

Yes, it's technically a fruit, but that doesn't mean it deserves to be juiced. This watery, vaguely salty concoction is only for the desperate.

HEALING PTS	MORALITY	PURITY	FATNESS	BASE VALUE
40	-	-	0.1%%	14 Gold
EXPERIENCE	SKILL EXPERIENCE	STRENGTH EXPERIENCE	WILL EXPERIENCE	
5	-	-	-	

DURIAN FRUIT JUICE
★

The sensory experience of this exotic, spiny fruit has been likened to 'custard passed through a sewer pipe' or 'eating one's favorite ice cream while sitting on the toilet.' The juice is not much better.

HEALING PTS	MORALITY	PURITY	FATNESS	BASE VALUE
20	-	-5.0	0.1%	8 Gold
EXPERIENCE	SKILL EXPERIENCE	STRENGTH EXPERIENCE	WILL EXPERIENCE	
-	-	-	-	

MYSTICAL JUICE
★★★★★

Squeezed from clouds, pixies and pure thoughts, this juice is both delectable and extremely healthy.

HEALING PTS	MORALITY	PURITY	FATNESS	BASE VALUE
320	-	15.0	0.1%	118 Gold
EXPERIENCE	SKILL EXPERIENCE	STRENGTH EXPERIENCE	WILL EXPERIENCE	
625	-	-	-	

QUALITY BANANA JUICE
★★★★

Bananas have no juice to squeeze? Never you mind such trivial details—this sweet concoction is healthful and delicious.

HEALING PTS	MORALITY	PURITY	FATNESS	BASE VALUE
160	-	10.0	0.1%	49 Gold
EXPERIENCE	SKILL EXPERIENCE	STRENGTH EXPERIENCE	WILL EXPERIENCE	
125	-	-	-	

RANCID WATER

★

This water has a rather sludgy consistency and smells faintly of eggs. You'd better be thirsty.

HEALING PTS	MORALITY	PURITY	FATNESS	BASE VALUE
15	-	-5.0	-	7 Gold
EXPERIENCE	SKILL EXPERIENCE	STRENGTH EXPERIENCE	WILL EXPERIENCE	
-	-	-	-	

SPRING WATER

★★★★

Clean and pure, collected from the springs in the mountain ranges to the north.

HEALING PTS	MORALITY	PURITY	FATNESS	BASE VALUE
120	-	15.0	-	30 Gold
EXPERIENCE	SKILL EXPERIENCE	STRENGTH EXPERIENCE	WILL EXPERIENCE	
-	-	-	-	

SUBLIME WATER

★★★★★

Crystal clear and extraordinarily pure, it tastes better than beer, chocolate and a sack of gold.

HEALING PTS	MORALITY	PURITY	FATNESS	BASE VALUE
240	-	20.0	-	52 Gold
EXPERIENCE	SKILL EXPERIENCE	STRENGTH EXPERIENCE	WILL EXPERIENCE	
-	-	-	-	

VALUE WATER

★★

It's warm and has a coppery taste, a bit like blood.

HEALING PTS	MORALITY	PURITY	FATNESS	BASE VALUE
30	-	5.0	-	11 Gold
EXPERIENCE	SKILL EXPERIENCE	STRENGTH EXPERIENCE	WILL EXPERIENCE	
-	-	-	-	

WELL WATER

★★★

Perfectly drinkable water from a town well.

HEALING PTS	MORALITY	PURITY	FATNESS	BASE VALUE
60	-	10.0	-	18 Gold
EXPERIENCE	SKILL EXPERIENCE	STRENGTH EXPERIENCE	WILL EXPERIENCE	
-	-	-	-	

MEAT & FISH

CANNED MUTTON PRODUCT

★

Will leave you as strong and healthy-looking as this gelatinized cube of compressed sheep parts.

HEALING PTS	MORALITY	PURITY	FATNESS	BASE VALUE
20	-	-20.0	5.0%	6 Gold
EXPERIENCE	SKILL EXPERIENCE	STRENGTH EXPERIENCE	WILL EXPERIENCE	
-	-	-	-	

CHICKEN-FRIED MUTTON

★★★

This fatty dish contains no actual chicken. One more reason they deserve chasing.

HEALING PTS	MORALITY	PURITY	FATNESS	BASE VALUE
80	-	-10.0	5.0%	25 Gold
EXPERIENCE	SKILL EXPERIENCE	STRENGTH EXPERIENCE	WILL EXPERIENCE	
-	-	25	-	

CRUNCHY CHICK

★

High in protein, low in morality.

HEALING PTS	MORALITY	PURITY	FATNESS	BASE VALUE
25	-5.0	-	-	28 Gold
EXPERIENCE	SKILL EXPERIENCE	STRENGTH EXPERIENCE	WILL EXPERIENCE	
-	-	-	-	

DUBIOUS WHITEFISH

★★

Anyone can fight balverines. The truly adventurous scrimp on seafood.

HEALING PTS	MORALITY	PURITY	FATNESS	BASE VALUE
40	-	-10.0	-	13 Gold
EXPERIENCE	SKILL EXPERIENCE	STRENGTH EXPERIENCE	WILL EXPERIENCE	
-	-	-	5	

FRESH SALMON

★★★★

Improves your Will and instills in you an inexplicable desire to swim upstream.

HEALING PTS	MORALITY	PURITY	FATNESS	BASE VALUE
160	-	-5.0%	-	61 Gold
EXPERIENCE	SKILL EXPERIENCE	STRENGTH EXPERIENCE	WILL EXPERIENCE	
-	-	-	125	

MAGNIFICENT TUNA

★★★★★

Caught exclusively by wizened old men, this dish tastes of epic struggle. Delicious, delicious struggle.

HEALING PTS	MORALITY	PURITY	FATNESS	BASE VALUE
320	-	-1.0%	-	172 Gold
EXPERIENCE	SKILL EXPERIENCE	STRENGTH EXPERIENCE	WILL EXPERIENCE	
-	-	-	625	

RANCID ANCHOVY

★

You could use it as bait if only other fish were dumb enough to find it appetizing.

HEALING PTS	MORALITY	PURITY	FATNESS	BASE VALUE
20	-	-15.0	-	7 Gold
EXPERIENCE	SKILL EXPERIENCE	STRENGTH EXPERIENCE	WILL EXPERIENCE	
-	-	-	-	

MUTTON CUTLETS

★★★★

Mighty taste for a mighty body. Fatty cuts for a... you get the idea.

HEALING PTS	MORALITY	PURITY	FATNESS	BASE VALUE
160	-	-5.0%	5.0%	60 Gold
EXPERIENCE	SKILL EXPERIENCE	STRENGTH EXPERIENCE	WILL EXPERIENCE	
-	-	125	-	

RANCID BEEF JERKY

★

Nothing elevates you in the eyes of your peers like being seen gnawing a cut of truly rank jerky.

HEALING PTS	MORALITY	PURITY	FATNESS	BASE VALUE
20	-	-20.0	2.5%	6 Gold
EXPERIENCE	SKILL EXPERIENCE	STRENGTH EXPERIENCE	WILL EXPERIENCE	
-	-	-	-	

MUTTON TENDERLOIN

★★★★★

This ambrosial, impossibly tender cut will imbue you with the strength of a hundred, um, sheep. Still, that's a lot of sheep.

HEALING PTS	MORALITY	PURITY	FATNESS	BASE VALUE
320	-	-1.0%	5.0%	172 Gold
EXPERIENCE	SKILL EXPERIENCE	STRENGTH EXPERIENCE	WILL EXPERIENCE	
-	-	625	-	

REVELATORY BEEF JERKY

★★★★★

Cured with the finest salts and aged in rosewood casks guarded by monks who have taken the vows of jerky abstinence.

HEALING PTS	MORALITY	PURITY	FATNESS	BASE VALUE
320	-	-	2.5%	172 Gold
EXPERIENCE	SKILL EXPERIENCE	STRENGTH EXPERIENCE	WILL EXPERIENCE	
-	-	625	-	

MYSTERY MEAT

★

Mystery meat.

HEALING PTS	MORALITY	PURITY	FATNESS	BASE VALUE
25	-	-5.0	5.0%	6 Gold
EXPERIENCE	SKILL EXPERIENCE	STRENGTH EXPERIENCE	WILL EXPERIENCE	
-	-	-	-	

SALTY BEEF JERKY

★★

It'll keep longer than you will.

HEALING PTS	MORALITY	PURITY	FATNESS	BASE VALUE
40	-	-15.0	2.5%	12 Gold
EXPERIENCE	SKILL EXPERIENCE	STRENGTH EXPERIENCE	WILL EXPERIENCE	
-	-	5	-	

ORGANIC JERKY

★★★★

Cows must submit to years of training and rigorous study to achieve organic jerkyhood.

HEALING PTS	MORALITY	PURITY	FATNESS	BASE VALUE
160	-	-5.0%	2.5%	61 Gold
EXPERIENCE	SKILL EXPERIENCE	STRENGTH EXPERIENCE	WILL EXPERIENCE	
-	-	125	-	

TRAVEL-READY BEEF JERKY

★★★

A passable table jerky, it tastes vaguely of salted meat.

HEALING PTS	MORALITY	PURITY	FATNESS	BASE VALUE
80	-	-10.0	2.5%	26 Gold
EXPERIENCE	SKILL EXPERIENCE	STRENGTH EXPERIENCE	WILL EXPERIENCE	
-	-	25	-	

PRE-SLICED MUTTON

★★

Paper thin with plenty of fat.

HEALING PTS	MORALITY	PURITY	FATNESS	BASE VALUE
40	-	-15.0	5.0%	12 Gold
EXPERIENCE	SKILL EXPERIENCE	STRENGTH EXPERIENCE	WILL EXPERIENCE	
-	-	5	-	

WESTCLIFF COD

★★★

Caught off the coast of Westcliff, where its bountiful presence should ensure it never goes extinct.

HEALING PTS	MORALITY	PURITY	FATNESS	BASE VALUE
80	-	-7.0	-	26 Gold
EXPERIENCE	SKILL EXPERIENCE	STRENGTH EXPERIENCE	WILL EXPERIENCE	
-	-	-	25	

CHEESE & NUTS

CRUCIBLE PEANUTS

★★★★

The peanuts of champions! Or at least the peanuts of the people who sit safely in the stands while the champions get mauled to death.

HEALING PTS	MORALITY	PURITY	FATNESS	BASE VALUE
160	-	10.0	-	36 Gold
EXPERIENCE	SKILL EXPERIENCE	STRENGTH EXPERIENCE	WILL EXPERIENCE	
-	-	-	-	

DAIRY FARM CHEESE

★★★

Nobody knows where the animals whose milk is used to make this cheese are kept. And as long as there's a steady supply to melt on toast or eat with a nice glass of wine, nobody cares.

HEALING PTS	MORALITY	PURITY	FATNESS	BASE VALUE
80	-	5.0	5.0%	21 Gold
EXPERIENCE	SKILL EXPERIENCE	STRENGTH EXPERIENCE	WILL EXPERIENCE	
-	-	-	-	

EXTRA-SALTED PEANUTS

★★★

Two peanuts were walking down the street, and they were assaulted. They had it coming.

HEALING PTS	MORALITY	PURITY	FATNESS	BASE VALUE
80	-	5.0	-	21 Gold
EXPERIENCE	SKILL EXPERIENCE	STRENGTH EXPERIENCE	WILL EXPERIENCE	
-	-	-	-	

FAIRFAX DELIGHT CHEESE

★★★★

Soft, pungent, and respectable, you and this cheese should get along fine.

HEALING PTS	MORALITY	PURITY	FATNESS	BASE VALUE
160	-	10.0	5.0%	36 Gold
EXPERIENCE	SKILL EXPERIENCE	STRENGTH EXPERIENCE	WILL EXPERIENCE	
-	-	-	-	

GOLD ROASTED PEANUTS

★★★★★

The layer of honeyed gold covering these delicious peanuts is so slight, it melts in your mouth.

HEALING PTS	MORALITY	PURITY	FATNESS	BASE VALUE
320	-	15.0	-	65 Gold
EXPERIENCE	SKILL EXPERIENCE	STRENGTH EXPERIENCE	WILL EXPERIENCE	
-	-	-	-	

HOWLING CHEESE

★★

Made with balverine milk. Just one more reason not having a nose can be an advantage in life.

HEALING PTS	MORALITY	PURITY	FATNESS	BASE VALUE
40	-	-	5.0%	13 Gold
EXPERIENCE	SKILL EXPERIENCE	STRENGTH EXPERIENCE	WILL EXPERIENCE	
-	-	-	-	

MIASMIC CHEESE

★

This foul melty goo is not technically cheese, but you'd be wise not to say that to its face.

HEALING PTS	MORALITY	PURITY	FATNESS	BASE VALUE
20	-	-5.0	5.0%	8 Gold
EXPERIENCE	SKILL EXPERIENCE	STRENGTH EXPERIENCE	WILL EXPERIENCE	
-	-	-	-	

NASTY NUTS

★

The Nasty brand of nuts is at least upfront about its singularly disgusting, and only barely nutty, product.

HEALING PTS	MORALITY	PURITY	FATNESS	BASE VALUE
20	-	-5.0	-	8 Gold
EXPERIENCE	SKILL EXPERIENCE	STRENGTH EXPERIENCE	WILL EXPERIENCE	
-	-	-	-	

SINGLE-SEED PEANUTS

★★

Even other peanuts don't want to be associated with these loser legumes.

HEALING PTS	MORALITY	PURITY	FATNESS	BASE VALUE
40	-	-	-	13 Gold
EXPERIENCE	SKILL EXPERIENCE	STRENGTH EXPERIENCE	WILL EXPERIENCE	
-	-	-	-	

UNICORN CHEESE

★★★★★

It's doubtful real unicorn milk is used to make this delicacy, but its exquisite taste and exorbitant price is enough to convince Albion's higher classes that no other cheese deserves to go on their sandwiches.

HEALING PTS	MORALITY	PURITY	FATNESS	BASE VALUE
320	-	15.0	5.0%	64 Gold
EXPERIENCE	SKILL EXPERIENCE	STRENGTH EXPERIENCE	WILL EXPERIENCE	
-	-	-	-	

TOFU, FRUIT & VEGETABLES

GOLDEN APPLE
★★★★★

Though containing no actual gold, the healthy effects of this delicious fruit are just as precious.

HEALING PTS	MORALITY	PURITY	FATNESS	BASE VALUE
320	-	15.0	-	186 Gold

EXPERIENCE	SKILL EXPERIENCE	STRENGTH EXPERIENCE	WILL EXPERIENCE
625	-	-	-

CRISP CELERY
★★★

A crunchy, fibrous vegetable which requires more calories to digest than it provides.

HEALING PTS	MORALITY	PURITY	FATNESS	BASE VALUE
80	-	5.0	-5.0%	21 Gold

EXPERIENCE	SKILL EXPERIENCE	STRENGTH EXPERIENCE	WILL EXPERIENCE
-	-	-	-

HOLY TOFU
★★★★★

Coagulated and pressed in holy water, but the flavor is nothing special.

HEALING PTS	MORALITY	PURITY	FATNESS	BASE VALUE
320	5.0	25.0	-	66 Gold

EXPERIENCE	SKILL EXPERIENCE	STRENGTH EXPERIENCE	WILL EXPERIENCE
-	-	-	-

DIVINE CARROT
★★★★★

This mammoth root glows with a supernatural aura.

HEALING PTS	MORALITY	PURITY	FATNESS	BASE VALUE
320	-	15.0	-	175 Gold

EXPERIENCE	SKILL EXPERIENCE	STRENGTH EXPERIENCE	WILL EXPERIENCE
-	625	-	-

HOMEGROWN CARROT
★★★

Stiff, straight, and healthy, it's probably inappropriate to carry in your pocket.

HEALING PTS	MORALITY	PURITY	FATNESS	BASE VALUE
80	-	5.0	-	26 Gold

EXPERIENCE	SKILL EXPERIENCE	STRENGTH EXPERIENCE	WILL EXPERIENCE
-	25	-	-

EXPIRED CELERY
★

If you're brave enough to eat this you'll be rewarded with negative net calories... and perhaps an upset stomach.

HEALING PTS	MORALITY	PURITY	FATNESS	BASE VALUE
20	-	-5.0	-5.0%	10 Gold

EXPERIENCE	SKILL EXPERIENCE	STRENGTH EXPERIENCE	WILL EXPERIENCE
-	-	-	-

HYDROPONIC CARROT
★★★★

The resounding crack of this crisp imperator focuses on the mind.

HEALING PTS	MORALITY	PURITY	FATNESS	BASE VALUE
160	5.0	10.0	-	63 Gold

EXPERIENCE	SKILL EXPERIENCE	STRENGTH EXPERIENCE	WILL EXPERIENCE
-	125	-	-

FERMENTED TOFU
★

This rancid curd is supposedly a delicacy in some parts of Albion. It's covered in sticky slime and has the complex yet playful aroma of a dumpster in July.

HEALING PTS	MORALITY	PURITY	FATNESS	BASE VALUE
20	5.0	5.0	-	9 Gold

EXPERIENCE	SKILL EXPERIENCE	STRENGTH EXPERIENCE	WILL EXPERIENCE
-	-	-	-

LUSH CELERY
★★★★

Too snobbish to be seen lying among other salad ingredients, this celery is more often seen languidly soaking its stalk in an expensive cocktail.

HEALING PTS	MORALITY	PURITY	FATNESS	BASE VALUE
160	-	10.0	-5.0%	37 Gold

EXPERIENCE	SKILL EXPERIENCE	STRENGTH EXPERIENCE	WILL EXPERIENCE
25	-	-	-

FLACCID CELERY
★★

Having lost its crunch, this floppy stalk is as healthy as it is unpleasant.

HEALING PTS	MORALITY	PURITY	FATNESS	BASE VALUE
40	-	-	-5.0%	14 Gold

EXPERIENCE	SKILL EXPERIENCE	STRENGTH EXPERIENCE	WILL EXPERIENCE
-	-	-	-

MEALY APPLE
★★

A lone worm inhabits this apple. It's not a feature, it's just a bug.

HEALING PTS	MORALITY	PURITY	FATNESS	BASE VALUE
40	-	-	-	15 Gold

EXPERIENCE	SKILL EXPERIENCE	STRENGTH EXPERIENCE	WILL EXPERIENCE
5	-	-	-

MUSHY TOFU

★★

On its way out, but still nutritious and cleansing.

HEALING PTS	MORALITY	PURITY	FATNESS	BASE VALUE
40	5.0	10.0	-	14 Gold
EXPERIENCE	SKILL EXPERIENCE	STRENGTH EXPERIENCE	WILL EXPERIENCE	
-	-	-	-	

SHRIVELED CARROT

★

In a certain light, it still looks orange. But then, so do you.

HEALING PTS	MORALITY	PURITY	FATNESS	BASE VALUE
20	-	-5.0	-	10 Gold
EXPERIENCE	SKILL EXPERIENCE	STRENGTH EXPERIENCE	WILL EXPERIENCE	
-	-	-	-	

ORGANIC TOFU

★★★★

The food of choice for hippies everywhere.

HEALING PTS	MORALITY	PURITY	FATNESS	BASE VALUE
160	5.0	20.0	-	38 Gold
EXPERIENCE	SKILL EXPERIENCE	STRENGTH EXPERIENCE	WILL EXPERIENCE	
25	-	-	-	

SILKEN TOFU

★★★

Though a tactile delight for the tongue, and healthy gift for your body, neither will get much taste from this tofu.

HEALING PTS	MORALITY	PURITY	FATNESS	BASE VALUE
80	5.0	15.0	-	23 Gold
EXPERIENCE	SKILL EXPERIENCE	STRENGTH EXPERIENCE	WILL EXPERIENCE	
-	-	-	-	

PUNY CARROT

★★

Well on its way to getting beaten up by cocktail carrots.

HEALING PTS	MORALITY	PURITY	FATNESS	BASE VALUE
40	-	-	-	15 Gold
EXPERIENCE	SKILL EXPERIENCE	STRENGTH EXPERIENCE	WILL EXPERIENCE	
-	5	-	-	

SUBLIME CELERY

★★★★★

This blessed stalk of righteousness is sure to help shed the pounds.

HEALING PTS	MORALITY	PURITY	FATNESS	BASE VALUE
320	-	15.0	-5.0%	66 Gold
EXPERIENCE	SKILL EXPERIENCE	STRENGTH EXPERIENCE	WILL EXPERIENCE	
-	-	-	-	

ROTTEN APPLE

★

One thing you never want to hear from an apple: silence.

HEALING PTS	MORALITY	PURITY	FATNESS	BASE VALUE
20	-	-5.0	-	10 Gold
EXPERIENCE	SKILL EXPERIENCE	STRENGTH EXPERIENCE	WILL EXPERIENCE	
-	-	-	-	

RUSSET APPLE

★★★

An apple a day keeps the Guildmaster away.

HEALING PTS	MORALITY	PURITY	FATNESS	BASE VALUE
80	-	5.0	-	27 Gold
EXPERIENCE	SKILL EXPERIENCE	STRENGTH EXPERIENCE	WILL EXPERIENCE	
25	-	-	-	

SHINY APPLE

★★★★

Someone has buffed this baby to a blinding sheen. The crack as your teeth break the skin will be heard for miles.

HEALING PTS	MORALITY	PURITY	FATNESS	BASE VALUE
160	-	10.0	-	66 Gold
EXPERIENCE	SKILL EXPERIENCE	STRENGTH EXPERIENCE	WILL EXPERIENCE	
125	-	-	-	

DESSERTS

AMAZING APPLE PIE
★★★

"Delicious" doesn't do justice to this pie. It can fully heal a Hero in the midst of combat, and it actually makes you lose weight instead of gain it! As if that weren't enough, the special combination of magical spices gives you a hefty experience bonus.

HEALING PTS	MORALITY	PURITY	FATNESS	BASE VALUE
160	-	-	-90.0%	80 Gold
EXPERIENCE	SKILL EXPERIENCE	STRENGTH EXPERIENCE	WILL EXPERIENCE	
100	-	-	-	

APPLE PIE POCKET
★★★

This bland, portable pastry has all the fat of a regular pie with half the flavor.

HEALING PTS	MORALITY	PURITY	FATNESS	BASE VALUE
160	-	-	10.0%	58 Gold
EXPERIENCE	SKILL EXPERIENCE	STRENGTH EXPERIENCE	WILL EXPERIENCE	
100	-	-	-	

BITS O' BEEF PIE
★★★

If the meat seems a bit sparse, take smaller bites.

HEALING PTS	MORALITY	PURITY	FATNESS	BASE VALUE
160	-	-10.0	10.0%	56 Gold
EXPERIENCE	SKILL EXPERIENCE	STRENGTH EXPERIENCE	WILL EXPERIENCE	
-	-	100	-	

COUNTRY BLUEBERRY PIE
★★★

A little dented and worn, this pre-owned pie is a good starter pastry.

HEALING PTS	MORALITY	PURITY	FATNESS	BASE VALUE
160	-	-	10.0%	56 Gold
EXPERIENCE	SKILL EXPERIENCE	STRENGTH EXPERIENCE	WILL EXPERIENCE	
-	-	-	100	

CRABAPPLE PIE
★★

It doesn't taste like good crab, either.

HEALING PTS	MORALITY	PURITY	FATNESS	BASE VALUE
80	-	-5.0	10.0%	24 Gold
EXPERIENCE	SKILL EXPERIENCE	STRENGTH EXPERIENCE	WILL EXPERIENCE	
20	-	-	-	

CRUMBLY BLUEBERRY PIE
★★

Tastes like being the last person to know about a party.

HEALING PTS	MORALITY	PURITY	FATNESS	BASE VALUE
80	-	-5.0	10.0%	24 Gold
EXPERIENCE	SKILL EXPERIENCE	STRENGTH EXPERIENCE	WILL EXPERIENCE	
-	-	-	20	

EPIPHANIC BLUEBERRY PIE
★★★★

Staring transfixed into the indigo glow, you gain a deeper understanding of the universe.

HEALING PTS	MORALITY	PURITY	FATNESS	BASE VALUE
640	-	10.0	10.0%	496 Gold
EXPERIENCE	SKILL EXPERIENCE	STRENGTH EXPERIENCE	WILL EXPERIENCE	
-	-	-	2500	

ERUDITE APPLE PIE
★★★★★

Humanity's first disobedience: Definitely the best one.

HEALING PTS	MORALITY	PURITY	FATNESS	BASE VALUE
640	-	10.0	10.0%	534 Gold
EXPERIENCE	SKILL EXPERIENCE	STRENGTH EXPERIENCE	WILL EXPERIENCE	
2500	-	-	-	

FILET MIGNON PIE
★★★★★

The soft flaky shell can barely contain the divine cuts of tender beef stuffed inside.

HEALING PTS	MORALITY	PURITY	FATNESS	BASE VALUE
640	-	-1.0	10.0%	493 Gold
EXPERIENCE	SKILL EXPERIENCE	STRENGTH EXPERIENCE	WILL EXPERIENCE	
-	-	2500	-	

FRESH BAKED BLUEBERRY PIE
★★★★

Reminds you of childhood. Not yours, obviously. A good childhood.

HEALING PTS	MORALITY	PURITY	FATNESS	BASE VALUE
320	-	5.0	10.0%	152 Gold
EXPERIENCE	SKILL EXPERIENCE	STRENGTH EXPERIENCE	WILL EXPERIENCE	
-	-	-	500	

HOLLOW MAN FLESH PIE
★

The term "savoury" was never so ironically applicable.

HEALING PTS	MORALITY	PURITY	FATNESS	BASE VALUE
40	-	-20.0	10.0%	11 Gold
EXPERIENCE	SKILL EXPERIENCE	STRENGTH EXPERIENCE	WILL EXPERIENCE	
-	-	-	-	

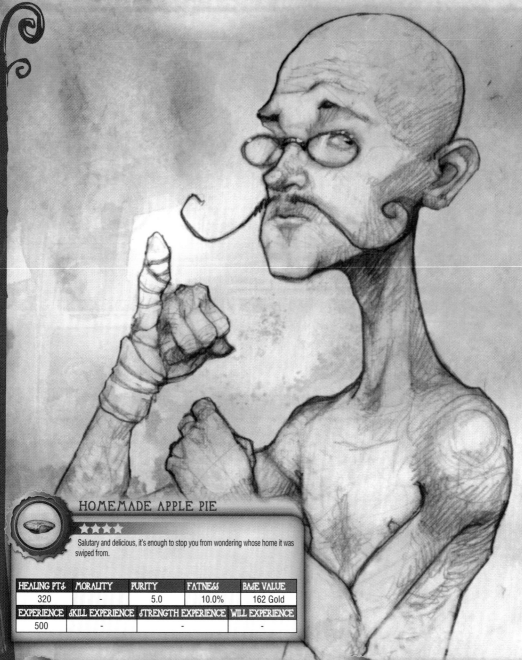

HOMEMADE APPLE PIE

★★★★

Salutary and delicious, it's enough to stop you from wondering whose home it was swiped from.

HEALING PTS	MORALITY	PURITY	FATNESS	BASE VALUE
320	-	5.0	10.0%	162 Gold
EXPERIENCE	SKILL EXPERIENCE	STRENGTH EXPERIENCE	WILL EXPERIENCE	
500	-	-	-	

KIDNEY AND 'FRIENDS' PIE

★★

Some people consider this fatty meat pie a delicacy. And that's very sad.

HEALING PTS	MORALITY	PURITY	FATNESS	BASE VALUE
80	-	15.0	10.0%	24 Gold
EXPERIENCE	SKILL EXPERIENCE	STRENGTH EXPERIENCE	WILL EXPERIENCE	
-	-	20	-	

RANCID BLUEBERRY PIE

★

The blueberries in this pie are so sour they're more likely to dissolve your teeth than turn them blue.

HEALING PTS	MORALITY	PURITY	FATNESS	BASE VALUE
40	-	-10.0	10.0%	11 Gold
EXPERIENCE	SKILL EXPERIENCE	STRENGTH EXPERIENCE	WILL EXPERIENCE	
-	-	-	-	

RANCID APPLE PIE

★

You can eat around the worms, but remember they're thinking the same thing about you.

HEALING PTS	MORALITY	PURITY	FATNESS	BASE VALUE
40	-	-10.0	10.0%	11 Gold
EXPERIENCE	SKILL EXPERIENCE	STRENGTH EXPERIENCE	WILL EXPERIENCE	
-	-	-	-	

SAVORY STEAK PIE

★★★★

If you see this mouthwatering pie and fret about weight gain, you need to reexamine your priorities.

HEALING PTS	MORALITY	PURITY	FATNESS	BASE VALUE
320	-	-5.0	10.0%	152 Gold
EXPERIENCE	SKILL EXPERIENCE	STRENGTH EXPERIENCE	WILL EXPERIENCE	
-	-	500	-	

Potions

Potions aren't as easily found as food and drinks and can cost thousands more, but they come with none of the adverse side-effects. The Hero who relies on a strict potion diet can say goodbye to being fat and ugly without having to ever punish their taste buds with the righteous diet of tofu and carrots.

(1) Name: This is the name of the potion. These names often provide a pretty clear indication to the benefits.

(2) Stars: Every potion has a star value. This is your guide to the relative rarity and value of a particular potion. The more stars the potion has, the stronger its impact.

(3) Image: This shows you what the potion looks like—or at least what the bottle it comes in looks like.

(4) Healing Pts: The amount of health consuming this potion will replenish.

(5) Other: A few of the potions have very specific, unusual effects. These will be listed here.

(6) Base Value: This is your guide to the monetary value of the potions. The base value ignores economic variables and serves as a general guide to the price of the item.

(7) Experience: Not every potion is meant to heal; some offer heaps of experience instead! Potions may provide increases in general experience, Skill Experience, Strength Experience, or Will Experience. Quickly collect the experience orbs that appear after you drink the potion.

(8) Description: A brief description of the potion. Note that some potions have effects that aren't discussed in the tables so be sure to read the descriptions if you have any questions.

(1) PERCOLATED JAVA POTION

★★★ (2)

(8) The java of choice from Oakridge to Wraithmarsh for villagers with a surplus of work to do and a deficit of taste. Java potions cause your health to restore gradually for a limited period of time, as well as giving you an experience boost.

(4) HEALING PTS		(5) OTHER		(6) BASE VALUE
200		-		75 Gold
(7) EXPERIENCE	SKILL EXPERIENCE	STRENGTH EXPERIENCE		WILL EXPERIENCE
-	50	50		50

HEALTH POTIONS

CHILDREN'S HEALTH POTION

★★

Tastes like cherries mixed with turpentine. For your 'owie' level injuries.

HEALING PTS	OTHER	BASE VALUE	
400	-	77 Gold	
EXPERIENCE	SKILL EXPERIENCE	STRENGTH EXPERIENCE	WILL EXPERIENCE
-	-	-	-

CURE-ALL HEALTH POTION

★★★★

For those persistent nagging injuries, like balverine gouges and sword wounds, it pays to spring for the good stuff.

HEALING PTS	OTHER	BASE VALUE	
600	-	109 Gold	
EXPERIENCE	SKILL EXPERIENCE	STRENGTH EXPERIENCE	WILL EXPERIENCE
-	-	-	-

LIVE FOREVER HEALTH POTION

★★★★★

Like being shot in the face at point-blank range with healthiness. The very strongest health potion available.

HEALING PTS	OTHER	BASE VALUE	
700	-	125 Gold	
EXPERIENCE	SKILL EXPERIENCE	STRENGTH EXPERIENCE	WILL EXPERIENCE
-	-	-	-

PLACEBO HEALTH POTION

★

It actually makes you feel better, plus it taste like sugar! As weak as health potions come.

HEALING PTS	OTHER	BASE VALUE	
200	-	43 Gold	
EXPERIENCE	SKILL EXPERIENCE	STRENGTH EXPERIENCE	WILL EXPERIENCE
-	-	-	-

STANDARD HEALTH POTION

★★★

Take orally. Do not exceed recommended dosage. Do not attempt to operate heavy weaponry after use. If pain continues, buy more potion.

HEALING PTS	OTHER	BASE VALUE	
500	-	93 Gold	
EXPERIENCE	SKILL EXPERIENCE	STRENGTH EXPERIENCE	WILL EXPERIENCE
-	-	-	-

JAVA POTIONS

Java potions regenerate health gradually over time. It takes 10 seconds for effects to fully be felt.

INSTANT JAVA POTION

★

Made from beans that were crushed to a fine powder and robbed of all but a trace of their natural essence, which would be criminal had the beans not been canephora rubbish to start with. Java potions cause your health to restore gradually for a limited period of time, as well as giving you an experience boost.

HEALING PTS	OTHER	BASE VALUE	
50	-	15 Gold	
EXPERIENCE	SKILL EXPERIENCE	STRENGTH EXPERIENCE	WILL EXPERIENCE
-	2	2	2

MUSTELA JAVA POTION

★★★★★

The beans that constitute this specially-branded java potion have been eaten and subsequently evacuated by rare Samarkandian weasels. The gastrointestinal processes result in a radically stronger, smoother potion that will appeal to serious connoisseurs of the mighty bean. Java potions cause your health to restore gradually for a limited period of time, as well as giving you an experience boost.

HEALING PTS	OTHER	BASE VALUE	
800	-	751 Gold	
EXPERIENCE	SKILL EXPERIENCE	STRENGTH EXPERIENCE	WILL EXPERIENCE
-	1250	1250	1250

OBSIDIAN JAVA POTION

★★★★

Created by forcing hot water through beans heavily roasted in the Fairfax tradition, this potent java requires the use of a specialized machine made from decommissioned clockwork rifles. Java potions cause your health to restore gradually for a limited period of time, as well as giving you an experience boost.

HEALING PTS	OTHER	BASE VALUE	
400	-	219 Gold	
EXPERIENCE	SKILL EXPERIENCE	STRENGTH EXPERIENCE	WILL EXPERIENCE
-	250	250	250

PERCOLATED JAVA POTION

★★★

The java of choice from Oakridge to Wraithmarsh for villagers with a surplus of work to do and a deficit of taste. Java potions cause your health to restore gradually for a limited period of time, as well as giving you an experience boost.

HEALING PTS	OTHER	BASE VALUE	
200	-	75 Gold	
EXPERIENCE	SKILL EXPERIENCE	STRENGTH EXPERIENCE	WILL EXPERIENCE
-	50	50	50

SLEEPY BEAN JAVA POTION

★★

Light, acrid java carelessly brewed. There's more energy in a languid limpet. Java potions cause your health to restore gradually for a limited period of time, as well as giving you an experience boost.

HEALING PTS	OTHER	BASE VALUE	
100	-	31 Gold	
EXPERIENCE	SKILL EXPERIENCE	STRENGTH EXPERIENCE	WILL EXPERIENCE
-	10	10	10

WILL POTIONS

ATTENUATED WILL POTION
★★

This low grade Will potion will enhance your arcane powers enough to repel vicious dragon-squirrels.

HEALING PTS		OTHER	BASE VALUE
-		-	141 Gold

EXPERIENCE	SKILL EXPERIENCE	STRENGTH EXPERIENCE	WILL EXPERIENCE
-	-	-	500

CONCENTRATED WILL POTION
★★★★

A vigorous, potent Will potion, for the Hero who's a little more than 'power-hungry' but not yet ready for 'power-mad.'

HEALING PTS		OTHER	BASE VALUE
-		-	2478 Gold

EXPERIENCE	SKILL EXPERIENCE	STRENGTH EXPERIENCE	WILL EXPERIENCE
-	-	-	12500

CRUSHED WHEAT WILL POTION
★

The recipe for this Will potion was devised by an Old Kingdom scholar to help her find loose change in seat cushions.

HEALING PTS		OTHER	BASE VALUE
-		-	36 Gold

EXPERIENCE	SKILL EXPERIENCE	STRENGTH EXPERIENCE	WILL EXPERIENCE
-	-	-	100

INFUSED WILL POTION
★★★

An adequate Will potion to help you move past the awkward 'Fun at dinner parties' level of ability.

HEALING PTS		OTHER	BASE VALUE
-		-	585 Gold

EXPERIENCE	SKILL EXPERIENCE	STRENGTH EXPERIENCE	WILL EXPERIENCE
-	-	-	2500

UNDILUTED WILL POTION
★★★★★

An unconscionably powerful Will potion. You may not have any immediate intention to tear reality asunder and destroy the cosmos, but it's nice to keep your options open.

HEALING PTS		OTHER	BASE VALUE
-		-	10534 Gold

EXPERIENCE	SKILL EXPERIENCE	STRENGTH EXPERIENCE	WILL EXPERIENCE
-	-	-	62500

SKILL POTIONS

ADEPT SKILL POTION
★★★★

Inject knowledge directly into your nerves and muscles with this highly potent brew.

HEALING PTS		OTHER	BASE VALUE
-		-	2478 Gold

EXPERIENCE	SKILL EXPERIENCE	STRENGTH EXPERIENCE	WILL EXPERIENCE
-	12500	-	-

CLUMSY SKILL POTION
★

Tying your shoelaces requires more adroitness than the meager experience brewed into this potion.

HEALING PTS		OTHER	BASE VALUE
-		-	36 Gold

EXPERIENCE	SKILL EXPERIENCE	STRENGTH EXPERIENCE	WILL EXPERIENCE
-	100	-	-

EXPERT SKILL POTION
★★★★★

The specially treated remains of over a dozen grandmasters of dexterity have been distilled into this extraordinary concoction.

HEALING PTS		OTHER	BASE VALUE
-		-	10534 Gold

EXPERIENCE	SKILL EXPERIENCE	STRENGTH EXPERIENCE	WILL EXPERIENCE
-	62500	-	-

FUMBLING SKILL POTION
★★

Always dropping things? Tired of hitting your thumb with a hammer? This skill potion could be the answer for you.

HEALING PTS		OTHER	BASE VALUE
-		-	141 Gold

EXPERIENCE	SKILL EXPERIENCE	STRENGTH EXPERIENCE	WILL EXPERIENCE
-	500	-	-

PRACTICED SKILL POTION
★★★

It's the liquid equivalent of practicing for a week. It's no wonder it tastes like sweat.

HEALING PTS		OTHER	BASE VALUE
-		-	585 Gold

EXPERIENCE	SKILL EXPERIENCE	STRENGTH EXPERIENCE	WILL EXPERIENCE
-	2500	-	-

STRENGTH POTIONS

XP POTIONS

BALVERINE STRENGTH POTION

★★★

The high impact combat drink your muscles crave! Contains no actual balvorn byproducts.

HEALING PTS		OTHER	BASE VALUE
-		-	585 Gold

EXPERIENCE	SKILL EXPERIENCE	STRENGTH EXPERIENCE	WILL EXPERIENCE
-	-	2500	-

BEETLE STRENGTH POTION

★

Harness the astounding power of sugar to build yourself up to Beetle Strength! Warning: Beetle Strength is not proportional.

HEALING PTS		OTHER	BASE VALUE
-		-	36 Gold

EXPERIENCE	SKILL EXPERIENCE	STRENGTH EXPERIENCE	WILL EXPERIENCE
-	-	100	-

HOBBE STRENGTH POTION

★★

The combat drink of short angry champions! 100% natural state ingredients.

HEALING PTS		OTHER	BASE VALUE
-		-	141 Gold

EXPERIENCE	SKILL EXPERIENCE	STRENGTH EXPERIENCE	WILL EXPERIENCE
-	-	500	-

THUNDER'S STRENGTH POTION

★★★★★

The most powerful potion modern alchemists have ever concocted. They claim it contains traces of the powdered bones of the Hero known as Thunder.

HEALING PTS		OTHER	BASE VALUE
-		-	10534 Gold

EXPERIENCE	SKILL EXPERIENCE	STRENGTH EXPERIENCE	WILL EXPERIENCE
-	-	62500	-

TROLL STRENGTH POTION

★★★★

Get big faster with the combat drink favored by the Crucible champs! Disclaimer: Contents neither endorsed nor recommended by the Crucible Regulatory Association of Albion.

HEALING PTS		OTHER	BASE VALUE
-		-	2478 Gold

EXPERIENCE	SKILL EXPERIENCE	STRENGTH EXPERIENCE	WILL EXPERIENCE
-	-	12500	-

BAD XP POTION

★

Staggeringly weak experience potion. On the Hoggins-McGuffy Experience Scale, it barely registers a 'burned my tongue on some hot tea.'

HEALING PTS		OTHER	BASE VALUE
-		-	39 Gold

EXPERIENCE	SKILL EXPERIENCE	STRENGTH EXPERIENCE	WILL EXPERIENCE
100	-	-	-

CONCENTRATED XP POTION

★★★

A moderate experience potion. On the Huggins-McGuffy Experience Scale, it's approximately equivalent to 'followed my favorite bard on his national tours.'

HEALING PTS		OTHER	BASE VALUE
-		-	643 Gold

EXPERIENCE	SKILL EXPERIENCE	STRENGTH EXPERIENCE	WILL EXPERIENCE
2500	-	-	-

ENRICHED XP POTION

★★★★

A strong, potent experience potion. On the Hoggins-McGuffy Experience Scale, it's six times more experiential than 'backpacked through the Albion hinterlands.'

HEALING PTS		OTHER	BASE VALUE
-		-	2725 Gold

EXPERIENCE	SKILL EXPERIENCE	STRENGTH EXPERIENCE	WILL EXPERIENCE
12500	-	-	-

PURE EXPERIENCE EXTRACTED

★★★★★

Almost terrifyingly strong experience potion. On the Hoggins-McGuffy Experience Scale, it's worth 17 'laughed in the face of death and lived to tell the tales.'

HEALING PTS		OTHER	BASE VALUE
-		-	11587 Gold

EXPERIENCE	SKILL EXPERIENCE	STRENGTH EXPERIENCE	WILL EXPERIENCE
62500	-	-	-

WATERED DOWN XP POTION

★★

A weak experience potion. On the Hoggins-McGuffy Experience Scale, it's roughly equivalent to 'ran into an old friend at the market.'

HEALING PTS		OTHER	BASE VALUE
-		-	154 Gold

EXPERIENCE	SKILL EXPERIENCE	STRENGTH EXPERIENCE	WILL EXPERIENCE
500	-	-	-

SPECIAL POTIONS

POTION OF LIFE
★★★★★

The same sect of Old Kingdom alchemists who are said to have solved the secret of immortality also created the recipe for this life-prolonging potion. Few have the knowledge or the skill to brew it successfully now.

HEALING PTS	OTHER	BASE VALUE
1000	Health Meter Extension: 50	2800 Gold

EXPERIENCE	SKILL EXPERIENCE	STRENGTH EXPERIENCE	WILL EXPERIENCE
-	-	-	-

RESURRECTION PHIAL
★

It's a good idea to keep one of these invaluable potions in your inventory. Should your health drop to zero, the Resurrection Phial will automatically revive you, while preventing any of the inconveniences associated with defeat, such as experience loss and scarring. Smells faintly of lavender.

HEALING PTS	OTHER	BASE VALUE
-	-	1200 Gold

EXPERIENCE	SKILL EXPERIENCE	STRENGTH EXPERIENCE	WILL EXPERIENCE
-	-	-	-

Gifts

Although we expect some Heroes to indeed choose a life of celibacy (and loneliness), most will eventually want to settle down and start a family–or at least get some nookie. That's where gifts come into play. The best way to make someone like you is to give them gifts of their liking. Check their list of likes and dislikes and try to give them a gift that matches their interests. After all, the gift you give a barmaid should be different than the ones you give your children. Don't just give any gift to anyone without first thinking about the result. Each gift has the capacity to increase/decrease their feelings about you so choose wisely. The gift you give can be one of friendliness, childishness, poshness, or romance. Naturally, gifts with higher poshness and romance ratings will go a long way towards helping you find a mate.

TOYS

You won't have much need for these gifts until you have a family (or two), but it's always a good idea to keep the kids happy once you do. Your adventuring will likely take you away from home for several days at a spell. Bring the kids home some toys to make up for all the times they have to tuck themselves into bed at night, wondering when they'll ever see you again.

GIFT	STARS	FRIENDLINESS	CHILDISHNESS	POSHNESS	ROMANCE	BASE VALUE
Autograph Card	★	5.00%	-	-	-	10
Garth Doll	★★★★★	-	20.00%	-	-	400
Hammer Doll	★★★★★	-	20.00%	-	-	400
Hero Doll	★★★★★	-	20.00%	-	-	400
Lucien Doll	★★★★★	-	20.00%	-	-	400
Porcelain Doll	★★★	-	20.00%	-	-	25
Ragdoll	★★★	-	20.00%	-	-	25
Reaver Doll	★★★★★	-	20.00%	-	-	400
Teddy Bear	★★★	-	20.00%	-	-	25
Theresa Doll	★★★★★	-	20.00%	-	-	400
Toy Bow	★★★	-	20.00%	-	-	25
Toy Gun	★★★	-	20.00%	-	-	25
Toy Horse	★★★	-	20.00%	-	-	25
Toy Mace	★★★	-	20.00%	-	-	25
Toy Music Box	★★★	-	20.00%	-	-	25
Toy Sword	★★★	-	20.00%	-	-	25

FLOWERS, PERFUME & CANDY

Regardless of your gender or sexual orientation, the object of your lustful desires will no doubt appreciate a gift of this variety. After all, everyone likes getting flowers and candy! Best of all, even the cheaper gifts—the ones with the negative poshness ratings—pack a hefty romantic punch. Save the candy for those you wish to befriend and give out the flowers and perfume to those you wish to bed.

GIFT	STARS	FRIENDLINESS	CHILDISHNESS	POSHNESS	ROMANCE	BASE VALUE
Cheap Flowers	★★	-	-	-10.00%	22.50%	50
Deepest Dark Chocolates	★★★★★	20.00%	-	20.00%	-	150
'Eau D'Hobbe' Perfume	★	-	-	-20.00%	22.50%	30
Fake Flowers	★	-	-	-20.00%	22.50%	25
Freshly Picked Flowers	★★★	-	-	-	22.50%	100
Gilded Flowers	★★★★★	-	-	20.00%	22.50%	400
Gravel Chocolate	★	20.00%	-	-20.00%	-	20
Honey-scented Flowers	★★★★	-	-	10.00%	22.50%	200
Love Potion No. 9.042	★★★★	-	-	10.00%	22.50%	240
Milk Chocolate	★★★	20.00%	-	-	-	80
Mudbrick Chocolate	★★	20.00%	-	-10.00%	-	40
'Permutation' Perfume	★★	-	-	-10.00%	22.50%	60
Pixie Tears' Perfume	★★★★★	-	-	20.00%	22.50%	480
Pure Chocolate	★★★★	20.00%	-	10.00%	-	160
'Scanque' Perfume	★★★	-	-	-	22.50%	120
Superior Chocolate	★★★★★	20.00%	-	20.00%	-	320

GEMSTONES & JEWELRY

Nothing says forever like a Forever Ring. Jewelry shouldn't be given out to just anyone. Hold onto any rings you get so you can use them to get engaged and continue to collect jewelry to give to your spouse(s) when you come home from a long quest. You'll be happy to know that even the cheapest of jewelry gets the romantic juices flowing. Save your money and refrain from buying the most expensive items unless your spouse is about to leave you or, worse, your mistress is.

GIFT	STARS	FRIENDLINESS	CHILDISHNESS	POSHNESS	ROMANCE	BASE VALUE
Amethyst	★★	10.00%	-	10.00%	-	400
Beggar's Ring	★	-	-	-	22.50%	50
Civil Ring	★★★	-	-	-	22.50%	200
Diamond	★★★★★	20.00%	-	25.00%	-	6250
Economy Value Necklace	★★	-	-	-10.00%	22.50%	200
Emerald	★★★	20.00%	-	15.00%	-	1000
Eternal Love Ring	★★★★★	-	-	-	22.50%	800
Forever Ring	★★★★	-	-	-	22.50%	400
Jet	★	20.00%	-	5.00%	-	160
Mood Ring	★★	-	-	-	22.50%	100
Mysterious Ring	★★★★★	-	-	-	22.50%	1000
Precious Necklace	★★★★	-	-	10.00%	22.50%	800
Pretty Necklace	★★★	-	-	-	22.50%	400
Ruby	★★★★	20.00%	-	20.00%	-	2500
Rusty Necklace	★	-	-	-20.00%	22.50%	100
Solid Gold Necklace	★★★★★	-	-	20.00%	22.50%	1600

Trophies

There is no room for humility in the life of a Hero! If you're to receive the renown you deserve, then you must flaunt the trophies you collect during your questing. Show these trophies off in public to win the admiration of the citizenry or, better yet, display them on the walls of your home so all who pass through your door will know exactly how fantastic you really are!

QUEST TROPHIES

TROPHY	STARS	RENOWN	BASE VALUE	QUEST	AREA	CHAPTER
Banshee Rags	★★★★	4	4000	Evil in Wraithmarsh	Wraithmarsh	Late Adulthood
Broken Spire Collar	★★★	3	3000	The Hero of Will	Tattered Spire	Late Adulthood
Captain Dread's Sword	★★★	3	3000	Treasure Island of Doom!	Sinkhole	Late Adulthood
Crucible Trophy	★★★★★	5	5000	The Crucible	Westcliff	Early Adulthood
Dash's Goggles	★★	2	2000	A Bridge Too Far	Rookridge	Early Adulthood
Golden Oak Leaf	★★	2	2000	The Hero of Strength	Oakfield	Early Adulthood
Hobbe Leg	★★	2	2000	Hobbe Squatters	Oakfield	Late Adulthood
Hobbe Staff Head	★★★	3	3000	The Rescue	Hobbe Cave	Happily Ever After
Hollow Man Head	★★★	3	3000	The Summoners	Bowerstone Cemetery	Early Adulthood
Lucien's Contract	★★★★	4	4000	The Hit	Forsaken Fortress	Happily Ever After
Mutton of Eternal Hope	★★★	3	3000	T.O.B.Y.	Bloodstone	Late Adulthood
Rod of Life	★★★	3	3000	Love Hurts	Bowerstone Cemetery	Late Adulthood
Sex Change Souvenir	★★★★	4	4000	Castle Fairfax	Fairfax Gardens	Happily Ever After
Shard Shard	★★★★★	5	5000	Bloodstone Assault	Bloodstone	Late Adulthood
Silver Bullet	★★★	3	3000	Westcliff Shooting Range	Westcliff	Early Adulthood
Son of Chesty	★★★★	4	4000	Brightwood Tower	Brightwood	Happily Ever After
Temple of Light Seal	★★★★	4	4000	Defender of the Light	Oakfield	Early Adulthood
Temple of Shadows Seal	★★★★	4	4000	The Oakfield Massacre	Rookridge	Early Adulthood
Thag's Head	★	1	1000	The Bandit	Bower Lake	Early Adulthood
Troll's Eyeball	★★★	3	3000	Something Rotten	Rookridge	Late Adulthood

Augments

The augments listed here can be installed into any weapon with an empty augment slot to give it a powerful boost in power. Augments are pretty rare in the wild, but they can be purchased from stone cutters around Albion. These magical gems can provide some extremely helpful upgrades to your weaponry, but many also come with a rather nasty side-effect. Be sure to understand the effects of the augment well before installing it into a weapon. Experiment with combining different augments in the same weapon to stack their powers.

WEAPON AUGMENTS

AUGMENT	STARS	BASE VALUE	EFFECT
Bewitching	★	900	This is a magical augment which will make you more attractive without the need for cosmetic surgery.
Cursed Warrior	★★★	2680	Your practical and studied approach to battle earns you more experience than usual during combat. However, your devotion to it consumes you, gradually depleting your health to dangerous levels.
Devastation	★★★★	4690	Increases your skill with the augmented weapon, causing additional damage.
Discipline	★★★★	4690	Your practical and studied approach to battle earns you more experience than usual during combat.
Fear Itself	★	875	Wielding a weapon with this augment attached will instill terror in the hearts of any citizens who see you.
Flame	★★★	2680	This augment allows you to scorch your enemies with mystical fire damage. Additionally, its name is catchy and violates no copyrights.
Ghoul	★★★★	4690	Each weapon hit drains health from your opponent and transfer it to you.
Gnarly	★★	1530	You are more resistant to damage, yet oddly, you scar more easily.
Gold Burden	★★★	2680	You will earn gold for every kill you make, but you will deal out less damage and receive more as a consequence.
Golden Touch	★★★★★	8200	This bloodthirsty augment will reward you with gold for every kill you make.
Killerwatt	★★★	2680	Your weapon causes electrical damage instead of normal.
Life Sucks	★★★	2680	With every strike, you will absorb some of the life essence of your target, however you cause less damage in combat and take more.
Lucky Charm	★★★★	4690	You dish out more damage and take less yourself.
Piercing Agony	★★★	2680	You will inflict much greater damage than usual, but your health will constantly deplete down to dangerous levels in return.
Slash & Burn	★★	1530	You will inflict fire instead of normal damage to enemies, but the mystical flames will make you prone to scarring.
Stoneskin	★★	3060	Your skin becomes extremely resistant to scarring.
Storm Scar	★★	1530	You will cause electrical damage to your enemies, but the energies will leave you scarred.

Dyes

The world of Albion is too bright a place for everyone to be seen wearing the same clothes. Use these dyes (often found in dig spots) to transform the color of your clothes and hair! Dyes can be applied to numerous pieces of clothing and give you the opportunity to create a custom look. Dyes with the higher star rating are more valuable and can help improve the Hero's attractiveness.

CLOTHING & HAIR DYES

DYE	STARS	BASE VALUE
Apocalyptic Pink Dye	★★★★★	1000
Aquapos Dye	★★★★★	1000
Banana Pudding Dye	★	250
Barely Blue Dye	★	250
Burning Orange Dye	★★★★★	1000
Carotene Orange Dye	★	250
Cloudless Sky Dye	★	250
Compost Brown Dye	★	250
Diver's Dye	★	250
Envy Green Dye	★★★★★	1000
Fishtankarous Dye	★	250
Freshwater Springs Dye	★	250
Gables Green Dye	★	250
Gangreen Dye	★	250
Greypefruit Dye	★	250
Greypricot Dye	★	250
Impermissible Carmine Dye	★	250
Insatiable Butcher Pink Dye	★	250
Java Dye	★	250
Kangarouge Dye	★	250
Kilowhite Dye	★	250

DYE	STARS	BASE VALUE
Leathery Tan Dye	★	250
Liquid Gold Dye	★★★★★	1000
Mansfield Green Dye	★	250
Moonless Midnight Dye	★	250
Peacock Dye	★★★★★	1000
Periwinkle Dye	★	250
Piratical Orange Dye	★	250
Pomegreynate Dye	★	250
Red Letter Dye	★	250
Regal Purple Dye	★★★★★	1000
Scarlet Slime Dye	★★★★★	1000
Shiner Dye	★	250
Soylent Dye	★	250
Sunshine Yellow Dye	★	250
Swarthy Revenge Indigo Dye	★★★★★	1000
Sweet Cream Dye	★	250
True Blue Dye	★	250
Valiant Avenger Pink Dye	★	250
Vermillipede Dye	★	250
Viole Dye	★	250
Yellowbelly Dye	★	250

Furniture

Everyone wants a roof over their head, but they prefer there to be some beds, chairs, and tables under that roof with them. Give your family the comforts they deserve by outfitting your home with any of these lines of furniture. Hold off on buying a home and starting a family until you can at least afford furniture from the "average" line, else you're bound to hear them complaining about the squalor you force them to live in. You can replace the furniture in a home you own by accessing the real estate sign and selecting "Redecorate" mode. Now all of the exchangeable furniture can be targeted and swapped with pieces from your inventory.

BROKEN SERIES

FURNITURE	STARS	BASE VALUE
Broken Bedside Table	★	10
Broken Bookcase	★	30
Broken Closet	★	45
Broken Comfy Chair	★	20
Broken Cupboard	★	40
Broken Dining Table	★	40
Broken Double Bed	★	50
Broken Drawers	★	20
Broken Dresser	★	35
Broken Sink	★	15
Broken Stove	★	15

WORN SERIES

FURNITURE	STARS	BASE VALUE
Worn Bedside Table	★★	20
Worn Bookcase	★★	60
Worn Closet	★★	90
Worn Comfy Chair	★★	40
Worn Cupboard	★★	80
Worn Dining Table	★★	80
Worn Double Bed	★★	100
Worn Dresser	★★	70

AVERAGE SERIES

FURNITURE	STARS	BASE VALUE
Average Bedside Table	★★★	40
Average Bookcase	★★★	120
Average Closet	★★★	180
Average Comfy Chair	★★★	80
Average Cupboard	★★★	160
Average Dining Table	★★★	160
Average Double Bed	★★★	200
Average Drawers	★★★	80
Average Dresser	★★★	140
Average Sink	★★★	60
Average Stove	★★★	60

DECORATIVE SERIES

FURNITURE	STARS	BASE VALUE
Decorative Bedside Table	★★★★	80
Decorative Bookcase	★★★★	240
Decorative Closet	★★★★	360
Decorative Comfy Chair	★★★★	160
Decorative Cupboard	★★★★	320
Decorative Dining Table	★★★★	320
Decorative Double Bed	★★★★	400
Decorative Dresser	★★★★	280

LUXURY SERIES

FURNITURE	STARS	BASE VALUE
Luxury Bedside Table	★★★★★	160
Luxury Bookcase	★★★★★	480
Luxury Closet	★★★★★	720
Luxury Comfy Chair	★★★★★	320
Luxury Cupboard	★★★★★	640
Luxury Dining Table	★★★★★	640
Luxury Double Bed	★★★★★	800
Luxury Drawers	★★★★★	320
Luxury Sink	★★★★★	240
Luxury Stove	★★★★★	240

SPECIAL SERIES

FURNITURE	STARS	BASE VALUE
Dresser for Successor	★★★★★	560
Good Night Child's Bed	★★★	100
Lullaby Child's Bed	★★★★	200
Nightmare Child's Bed	★	25
Restless Night Child's Bed	★★	50
The Sleepmaster	★★★★★	1200
Sweet Dreams Child's Bed	★★★★★	400

Clothing

There are plenty of quality tailors scattered throughout the cities of Albion and each of them are capable of crafting some fine, handmade clothing. Outfit your Hero any way you see fit, but keep in mind that these choices will go a long way towards impacting the first impression others form of you. Dress in a way that matches your desired outcome on the morality scale, as this will certainly affect your progress in that area. Note that all clothes can be worn by both males and females. Many items are unisex, but those that are designed specifically for one sex carry a cross-dressing rating should the other sex wear them. Heroes wishing to experiment with gender play should consider wearing clothes of the opposite sex, especially if looking to start a same-sex relationship.

OUTFITS

BANDIT
Nobody knows where bandits buy their clothes, but they probably stitch and sew them themselves, when no one's looking.

CHICKEN SUIT
Transform yourself into what you've always wanted to become. Stand in front of the mirror, and ask yourself: "Would you chase me? I'd chase me. I'd chase me hard."

FEMALE GYPSY
Want to fit in at the Bower Lake camp? Wear this!

BOOR-ZHWAH
Become a part of Albion's bourgeoisie, a place from which you can look upon the lower classes with disdain and the upper classes with envy.

EXPLORER
The intrepid explorers who have ventured beyond the lands of Albion have traditionally favored this outfit. Nobody knows how useful it is to the trade, since few of them come back alive.

FEMALE LOWER CLASS
Mingle with the rabble with this cheap slum-dweller outfit.

FEMALE UPPER CLASS

Being a fancy lady, you're too posh to wear anything but the best. This outfit marks you out as one of Albion's elite. In the gold-stakes if nothing else.

MALE GYPSY

The perfect outfit for those who have a sky for a blanket and the earth for their bed.

RANGER

Seldom seen these days, Rangers are at home in the woods, wrestling trees and snuggling up to weeds and rocks.

HAL'S OUTFIT

This "Halo" themed outfit is available only to owners of the Collector's Edition of "Fable 2".

Long ago, when Albion was still under rule of the Old Kingdom, a rift in space opened a portal between dimensions. Through the rift stepped a warrior of immense power, clad in green armor and carrying a striking crystal sword. Though he never revealed his real name, he was known to all as Hal.

MALE LOWER CLASS

Mingle with the rabble with this cheap slum-dweller outfit.

SHADOW-WORSHIPPER

The posh twits at the Temple of Shadows may only be playing at being evil, but the aura of malice this outfit emanates is unmistakable.

HARLOT

You too can join the oldest profession in the world. Yes, older even than puppeteering.

MALE MIDDLE CLASS

Become a part of Albion's bourgeoisie, a place from which you can look upon the lower classes with disdain and the upper classes with envy.

SPIRE GUARD

Want to be a member of Lucien's army? This outfit is ideal for both guarding prisoners in the Spire and razing town's in Lucien's name across Albion.

HIGHWAYMAN OUTFIT

The Highwaymen's Guild is very selective about who becomes a member. But who needs membership when you can dress up like them?

MALE UPPER CLASS

You're too posh to wear anything but the best. This outfit marks you out as one of Albion's elite. In the gold-stakes if nothing else.

WILL USER

Don't allow non-Will-conducive clothes to cramp your magical style, this outfit is the choice of all serious spellcasters.

HOT DATE

Sexy and enticing, or a horrifying abomination? Put it on and decide for yourself.

MONK

It's no wonder the soft robes of this outfit are favored by the monks from the Temple of Light.

WIZARD

This wizard robe and hat allows the right wearer to cast Lvl. 3 Eroticism.

HEADGEAR

Introduction

Cast of Characters

The Hero's Way

Quest Guide

Albion Atlas

Weapons of Yore

Items & Clothing

Pub Games, Jobs
& More

Enemies of Albion

Stats are for Male/Female Heroes when appropriate.

NAME	STARS	ATTRACTIVENESS	AGGRESSIVENESS	POSHNESS	CROSS-DRESSING	OTHER	BASE VALUE
All-Weather Chapeau	★★★	5.0%	-	2.5%	-	-	67
Archmage Cap	★★★★★	10.0%	-	-	-	-	300
Bandit Bandana	★★★	-	5.0%/5.0%	-	-	-	45
Bandit Skullcap	★★★	-	5.0%	-	-	-	45
Chicken Suit Headpiece	★★★	-	-	-	-	Ridiculousness: 20.0%	225
Gossamer Head Wrap	★★	-	-	-	5.0%/0.0%	-	37
Hal's Helmet*	★★★★	5.0%	2.5%	-	-	-	270
Highwayman Hat	★★★★	5.0%	5.0%	-	-	-	180
Lover's Plume	★★★	0.0%/5.0%	-	-	10.0%/0.0%	Raunchiness: 5.0%	120
Merchant's Cap	★★★	-	-	-	-	Raunchiness: 5.0%	120
Noble Gent's Hat	★★★★★	15.0%	-	5.0%	-	-	270
Noble Lady's Hat	★★★★★	0.0%/15.0%	-	0.0%/5.0%	10.0%/0.0%	-	270
Pauper Bonnet	★	-2.5%	-	-2.5%	10.0%/0.0%	-	22
Pauper Hat	★	-2.5%	-	-2.5%	-	-	22
Powdered Wig	★★★★★	0.0%/10.0%	-	0.0%/2.5%	10.0%/0.0%	-	270
Rural Kerchief	★★	-	-	-	5.0%/0.0%	-	37
Spire Guard Headband	★★★★	-	5.0%	-	-	-	210
Striped Bandana	★★	-	-	-	-	-	37
Urban Capotain	★★★	0.0%/5.0%	-	0.0%/2.5%	10.0%/0.0%	-	67
Wizard Hat	★★★★	10.0%	-	-	-	-	240
Yokel Hat	★★	-	-	-	-	-	37

COATS

NAME	STARS	ATTRACTIVENESS	AGGRESSIVENESS	POSHNESS	CROSS-DRESSING	OTHER	BASE VALUE
Archmage Robe	★★★★	10.0%	5.0%	-	-	-	640
Assassin Coat	★★★	-	-	-	-	Evil: 5.0%	240
Chicken Suit Body	★★★	-	-	-	-	Ridiculousness: 20.0%	600
Crop Top Jacket	★★★	0.0%/10.0%	-	-	10.0%/0.0%	-	240
Cuffed Overcoat	★★★	5.0%	-	5.0%	-	-	180
Double Belted Jacket	★★★	0.0%/5.0%	-	0.0%/5.0%	10.0%/0.0%	-	180
Explorer Coat	★★★	5.0%	-	-	-	-	240
Hal's Body Armour*	★★★★	10.0%	5.0%	-	-	-	720
Highroller's Coat	★★★	5.0%	-	-	-	-	400
Highwayman Coat	★★★★	10.0%	5.0%	-	-	-	480
Monk Robes	★★★	-	-	-	-	Good: 10.0%	200
Noble Gent's Coat	★★★★★	15.0%	-	10.0%	-	-	720
Patchy Coat	★	-5.0%	-	-5.0%	10.0%/0.0%	-	60
Ranger Coat	★★★	-	-	-	-	-	200
Shadow-Worshipper Robes	★★★	-	-	-	-	Evil: 10.0%	240
Spire Guard Coat	★★★★	-	10.0%	-	-	-	560
Will User Robe	★★★★★	15.0%	-	5.0%	-	-	800

UPPER BODY

NAME	STARS	ATTRACTIVENESS	AGGRESSIVENESS	POSHNESS	CROSS-DRESSING	OTHER	BASE VALUE
Bandit Shirt	★★★	-	10.0%	-	-	-	90
Corset	★★★	0.0%/10.0%	-	-	-10.0%/0.0%	-	180
Embroidered Day Tunic	★★★	0.0%/5.0%	-	0.0%/5.0%	10.0%/0.0%	-	135
Explorer Shirt	★★★	-	-	-	-	-	180
Gypsy Male Shirt	★★	-	-	-	-	-	75
Knotted Shirt	★★★	-	-	-	-	Raunchiness: 10.0%	240
Noble Blouse	★★★★★	0.0%/15.0%	-	0.0%/10.0%	10.0%/0.0%	-	540
Noble Gent's Shirt	★★★★★	15.0%	-	10.0%	-	-	540
Pauper Blouse	★	-5.0%	-	-5.0%	10.0%/0.0%	-	45
Pauper Shirt	★	-5.0%	-	-5.0%	-	-	45
Sun Vest	★★	-	-	-	10.0%/0.0%	-	75
Tart Bodice	★★★	-	-	-	10.0%/0.0%	Raunchiness: 10.0%	240
Vintage Vest & Shirt	★★★	5.0%	-	5.0%	-	-	135

HANDS

NAME	STARS	ATTRACTIVENESS	AGGRESSIVENESS	POSHNESS	CROSS-DRESSING	OTHER	BASE VALUE
Bandit Gloves	★★★	-	2.5%	-	-	-	15
Felt-Lined Carriage Gloves	★★★	2.5%	-	2.5%	-	-	22
Hal's Gauntlets*	★★★★	1.0%	1.0%	-	-	-	90
Highwayman Gloves	★★★★	1.0%	2.5%	-	-	-	60
Monk Gloves	★★★★	-	-	-	-	Good: 2.5%	25
Pauper Gloves	★	-2.5%	-	-2.5%	-	-	7
Spire Guard Gloves	★★★★	-	2.5%	-	-	-	70
Tart Gloves	★★★	-	-	-	2.5%/0.0%	Raunchiness: 2.5%	40

LOWER BODY

NAME	STARS	ATTRACTIVENESS	AGGRESSIVENESS	POSHNESS	CROSS-DRESSING	OTHER	BASE VALUE
Bandit Trousers	★★★	-	5.0%	-	-	-	60
Classic Chequered	★★★	5.0%	-	5.0%	-	-	90
Explorer Trousers	★★★	-	-	-	-	-	120
Gypsy Male Trousers	★★	-	-	-	-	-	50
Hal's Leg Armour	★★★★	5.0%	2.5%	-	-	-	360
Harlequin Trousers	★★★	-	-	-	-	Raunchiness: 10.0%	160
Highwayman Trousers	★★★★	4.0%	5.0%	-	-	-	240
Hot Pants	★★★	0.0%/5.0%	-	-	5.0%/0.0%	-	120
Layered Skirt	★★	-	-	-	10.0%/0.0%	-	50
Noble Gent's Trousers	★★★★★	10.0%	-	10.0%	-	-	360
Noble Skirt	★★★★★	0.0%/10.0%	-	0.0%/10.0%	10.0%/0.0%	-	360
Pauper Skirt	★	-5.0%	-	-5.0%	10.0%/0.0%	-	30
Pauper Trousers	★	-5.0%	-	-5.0%	-	-	30
Pauper Trousers	★	-5.0%	-	-5.0%	-	-	30
Ranger Trousers	★★★	-	-	-	-	-	100
Signature Skirt	★★★	0.0%/5.0%	-	0.0%/5.0%	10.0%/0.0%	-	90
Spire Guard Trousers	★★★★	-	5.0%	-	-	-	280
Tart Skirt	★★★	-	-	-	10.0%/0.0%	Raunchiness: 10.0%	160
Will User Trousers	★★★★★	5.0%	-	-	-	-	400

FEET

NAME	STARS	ATTRACTIVENESS	AGGRESSIVENESS	POSHNESS	CROSS-DRESSING	OTHER	BASE VALUE
Bandit Boots	★★★	-	2.5%	-	-	-	30
Buckled Loafers	★★★	2.5%	-	2.5%	-	-	45
Chicken Suit Feet	★★★	-	-	-	-	Ridiculousness: 5.0%	150
Clogs	★★	-	-	-	-	-	25
Explorer Boots	★★★	-	-	-	-	-	60
Hal's Boots	★★★★	1.0%	1.0%	-	-	-	180
Highwayman Boots	★★★★	2.0%	2.5%	-	-	-	120
Leather Boots	★★	-	-	-	5.0%/0.0%	-	25
Mid-Calf Bootie	★★★	0.0%/2.5%	-	0.0%/2.5%	5.0%/0.0%	-	45
Monk Boots	★★★	-	-	-	-	Good: 2.5%	50
Noble Gent's Boots	★★★★★	5.0%	-	5.0%	-	-	180
Noble Lady's Boots	★★★★★	0.0%/5.0%	-	0.0%/5.0%	5.0%/0.0%	-	180
Pauper Boots	★	-2.5%	-	-2.5%	-	-	15
Spire Guard Boots	★★★★	-	2.5%	-	-	-	140
Tart Boots	★★★	-	-	-	5.0%/0.0%	Raunchiness: 5.0%	80
Thigh Boots	★★★	0.0%/5.0%	-	-	5.0%/0.0%	-	60

MASKS

NAME	STARS	ATTRACTIVENESS	AGGRESSIVENESS	POSHNESS	CROSS-DRESSING	OTHER	BASE VALUE
Ballroom Mask	★★★★	1.0%	-	2.5%	-	-	120
Eye Patch	★	-	2.5%	-	-	-	90
Highwayman Mask	★	1.0%	1.0%	-	-	-	100
Shadow-Worshipper	★	-	-	-	-	Evil: 10.0%	120

Pub Games, Jobs, and More

When it comes to earning money in Albion, you just might be surprised at the number of ways and ease at which it can be done. Heroes in search of building their bank account can take on a temporary job, accept various mini-quests, or even test their luck at any of the different Pub Games found in Albion and online with Xbox Live Arcade. This chapter peels the cover off each of these money-making ventures and shows how to make money with each.

PUB GAMES

Whether you're looking to play strictly for enjoyment or are hoping to win a little money, the Game Masters in Albion have an assortment of tried and true *Pub Games* available for you to play. These games are all Albion-inspired takes on modern games that will likely seem familiar. Each game requires a different level of strategy, from "quite a lot" to "none at all," depending on your mood. Many of these games are house-advantage games, meaning that the long-term odds are against the player. If you were to play such a game for a long enough period, you'd probably wind up in the red. However, in the short term you could get incredibly lucky indeed.

Money & Debt

It's important to understand that every time you play these games, you are always playing on credit. When you join the game, you borrow enough chips to play the game (and can re-borrow as often as you like) and you never have to pay for your chips with cash. When you leave a game, any chips you have will go towards paying your debt first. If your debt is paid, then any additional chips end up in your pocket as gold.

You never have to pay your debt with gold if you don't wish to. However, a severe gambling debt can be a problem in the world of Albion and, should it grow large enough, you may be charged with a crime and fined. To reduce your debt, you can pay it down whenever you visit a game master.

Note that in Albion, gambling debt does not interfere with your primary gold balance; that is, beginning *Fable II* with a gambling debt from the XBLA version of *Pub Games* does not mean that you won't have gold in your pocket! It does, however, mean that you owe money to Game Masters, and this will affect your ability to cash money out of those games. As mentioned above, carrying too much gambling debt is considered a crime.

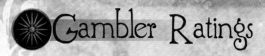

Gambler Ratings

As a gambler in the world of Albion, you earn a star rating based on how much gambling you do. You earn one point for each gold piece that you bet, and you increase in star levels based on your total points earned. These star levels unlock bigger games, and also allow you to borrow money in larger blocks.

You begin your gambling career with a rating of one star, and access to only the lowest-limit games. At 3000 points, you are promoted to the two-star level and so forth. Your Credit Limit represents the largest block of money that you can borrow at once. You actually have unlimited credit, so you can borrow this amount again and again. Also, if you have plenty of gold on hand, your credit limit is always equal to your total gold, or your level-based limit, whichever is greater.

PUB GAMES GAMBLER RATINGS		
Level	Points Required	Credit Limit
★	0	400
★★	3000	800
★★★	15,000	1500
★★★★	75,000	2500
★★★★★	300,000	4000

Fortune's Tower Merchant Directory

Fortune's Tower is a press-your-luck style card game that is a mix of the classic games of Solitaire and Blackjack. Of the three different Pub Games, Fortune's Tower contains the largest element of strategy and gives the player the most control over winning and losing. It's important to always consider how many Hero Cards are still remaining, and most importantly, whether or not the Gate Card is still in play. Knowing when to cash out is where the strategy comes in.

Rules

- A game of pressing your luck, played with a deck of cards ranked from 1 through 7 plus four 'Hero' cards.
- Decks contain 8, 9, or even 10 sets of each numbered card plus the four Heroes.
- Bets must be a multiple of 15 gold. Use the Left Thumbstick to increase or decrease your initial bet.
- The dealer begins the game by dealing three cards. The first is face down and is called the 'Gate Card.' The next two are face up and placed in a second row. There can be as many as eight rows if you reach the bottom of the tower.
- After each row is dealt you can either take the dealer's offer (equal to the total value of cards in the row) or you can choose to have another row dealt.
- Vertical pairs can end your game, so you don't want to see cards of the same rank touching one another from different rows (in contrast, horizontal pairs are a pleasant sight, as it reduces the chance of a vertical pair).
- The first time you draw a vertical pair, the dealer will replace the lower card within the pair with the Gate Card, thereby saving your game. A second vertical pair ends the game and you won't receive any gold.
- Hero cards aren't worth any gold since they have no face value, but their presence protects the entire row from misfortune. Drawing a Hero card not only protects against vertical pairs, but even keeps your Gate Card safe.
- Press the A Button to push on and have the dealer deal another row or press the B Button to cash out and take the dealer's offer.
- When an entire row matches, this is called a 'set.' A set gives a bonus multiplier equal to the row number with which it takes place. This multiplier remains in play until Misfortune is caused or you cash out. Multipliers can go as high as x8.
- Finish row eight without busting or using the Gate Card to win the jackpot. The jackpot pays the value of every card on the table, times any multipliers you may have.
- Each table has its own unique betting limit. Increase your bet in multiples of 15 to win even more gold. For example, betting 60 gold earns you 4x the gold you'd win by betting just 15 gold.

MISFORTUNE

The term "Misfortune" simply refers to losing at Fortune's Tower before you had a chance to cash out. This happens whenever you have one or more vertical pairs and no Gate Card or Hero Card to save you from defeat.

Variants and Odds

All Fortune's Tower games play by the same rules. However, there are three different decks, known as the Ruby, Emerald, and Diamond decks. The difference in the decks is the quantity of the number cards. Since Hero cards are the best cards for the player, having proportionally fewer of these cards makes the Ruby and Emerald decks slightly worse for the player than the Diamond deck.

> **Ruby Decks:** Contain 4 Heroes and 70 number cards.
>
> **Emerald Decks:** Contain 4 Heroes and 63 number cards.
>
> **Diamond Decks:** Contain 4 Heroes and 56 number cards.

With basic strategy (described below) players can expect the following approximate returns in the long run: Ruby deck (92%), Emerald deck (93.3%), and Diamond deck (99.4%).

Basic Strategy

Since Fortune's Tower is a press-your-luck game, you are essentially making a new bet on each round. You are risking the value of the row (which you could take right now) in exchange for the expected value of the next row, which might be better or worse.

Despite this complexity, there is a simple strategy table for Fortune's Tower, which gives you the correct play most of the time. This table is based on two factors: the Gate card, and the value of the row.

To use these tables, simply look at the unmodified offer value (that is, the raw total of the values in the row, applying no multipliers). If that value is equal to or higher than the value on the table, you should take the dealer's offer; otherwise, you should push on. The first column under each deck represents the minimum cashout value if your Gate card is intact; the second, lower value is the minimum value if the Gate card has been used.

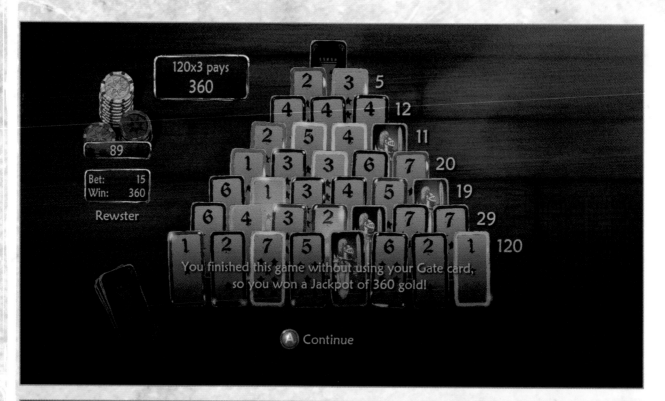

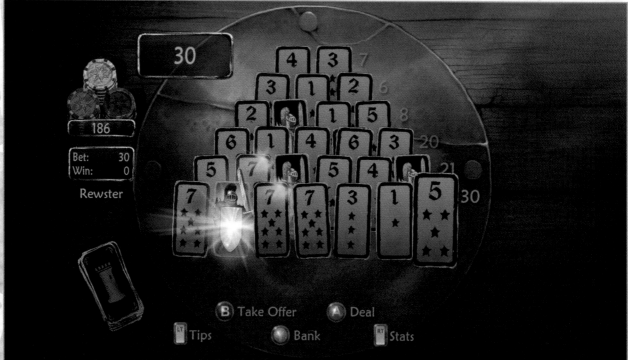

RUBY DECK		
Row	Gate Card Intact	Used Gate Card
2	12+	-
3	15+	9+
4	17+	9+
5	22+	11+
6	33+	11+
7	Never	12+
8	Always	Always

EMERALD DECK		
Row	Gate Card Intact	Used Gate Card
2	12+	-
3	15+	9+
4	18+	10+
5	24+	11+
6	35+	12+
7	Never	13+
8	Always	Always

DIAMOND DECK		
Row	Gate Card Intact	Used Gate Card
2	13+	-
3	16+	9+
4	20+	10+
5	26+	11+
6	38+	13+
7	Never	14+
8	Always	Always

For example, in the Ruby deck, you should cash out on Row 2 if the cards total 12 points or more. If you still have your Gate card on row 5, you should cash out with 22 or more. Notice that if your Gate card is intact on Row 7, you should always go for the Jackpot.

Again, these numbers are compared to the raw total value of the row, before you apply any modifiers for a larger bet, or for a bonus multiplier. It may seem tempting to behave differently when, for example, you have a 3x multiplier. However, that multiplier applies to all rows. This means that you are risking three times as much to win three times as much, so the correct play remains the same.

You will notice that there are many times where the best move is to cash out for less than you paid. Once your Gate Card is gone, the risk of misfortune is often too high to stick around.

ADVANCED STRATEGY

The basic strategy tables do not take into account any of the cards in play, only the raw total of the current row. You can use this extra information to improve your play. In fact, with perfect play on the Diamond deck, you may even have a slight edge over the house.

One of the interesting things about Fortune's Tower is that you can "count cards" just by looking at what's in play. Your decision to stay in the game or cash out can be informed by what's already been dealt.

Keystone

Keystone is a dice game that combines the betting strategies of Craps with the luck of Roulette. The object of the game is to place bets based on the numbers you expect to be rolled with the three dice before the Arch collapses. The Arch collapses if either 3 or 18 are removed or once both 10 and 11 have been rolled. With each roll of the dice another stone from the Arch is removed and it gets that much closer to collapsing. If a stone on the Arch has already been removed, then the one nearest it on the downward slope of the Arch is removed. Players place bets on the Arch (outside bets) that last for the entire length of the game and can also place inside bets which are one-roll only.

Rules

- A series of wagers are placed on the roll of three dice. Bet on single numbers, sets of numbers, or long strings of rolls.

- The outer arch contains 16 stones (3 through 18), one for each possible roll. Arch stones are removed one by one as the game proceeds.

- If the same number is rolled again, a lower Arch stone will be removed. The word 'lower' refers to the stones physically lower on the arch than that of the number rolled. The arrows under the Arch stones point in the direction of the stones that will be removed with repeat rolls.

- The game ends when the Arch collapses. This happens as soon as either of the 'Base' stones are removed (3 or 18) or if both of the Keystones (10 and 11) are removed. An average game lasts eight rounds.

- Playing Arch bets is a wager placed on one of the Arch stones. You are betting that the particular stone will be removed before the game ends. Arch bets can only be placed at the beginning of the game, and you must make at least one in order to start.

- Inside bets are single round bets. Different wagers have different odds, such as 8:10. In each case, the number on the right side shows how much you must bet, and the number on the left shows how much additional gold you will win if your wager is successful. We say "additional" because a winning bet also returns your initial outlay.

- Hold Left Trigger to see an odds overlay for the entire Keystone board. Note that betting on a specific three-of-a-kind bet, also known as a "hardways" bet in gambling parlance, pays off 400:2. This means that a single bet of 2 gold will return 402 gold (including your initial bet).

- The second number in each odds bet tells you the minimum bet for that space. You must always bet in multiples of the minimum bet. For example, 2 for inside bets or 5 for Arch bets.

- Trips means any three of a kind, a Pair means any two of a kind, and Run means a sequence such as 2-3-4 or 4-5-6. A bet on the Keystone space covers both 10 and 11 together.

- You can also bet black or red and diamond or circle, but note that 3, 10, 11, and 18 are neutral and yield a losing bet even if you cover all four of these squares.

- When applicable, a Jackpot rule allows players to be automatically paid on all Arch bets if the first roll, the "come out roll", is a 3 or 18. After the first roll, rolling a 3 or 18 still ends the game, but they won't cause a Jackpot. In a Jackpot game, all inside bets pay out normally, including bets on the first roll.

- Bloodstone is essentially the backwards version of Keystone in which you bet against the roll of the dice. Most bets will usually win a little, but they can sometimes lose a lot.

- Bloodstone bets are made with an oversized chip called a "lammer" which marks every space that you think the dice will not roll. You don't bet with chips because you'd need too many. Most bets will usually win.

Variants and Odds

Keystone has three major variants: Standard, Jackpot, and Bloodstone. In Standard Keystone all the normal Keystone rules apply. In Jackpot Keystone, there is an additional rule: if the first roll of the game is a 3 or an 18, then all Arch bets are instant winners. Bloodstone is quite different; it is essentially the basic game in reverse.

> **Standard:** No Jackpot rule is in effect; bet on stones you expect to be rolled.
>
> **Jackpot:** Pays all Arch bets if a 3 or 18 are rolled on first roll. Jackpots are very rare.
>
> **Bloodstone:** Reverse Keystone that requires you to place lamers on numbers you don't think will be rolled. Can win a little, but stand to lose a lot.

The payouts for each bet in Keystone are based on the likelihood of that event happening. You can compute the house advantage on any bet by comparing the true odds to the actual payout of the table. For example, the odds of rolling any trips (three of a kind) are 6 in 216: there is exactly one way to roll each three of a kind, out of a total of 216 possible rolls. This reduces to 1 roll in 36, which (if the game had no house advantage) should pay 35:1. A typical Keystone table pays 34:1 for this bet, which means that for every 36 gold the house should return to you, it gives you only 35. The payback on this bet is therefore 35/36, or 97.22%. Odds on the Keystone bets vary between bets, and from table to table. For any one-roll bet, you can compute the correct odds and house percentage as described above.

For the multi-roll bets, you need to know the odds of a particular stone being cleared (paid) before the end of the game, which are as follows:

ARCH BET ODDS BY GAME TYPE		
Arch Bet	Odds to Clear (Standard)	Odds to Clear (Jackpot)
3 or 18	21.4%	21.9%
4 or 17	31.7%	32.6%
5 or 16	42.9%	43.9%
6 or 15	52.8%	53.7%
7 or 14	60.3%	61.2%
8 or 13	64.7%	65.6%
9 or 12	63.8%	64.7%
10 or 11	74.4%	75.3%

Bloodstone uses similar odds calculations. For example, on the Trips bet, the odds of winning are 210 in 216 (all but the 6 ways to roll trips), which reduces to 35 in 36. If the bet pays 10/360, then on average you will collect 10 gold 35 times, and lose 360 gold once. The value of this bet is therefore 350/360, which is the same 97.22% we calculated above. The main difference is that in Bloodstone you are "laying odds" on this bet, meaning that you will usually win a little but sometimes lose a lot. In Keystone, the opposite is true: on the Trips bet you sometimes win a lot, but usually lose a little.

Basic Strategy

There is no single strategy that will consistently win or lose in Keystone, other than to stick to the individual bets with the lowest house percentage. However, there are some betting patterns that can be fun to play.

For example, you can choose to play the "High Game" or "Low Game," betting on all Arch stones on the left or right side of the arch. If you feel like a run of low rolls is coming, bet the entire low end and see how many you can eliminate before the end of the game.

A bet of three units on Pair, two units on Run, and one unit on Trips, is a fun set of bets. You will lose all six units less than half the time, roughly 44% of the rolls. You will get your money back when you hit the pair (or a little more, depending on the table), roughly 41% of the time. Trips will hit on one roll in 36, paying roughly six times your total bet, and a Run will hit roughly 11% of the time, paying roughly three times your total bet. The payback percentage on this set of bets is 96.2%.

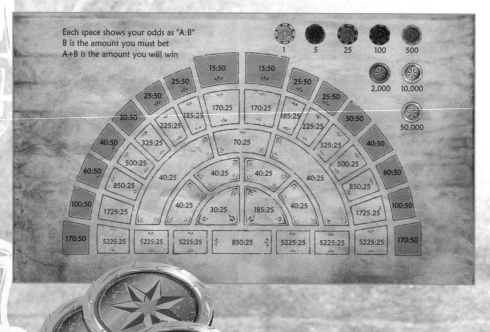

In Bloodstone, you want to make a lot of bets so that one bad roll won't necessarily cripple you. One fun set of bets is to cover all the even or odd numbers in the middle of the arch (for example, 6, 8, 10, 12, and 14). This way, you win all five bets on any odd roll, or on one of the long-shot even rolls (4, 16 and 18), and you lose a reasonable amount (at most, 22 bets) if one of your numbers hits.

✳ Spinnerbox

Spinnerbox is a rather unique take on the popular slot machines seen in today's casinos. Just like the real thing, your input is limited to deciding how much to bet and then pressing the A Button to spin the flit switches. What happens after that is up to chance. There is probably no faster way to burn through your hard-earned money than by playing Spinnerbox, as you can play a round in as little as 5 seconds if you continue to press A Button quickly. Of course, if you're lucky, then this also means that there's no faster way to get rich!

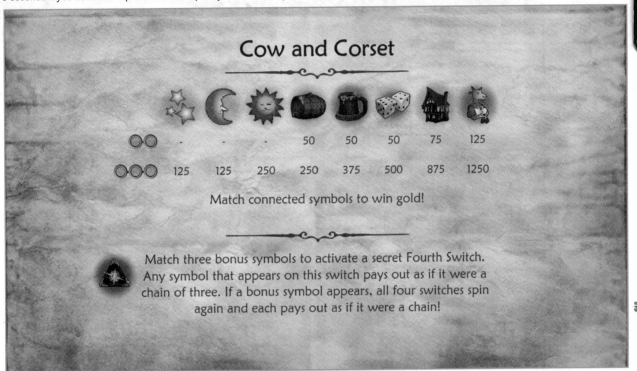

Cow and Corset

⊙⊙	-	-	-	50	50	50	75	125
⊙⊙⊙	125	125	250	250	375	500	875	1250

Match connected symbols to win gold!

Match three bonus symbols to activate a secret Fourth Switch. Any symbol that appears on this switch pays out as if it were a chain of three. If a bonus symbol appears, all four switches spin again and each pays out as if it were a chain!

Bet: 3
Win: 15

15

109

Ⓨ Adjust Bet   Ⓐ Spin
Payouts   Ⓧ Bank   Stats

The goal of Spinnerbox is to get a chain of matching—and touching—symbols. Some spinner boxes contain just three switches while others have four or even six. There are bonuses involved in each of the games, but scoring large payouts on the bigger boards is definitely less common than on the smallest board. Regardless the board you decide to play on, be sure to watch your money closely as it can disappear mighty quick playing this game.

Rules

- A spinner box is a decorative box containing several devices called 'flit switches.' A flit switch is a magical spinner that will randomly cycle through a variety of symbols. To play Spinnerbox, just place your bet and spin!

- A 'chain' is two or more adjacent symbols of the same type. When a chain appears, you'll win an amount of gold based on which symbols you get, and how much you bet.

- Some spinner boxes have three switches, some have four, and some have six. Bigger boxes mean better chains, as many as six of a kind!

- Some spinner boxes have symbols that enhance the game instead of simply paying out gold. These are called 'Bonus' symbols. On Cow and Corset, for example, when you get a chain of three bonus symbols, a fourth switch appears in the middle of the box. Whichever symbol appears on this single switch pays out as if it was three of a kind.

- On four-switch spinner boxes, every Coins symbol will earn you a free spin. You earn free spins whenever you get a chain of two or more Coins symbols. You can even earn more free spins while playing your original free spins.

- On Flower Garden, Crowns give you a payout multiplier, which applies to your next spin. Your multiplier grows with each Crown that appears, and keeps growing for as long as they keep popping up. The multiplier will reset if a spin produces no Crowns.

- Hold the Left Trigger to see a list of all payouts and bonus game rules for any spinner box. To see what different starting bets might pay, you can even change your wager while looking at this list.

Variants and Odds

The different Spinnerbox varieties become available as you continue to travel around Albion, raise your gambler rating, and encounter different Game Masters. There is no denying that you stand to win a lot of money while playing the games with more flit switches, but the occurrence of a three-of-a-kind on the three switch boards is too frequent to be ignored. Consider sticking to the simple version and bet the maximum every round. The fourth flit switch bonus will pay off huge!

Three Switch: Simple three switch spinner box with a bonus fourth switch that appears on three of a kind.

Four Switch: Four switches with Coins symbols mixed in to reward you with free spins.

Six Switch: A six-switch spinner box with Crown symbols that provide a winnings multiplier for your following spin.

As with a real slot machine, each spin is independent of the others, so you are equally likely to hit a jackpot on the next spin, whether your last spin was a winner or not. These games can be extremely volatile. That means that, in the short term, you can have wildly different results. In general, the higher the top award in a given machine, the higher the volatility of that machine, and the longer you would have to play it to come close to the expected payback. In the short term, this could mean big wins or big losses.

The different symbols on each Spinnerbox reel are not always set to appear with the same frequency. For example, on the Cow and Corset game, the bonus reel symbol appears more often than any other symbol. This ensures that the bonus game happens with a reasonably high frequency, which is roughly 1 game in 35.

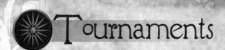

Tournaments

In the *Fable II Pub Games* for XBLA, you will find house-sponsored tournaments that have a built-in advantage for the player. In each tournament, the house adds additional money (and prizes) to the prize pool, making the tournament a long-term winning proposition. The hitch is that to unlock the high-level tournaments, you need to put in some time playing in the cash games, and raising your star rating.

In both the Fortune's Tower and Keystone tournaments, money management is as important as basic strategy. Notice where other players stand in the tournament (you can view all relevant stats by holding the Right Trigger). If you are in the lead, you may want to bet conservatively. If you are far behind, you need to play more aggressively. When a small win won't make the difference, you need to set yourself up for a big one. In the Spinnerbox tournament, there's no option to vary your bet, so the only winning strategy is try, try again!

To make the most gold over time, you should unlock the highest level tournaments. It's slow going, but the odds are in your favor. If you want the chance to make gold more quickly, try your luck at the high-limit cash games, but be prepared for big swings up and down!

Fortune's Tower Tournaments

This is a "shootout" tournament. First, you play 12 hands against four A.I. opponents, and the winner of the round (the player with the most chips) moves on to a final table. At the final table, all players' chips are reset, and all five players at this table will win a cash prize. To succeed in this format, you must do whatever it takes to win first place on the first table, and then you can focus on placing as high as possible at the second.

FORTUNE'S TOWER TOURNAMENTS			
Gambler Rating	Buy-In	Prize Pool	Item Bonus
1	0	500	Hairstyle Card
2	20	1500	"Dog Tricks! The Backflip"
3	80	4000	Highroller's Coat
4	200	9000	Potion of Will
5	500	18500	Championship Pistol

Cut Your Losses

The key to winning in Fortune's Tower tournaments is to manage your money as conservatively as possible and avoid the temptation to go for broke. We recommend starting with a bet only twice that of the minimum for the first hand then raising or lowering your bet based on the previous hand's performance. If you win the first hand, increase your bet, but if not, lower the bet. This way you resist the urge to chase a losing streak with too much good money and only bet more after you've already won a little.

Keystone Tournaments

This is a "duplicate" tournament. Players are divided into six tables, but the dice roll the same on every table. This is to keep the tournament fair and so that all players are competing on the same series of rolls. To win this tournament, you must have the most chips at the end of five full games.

KEYSTONE TOURNAMENTS			
Gambler Rating	Buy-In	Prize Pool	Item Bonus
1	0	750	Deepest Dark Chocolate
2	50	2400	Sleepmaster 3000
3	150	5700	Potion of Strength
4	400	13200	Face Tattoo
5	750	22500	Championship Cutlass

Trips or Bust

The AI players in a Keystone tournament tend to bet randomly. This means that, while most of them will lose, some of them will usually win. When they do hit a big win, it will be because of long-odds bets such as hardways and trips. To make sure that these players don't get ahead of you, concentrate on similar long shot bets so that you have a good chance of staying even with the players who get ahead. If you bet the absolute minimum, you can also win the Keystone tournament, but only if none of your opponents gets lucky!

Spinnerbox Tournaments

This game has 20 players, each of whom takes 100 spins on the same Spinnerbox game. To win, just have the most chips total at the end. You'll notice that the tournament game is quite a bit "looser" than a standard Spinnerbox game, paying back roughly 500%. This is because Tournament chips have no gold value, so you might as well have the fun of hitting a few jackpots on your way!

SPINNERBOX TOURNAMENTS			
Gambler Rating	Buy-In	Prize Pool	Item Bonus
1	0	400	Apple Pie
2	25	1300	"Hat, Headband, Moustache"
3	100	3500	Body Tattoo
4	250	8000	Potion of Skill
5	600	17000	Mysterious Ring

Play it Fast

Since you can't adjust your bet in a Spinnerbox tournament, there's little you can do other than press the A Button as quickly as you can in hopes of winning and at least complete the tournament rapidly so you can play again that much sooner.

JOBS

In addition to gambling at the Pub Games, there are also a number of jobs that you can do to earn money. Each of these jobs is quite simple; none require more than a single well-timed tap of the A Button. However, they can earn you huge money in little time. Although these jobs are intentionally simplistic, they are one of the better ways of earning money in the game. Each of these jobs offers quicker and safer access to riches than any of the Pub Games. They are also easier and faster than completing Bounty Hunter and Assassination Society missions. So keep your eyes peeled for job openings and work your way up to a 4- or 5-star woodcutter, blacksmith, or bartender and start really earning the money!

Sleep the Week Away

If the job you're looking for isn't currently available, find yourself a bed and sleep for seven days. Jobs become available every ten to twenty days or so and sleeping through a week is the best way to advance the calendar and hopefully get access to a job or side-job that wasn't previously available. Just remember that prolonged sleeping will lead to increased corruption. After all, sloth is one of the deadly sins!

 Blacksmith

Tap the A Button when the target is over the sweet spot to score a good hammer. Make a perfect sword to increase your gold multiplier.

Locations: Bowerstone Market, Westcliff, and Bloodstone

BLACKSMITH JOB GROWTH		
Skill Rating	Earning Requirement	Base Pay per Sword
★	0 Gold	4 Gold
★★	60 Gold	16 Gold
★★★	800 Gold	54 Gold
★★★★	8000 Gold	96 Gold
★★★★★	32000 Gold	150 Gold

The blacksmith job is the most difficult of the three jobs, especially once you rise to a higher level skill rating. The reason for this is that it takes five successful swings of the hammer to earn any money and the sweet spot's position on the meter and the speed at which the cursor moves changes with each swing. The cursor also alternates sides, thereby making it even trickier. You need to really concentrate when working as a blacksmith, more than with any other job, in order to get the gold multiplier to a high number. Don't be afraid to let the cursor go past the sweet spot on the initial pass if it's moving quickly. The sweet spot will shrink, but you'll be able to time your button press better on the second pass.

Strength Pays

You can earn more gold as a blacksmith by developing your Physique.

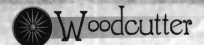

Woodcutter

Hit the A Button when the target is over the sweet spot to score a good chop. The faster you chop, the more gold you'll make. Score 10 chps in a row without missing to build up your gold multiplier.

Locations: Oakfield and Brightwood

WOODCUTTER JOB GROWTH		
Skill Rating	Earning Requirement	Base Pay per Log
★	0 Gold	1-3 Gold
★★	100 Gold	3-12 Gold
★★★	1000 Gold	11-27 Gold
★★★★	10000 Gold	10-48 Gold
★★★★★	40000 Gold	15-75 Gold

Working as a woodcutter has the benefit of earning money with every button press, but you need to successfully chop ten logs in order to raise the gold multiplier. Nevertheless, this is a considerably easier task than working as a blacksmith and you can earn money quite quickly. The position of the sweet spot will start to shift around a bit once you get a higher gold multiplier, especially at the higher skill levels, but you can always let the cursor pass and hit it on the second try. The sweet spot will expand and turn from green to yellow to orange before turning red. You can still successfully chop the log by stopping the cursor in any of these colors, but you will earn less money for not chopping in the green.

Bartender

Tap the A Button to serve a pint. The longer you pour, the better the head on the beer. But be careful not to spill! Pull 3 perfect pints in a row to increase your gold multiplier.

Locations: Oakfield, Bowerstone Market, Westcliff, Rookridge, and Bloodstone

BARTENDER JOB GROWTH			
Skill Rating	Earning Requirement	Base Pay per Pint	Dropped Mug Penalty
★	0 Gold	3 Gold	-2 Gold
★★	80 Gold	12 Gold	-8 Gold
★★★	800 Gold	27 Gold	-18 Gold
★★★★	8000 Gold	48 Gold	-32 Gold
★★★★★	32000 Gold	75 Gold	-50 Gold

There's no denying that being a bartender is the best job of the three. For starters, the sweet spot is always in the same spot and the meter fills in the same way with every pour. Secondly, it pays on every successful pour, and the gold multiplier increases every third pour. Although there is there is a penalty for breaking a mug if you are slow in pressing the A Button, there is plenty of margin for error to avoid this. Best of all, each of the bars has a vertical beam positioned directly to the right of your Hero as he/she is pulling beers. The left-hand edge of this beam matches up almost perfectly with the start of the green zone in the meter. Anticipate the meter getting to this point and press the A Button just right as it approaches the beam.

Bounty Hunter

Help rid Albion of dangerous creatures and criminals.

Bounty Hunter missions can provide a welcome source of quick and relatively painless money, so long as you don't mind traveling back and forth to areas you may not have been headed to. These jobs are given out by City Guards, typically in Bowerstone Market, and require you to travel to a specific location and slaughter a specific number of monsters or criminals that have become a problem for the locals. Once you receive the assignment, all you need to do is fast-travel to the area in question and kill the number of enemies specified in the lower right-hand corner of the screen. Once that's done, return to the City Guard to collect your payment. These jobs are randomly generated and the difficulty is dependent on the type and number of enemies you have to eliminate.

Assassination Society

Assassinate the Society's chosen target.

Assassination Society jobs will pop up periodically throughout your journey, but will be more common to those Heroes who begin their adventure by giving the Search Warrants to Arfur during the Childhood phase of the game. These missions are randomly generated and pay thousands of gold, but also carry a corruption penalty of -30 purity. That said, they can be quite fun to participate in so give them a try.

Each Assassination Society job begins with you receiving the contract from the society's contact. Check your Books & Documents section of your inventory and read the contract to learn who the mark is. The contract will specify who you must kill, where he/she can be located, why you're killing him, and also any specific rules for you to follow.

You're typically going to need to kill the mark where there are no witnesses. The easiest way to do this is to have him follow you someplace quiet. Consider buying a house somewhere in the area and, if appropriate, giving an engagement ring to the mark to guarantee he'll follow you. Once you have him alone, kill him. You'll need to return to the member who gave you the contract to get paid.

Slave Rescue

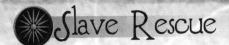

Find and rescue the slaves.

Slave Rescue quests provide a seemingly never-ending series of jobs for the moral Hero to participate in. These quests each require you to head to a particular area where slaves are being imprisoned and free them from their captives. These quests start out easy enough, but the difficulty will increase at random, depending on where the slaves are being held and what type of enemy is hoarding them. Fast-travel to the area, defeat the enemies guarding the cage and use the key the final enemy gives up to unlock the cage and free the prisoners. These quests provide quick sources of morality and renown and should not be overlooked.

Civilian Displacement

A hard labor agency is in need of new 'recruits'.

Civilian Displacement jobs are the exact opposite of the Slave Rescue assignments. Rather than trying to free a person from captivity, these missions require you to do the capturing. Meet the client to receive the order details and inspect the contract to see how many civilians are needed, what their occupation is, and what they look like. These missions are randomly generated and carry varying degrees of risk. Sometimes the order will be very specific, and other times it won't.

Once you know what type of person you're looking for, give the description some thought and go to the place where they're most likely to be. Most of the orders can be filled in Bowerstone Market, but you may need to look elsewhere on occasion. And regardless which area you head to find your recruit, always check the local pub first. Once you find the person fitting the description on the order, give them the Follow expression and lead them outside. Make sure they're following you, then fast-travel to the area specified in the quest description and make the delivery. Completing Civilian Displacement jobs pays thousands of gold, but further tilts your morality towards Evil.

CONTINUING QUESTS

The Archaeologist

The archaeologist at Fairfax Gardens offered you several quests during the Adolescence phase of the adventure (see Quest Guide for complete details), but that wasn't the last of her missions for you. Several more will become available during Adulthood and then even more in the sandbox portion of the game (after you complete the story). The table here lists each of the artifact locations and the renown you'll receive for completing them. Remember, all you need to do is to go to the region where the artifact is then follow your dog to the dig site. Retrieve the item and bring it to Belle at Fairfax Gardens to get a reward and another quest.

ARTIFACT DETAILS			
Artifact	Renown	Location	Availability
1	75	Bowerstone Old Town	Upon arrival in Bowerstone Market during Adolescence.
2	100	Rookridge	Upon arrival in Bowerstone Market during Adolescence.
3	125	Bowerstone Cemetery	Upon arrival in Bowerstone Market during Adolescence.
4	150	Oakfield	After returning from the Tattered Spire during Adulthood.
5	200	Bower Lake	After returning from the Tattered Spire during Adulthood.
6	250	Brightwood	After returning from the Tattered Spire during Adulthood.
7	300	Bandit Coast	After returning from the Tattered Spire during Adulthood.
8	350	Westcliff	After returning from the Tattered Spire during Adulthood.
9	450	Gemstone Grotto	After returning from the Tattered Spire during Adulthood.
10	500	Wraithmarsh	After defeating Lucien and returning from the Tattered Spire during Adulthood.
11	550	Bloodstone	After defeating Lucien and returning from the Tattered Spire during Adulthood.
12	600	Guild Cave	After defeating Lucien and returning from the Tattered Spire during Adulthood.
13	700	Reaver's Rear Passage	After defeating Lucien and returning from the Tattered Spire a second time.

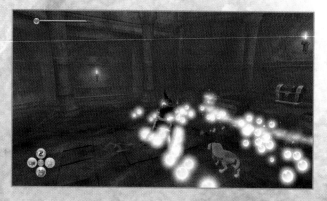

Belle won't be in her normal position when you return with the 13th artifact. Instead, she'll be standing in the excavation pit near a very large door. The final scroll will give her the code she needs to unlock the door, now she just wants you to head into the tomb and retrieve **The Archon's Dream** from the chest inside. Whether you choose to keep the gemstone or give it to Belle is up to you, but it is worth a small boatload of gold, so we suggest keeping it. Turn your safety off and slice her up.

Hobbes

VARIETY		HP	HOLY	EVIL	INFERNO	SHOCK	BLADES	CHAOS	VORTEX	FORCE PUSH	BLUNT	CUTTING	BULLET	ARROW
	Mentalist	2	---	---	---	---	---	O	O	O	---	---	---	---
	Caster	100	---	---	O	O	O	---	O	O	---	---	---	---
	Skeleton	125	O	X	X	O	---	O	O	O	O	---	---	---
	Ambusher	150	---	---	O	---	---	O	O	O	---	---	---	---
	Grunt	150	---	---	---	---	---	O	O	O	---	---	---	---
	Leader	350	---	---	---	---	---	O	O	O	---	---	---	---
	Elite Caster	400	---	---	O	O	O	---	O	O	---	---	---	---
	Sniper	400	---	---	O	O	---	O	O	O	---	---	---	---
	Crucible	440	---	---	---	---	---	O	O	O	---	---	---	---
	Ambusher Elite	500	---	---	O	---	---	O	O	O	---	---	---	---
	Elite Grunt	500	---	---	---	O	---	O	O	O	---	---	---	---
	Elite Skeleton	500	O	X	X	O	---	O	O	O	O	---	---	---
	Ambusher Leader	900	---	---	O	---	---	---	O	O	---	---	---	---
	Elite Leader	900	---	---	---	O	---	---	O	O	---	---	---	---
	Skeleton Super Elite	1000	O	X	X	O	---	O	O	O	O	---	---	---
	Hobbe Wizard	1800	---	---	O	O	O	X	O	O	---	---	---	---
	Hobbe Leader: Rescue	2500	---	---	---	O	---	X	X	X	---	---	---	---

Hobbes are small cave-dwelling creatures that rely on their fangs, claws, and maces to beat interlopers to death. Some say they turn small children into hobbes, while others think they just eat them. Either way, they are certainly nothing to be trifled with. Hobbes attack with vicious aggression and typically attack in groups. They are capable fighters, skilled at blocking melee attacks with surprising skill. As such, it is best to beat them back with ranged attacks and magic spells. Area-effect spells are particularly useful given their tendency to surround their prey. Use Force Push and Vortex to knock them about, then finish them off with a blast of Inferno or Shock.

Although there are many types of hobbes, most of them are pretty similar save for the ones on stilts and the various skeleton types. These two varieties of hobbes may seem quite different, but they do share one common feature—Inferno is all but useless against them. Skeleton hobbes are resistant to Inferno and the stilt-walking leaders can stride right through the flames without fear. For that reason, we recommend using Shock and blunt melee weapons to take out the skeletons and Sub-Targeted headshots to dispose of the stilt-using hobbes.

City Guards

Variety	HP	HOLY	EVIL	INFERNO	SHOCK	BLADES	CHAOS	VORTEX	FORCE PUSH	BLUNT	CUTTING	BULLET	ARROW
Guard: Grunt	600	X	O	---	---	---	---	---	---	---	---	---	---
Guard: Lieutenant	900	X	O	---	---	---	X	---	---	---	---	---	---
Body Guard	900	---	---	---	---	---	X	---	---	---	---	---	---
Guard: Elite Grunt	1300	X	O	---	---	---	---	---	---	---	---	---	---
Guard: Elite Lieutenant	1500	X	O	---	---	---	X	---	---	---	---	---	---

Only the most devilish of Heroes will bring blade to the innocent, let alone resist arrest long enough to force the city guards to call for backup. But if this is your plan, then know that the city guards (and body guards in the Assassination jobs) have little resistances and can be slain in any number of ways. They'll fight with guns and swords, but they have no match for your Inferno spell, nor could they withstand any other Level 3 surround spell. Let them have it, then get running before even more city guards arrive on the scene.

MONSTERS

Giant Beetles

Variety	HP	HOLY	EVIL	INFERNO	SHOCK	BLADES	CHAOS	VORTEX	FORCE PUSH	BLUNT	CUTTING	BULLET	ARROW
Weak Spitter	2	---	---	O	O	O	---	O	O	---	---	---	---
Weak Basic	2	---	---	O	O	O	---	O	O	---	---	---	---
Basic	10	---	---	---	---	---	---	---	---	O	---	---	---
Spitter	10	---	---	---	---	---	---	---	---	O	---	---	---
Armored Facehugger	60	---	---	---	---	---	---	---	---	O	---	---	---
Armored Spitter	75	---	---	---	---	---	---	---	---	O	---	---	---
Nocturnal Spitter	200	---	---	---	O	---	---	---	---	O	---	---	---
Nocturnal Facehugger	200	---	---	---	O	---	---	---	---	O	---	---	---
Armored Elite	700	---	---	---	---	---	---	---	---	---	---	---	---

Giant beetles rise up from the ground and attack in swarms as you near their underground hives. Most giant beetles do most of their damage by slamming into their prey while flying around or by trying to latching onto its face and pinching it repeatedly. These dive-bombing insects move slowly and don't inflict much damage, but they can bring down an inexperienced Hero if given the opportunity. They are extremely susceptible to all manner of attacks the weakest and can be defeated with a single slash of worst swords. Mash the buttons and rattle the Left Thumbstick back and forth to shake a Facehugger loose.

Some giant beetles hang back and attack from afar by spitting a toxic purple substance. These projectile attacks aren't terribly common and are also quite easy to avoid, especially once you have learned the Roll ability. These spitballs inflict more damage than the physical attacks so keep your eyes peeled for giant beetles lurking in the distance. Use your ranged weaponry to defeat them as soon as they're spotted.

Spire Guards

VARIETY		HP	HOLY	EVIL	INFERNO	SHOCK	BLADES	CHAOS	VORTEX	FORCE PUSH	BLUNT	CUTTING	BULLET	ARROW
	Basic	500	---	---	---	---	---	---	---	---	---	---	---	---
	Lieutenant	600	---	---	---	---	---	X	---	---	---	---	---	---
	Elite	1100	---	---	---	---	---	---	---	---	---	---	---	---
	Lieutenant Elite	1300	---	---	---	---	---	X	---	---	---	---	---	---
	Soldier	1500	---	---	---	---	---	X	X	X	---	---	---	---
	Commandant	2000	---	---	---	---	---	X	X	X	---	---	X	---
	Soldier Elite	2400	---	---	---	---	---	X	X	X	---	---	---	---

The Spire guards are an elite set of warriors who do Lucien's bidding, which explains their seemingly constant presence at Brightwood Tower. Spire guards are capable swordsmen with a knack for defense. Equipped with katana, the Spire guards are capable of attacking with surprising speed. Soldier and soldier elite level Spire guards are capable of unleashing a ground-based shockwave that sends a bolt of spikes through the ground in your direction. Never stand directly in front of these higher-level enemies.

The basic Spire guards don't have any particular weaknesses or resistances, but they are quite a bit harder to damage than other human enemies thanks to their training and thick armor. Stay on the move (rolling is the key to avoiding their sword slashes) and alternate between Flourishes and gunshot blasts. Use Force Push to keep them from getting too close and Time Control to buy yourself time to unleash a high-level magic spell.

Highwaymen

VARIETY		HP	HOLY	EVIL	INFERNO	SHOCK	BLADES	CHAOS	VORTEX	FORCE PUSH	BLUNT	CUTTING	BULLET	ARROW
	Basic	700	---	---	---	---	---	X	---	X	---	---	---	---
	Elite	1400	---	---	---	---	---	X	---	X	---	---	---	---
	Darius Zing	2500	---	---	---	---	---	X	X	X	---	---	---	---

Highwaymen are far tougher than everyday bandits and are equipped with both a sword and a rifle. They travel in packs and are fierce combatants who can defend as well if not better than Spire guards and attack with much greater force than bandits. Fortunately for the Hero, they should have more than enough firepower to deal with them by the time they make themselves known.

Highwaymen aren't as susceptible to Force Push or Chaos spells, but a Level 3 Inferno spell will all but wipe them out; just make sure to use Time Control or Raise Dead to buy you the time it takes to cast it. The speed of the highwaymen makes using ranged weaponry tough, especially if they get close to you, but a few well-aimed headshots can certainly put a dent in their plans!

HUMANS

--- = Normal   X = Resistance

O = Weakness   + = Immune

Bandits

VARIETY		HP	HOLY	EVIL	INFERNO	SHOCK	BLADES	CHAOS	VORTEX	FORCE PUSH	BLUNT	CUTTING	BULLET	ARROW
	Thag's Gang Grunt	53	---	---	---	---	---	---	O	O	---	---	O	O
	Turret	100	---	---	O	O	O	---	O	O	---	---	O	O
	Easy Grunt	100	---	---	---	---	---	---	---	---	---	---	---	---
	Regular Grunt	150	---	---	---	---	---	---	---	---	---	---	---	---
	Bandit Leader: Thag	400	---	---	---	---	---	X	X	X	---	---	---	---
	Lieutenant	600	---	---	---	---	---	---	---	---	---	---	---	---
	Elite Turret	700	---	---	O	O	O	---	O	O	---	---	O	O
	Elite Grunt	800	---	---	---	---	---	---	---	---	---	---	---	---
	Crucible Grunt	900	---	---	O	O	O	---	O	O	---	---	O	O
	Crucible Turret	900	---	---	O	O	O	---	O	O	---	---	O	O
	Elite Lieutenant	1000	---	---	---	---	---	---	---	---	---	---	---	---
	Crucible Lieutenant	1200	---	---	O	O	O	---	O	O	---	---	---	---
	Bandit Leader: Ripper	1200	---	---	---	---	---	---	---	---	---	---	---	---
	Bandit Leader: Fairfax	6000	---	---	---	---	---	+	X	X	---	---	---	---

Bandits are the lowest form of human enemy you'll encounter. These sword-wielding lowlifes prey on innocent, helpless travelers and imprison many of them as slaves. Although they travel in packs, they typically lack the coordination and intelligence necessary to develop any semblance of group strategy.

The Hero can make quick work of the bandits by taking advantage of their known weaknesses, of which there are several. For starters, most forms of bandits are vulnerable to ranged weaponry, thereby giving you a huge advantage if you can spot them early and snipe them from afar. If that's impossible and the bandits begin to swarm around you, look no further than the Inferno spell. Many of the bandits, particularly the higher powered ones, are vulnerable to all sorts of magic spells, but there's little denying the power of Inferno so light them up!

Enemies of Albion

This chapter contains all the information needed to defeat the enemies, both human and monstrous, that will try to stop you from freeing Albion of Lucien's tyranny. There are many different classes of enemy within each type and many of them not only have different levels of Hit Points (HP), but they are also vulnerable and resistant to different attacks. Consult the tables and the battle tactics provided here whenever you encounter a new foe so you know exactly how to exploit their weaknesses and avoid playing to their strengths. Note that Time Control and Raise Dead are universally applicable to all battle situations and work independently of the enemies you're fighting. See 'The Hero's Way' chapter for more information on how those spells work specifically.

The Crucible Champion

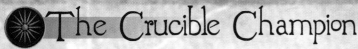

You are a Crucible champion. But there are still records to be broken and prizes to be won.

You'll be able to return to the Crucible at any time after escaping from the Tattered Spire. There are several reasons why you'd want to enter the Crucible again. For starters, it's unlikely that you managed eight perfect rounds on your initial visit so you still have **The Chopper** to win. Secondly, participating in the Crucible with either the Discipline or Golden Touch augment equipped can earn you far more experience or gold than you could anywhere else. Lastly, the Crucible is a lot of fun. And that's got to count for something, right? Follow these tips geared to high-level characters and breeze through all eight rounds and earn the legendary axe!

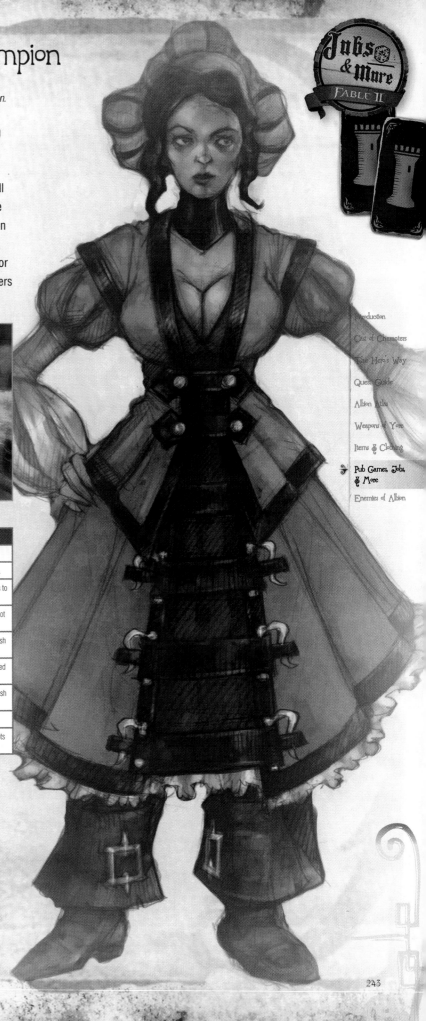

Round	Enemy Type	Tactic
1	Giant Beetles	Cast Level 4 Inferno and finish off the stragglers with melee attacks.
2	Hobbes	Cast Raise Dead and Inferno near the spawns, then use ranged attacks to finish off any survivors.
3	Hobbes	Use Level 3 or higher Force Push to knock them into the pit, and shoot explosives with ranged attacks.
4	Hollow Men	Cast Raise Dead and Level 4 or 5 Inferno to kill the majority, then finish off the others with melee attacks.
5	Bandits	Rush the far side and cast high level Raise Dead and attack with ranged weapon headshots.
6	Highwaymen	Use the switches to knock them into the pit and cast Level 3 Force Push along with ranged headshots.
7	Balverines	Cast Level 4 or 5 Inferno.
8	Troll	Cast high-level Shock or Inferno spells to take out multiple weak spots simultaneously.

Table title: CRUCIBLE TACTICS FOR HIGH LEVEL HEROES

Hollow Men

VARIETY		HP	HOLY	EVIL	INFERNO	SHOCK	BLADES	CHAOS	VORTEX	FORCE PUSH	BLUNT	CUTTING	BULLET	ARROW
	Easy	100	O	X	O	---	---	O	---	---	---	---	---	---
	Regular	160	O	X	O	---	---	O	---	---	---	---	---	---
	Elite	700	O	X	O	---	---	O	---	---	---	---	---	---
	Headless	1000	O	X	---	---	---	---	X	X	---	---	---	---
	Elder	1300	O	X	---	---	---	X	X	X	---	---	---	---
	Elder Elite	1500	O	X	---	---	---	X	X	X	---	---	---	---
	Leader/Gravekeeper	4000	O	X	---	X	---	X	X	X	---	---	---	---

The hollow men are quite unlike any other human-like creature the Hero has seen. They float nearby as twinkling lights, then plunge into the ground and erupt as ghastly reanimated corpses. Hollow men carry sickles and other crude melee weapons, and attack at close range. They are a slower form of enemy, but can be extremely dangerous as they tend to attack in large groups.

Most hollow men are incredibly susceptible to fire damage so make full use of the Inferno spell when battling them. A Level 2 Inferno cast targeted at an Easy or Regular level hollow man will kill it on the spot. Melee and ranged weapons are useful too, but neither are nearly as effective as a fireball targeted at their dried up skin and loose, sagging clothes! Those who follow a path of moral righteousness and obtain the Rising Sun legendary weapon will have an advantage against the elder hollow men during the latter stages of the story, as these much tougher hollow men aren't as vulnerable to most magic as the other hollow men are. Regardless of the type of hollow man you face, a Sub-Targeted headshot from a powerful weapon will almost always stop them cold!

Trolls

VARIETY		HP	HOLY	EVIL	INFERNO	SHOCK	BLADES	CHAOS	VORTEX	FORCE PUSH	BLUNT	CUTTING	BULLET	ARROW
	Forest (Weakspot)	140	---	---	O	O	O	X	X	X	---	---	---	---
	Rock (Weakspot)	180	---	---	---	---	---	X	X	X	---	---	---	---
	Swamp (Weakspot)	360	---	---	X	X	---	X	O	X	---	---	---	---

Trolls are unlike any creature you'll see elsewhere in Albion. They are massive creatures that spin in place heaving rocks and debris at their prey. Trolls are also capable of sending a massive shockwave across the ground; this is a targeted attack rather than area-of-effect. Each of the trolls has a number of weak spots on their body. These are what you must hit to weaken it. They aren't always visible, so take cover or stay on the run until they appear, then attack!

Getting close to a troll is simply out of the question. The beasts are far too strong to attempt a melee attack. It's possible, but the reward doesn't justify the risk. Instead, keep on the move circling around the troll while watching for it to attack. Move out of the way of the attack, then stop and either shoot one of the weakspots on its body or, better yet, take advantage of its vulnerability and cast a Level 2 or higher spell in hopes of damaging multiple weakspots at once! Forest trolls are susceptible to Inferno, Shock, and Blades, while swamp trolls are particularly vulnerable to the Vortex spell. Blades work with any of the trolls, and are quick to be summoned. Their auto-targeting feature is a nice bonus since they immediately go for the weak spots—even the hard to reach ones. A Blades spell also allows you to focus on your Hero's actions without constant recasting. It's typically easiest to use a combination of Time Control and ranged attacks.

Shards

VARIETY		HP	HOLY	EVIL	INFERNO	SHOCK	BLADES	CHAOS	VORTEX	FORCE PUSH	BLUNT	CUTTING	BULLET	ARROW
	Basic	1600	---	---	---	O	---	+	X	X	---	---	---	---
	Large	7000	---	---	---	O	---	+	X	X	---	---	O	O

Shards are large pyramid-shaped monstrosities that are sent from The Tattered Spire to deliver Spire guards to the battle. They emit powerful rays that teleport Spire guards into the area. Because of this, destroying Shards has to be a top priority whenever they appear. The outer shell of a Shard is impenetrable to attacks so you have to await the perfect moment and release your full fury. Eventually, the Shard will reveal its weak spot—a ball of white energy within. Hit that weak spot with full-powered spells and ranged attacks!

Balverines

VARIETY		HP	HOLY	EVIL	INFERNO	SHOCK	BLADES	CHAOS	VORTEX	FORCE PUSH	BLUNT	CUTTING	BULLET	ARROW
	Basic	140	---	---	O	O	O	X	X	X	---	---	---	---
	Blooded	180	---	---	---	---	---	X	X	X	---	---	---	---
	Sire	360	---	---	X	X	---	X	O	X	---	---	---	---

Balverines are among the most terrifying creatures in Albion. They appear as though they're half man and half wolf, but are far stronger and faster than either species alone. Balverines use their giant hands and long nails to claw and tear at their prey with rapid swipes. Balverines are not only ferociously aggressive, but they are capable of leaping high into the air (completely out of sight) and landing behind their opponent for a surprise attack.

The best way to fend off a balverine attack is with Inferno magic—their fur is highly flammable! There are other ways of dealing with balverines, though, especially if you've achieved 100% goodness and are using a weapon equipped with a Holy Augment. For starters, try using a fast melee weapon to attack in a chain. The balverine will leap into the air to break your attack. Quickly roll out of the way to avoid having it land behind you. Get up and renew the chain to finish it off! If you're in a situation when multiple balverines continue to appear, cast Raise Dead to summon the spirits of the deceased to fight on your behalf.

Banshees

VARIETY		HP	HOLY	EVIL	INFERNO	SHOCK	BLADES	CHAOS	VORTEX	FORCE PUSH	BLUNT	CUTTING	BULLET	ARROW
	Banshee Children	900	O	X	O	---	---	X	X	X	---	---	---	---
	Banshee	1400	O	X	O	---	---	X	X	X	---	---	---	---
	Queen	1800	O	X	O	---	---	X	X	X	---	---	---	---

Banshees are unlike other creatures you've encountered in that they float above the ground and use their powers to summon a cadre of tiny Shadow Children to attack. The banshee itself will use a brutal Soul Suck attack if you stray too close, but they tend to let their minions fight for them. Wipe out the shadow creatures with a Level 2 or 3 area spell, then take aim at the main attraction once it uncovers its face.

Banshees are immune to the Chaos spell and tend to be unaffected by area spells thanks to their ability to float. You can inflict significant damage with melee attacks and targeted spells, but the best ways to handle a Banshee are attacks with high-level ranged or melee weapons, or level 3+ targeted spells such as Blades. Stand back and wait for the banshee to let out a scream and uncover its face—this will happen once you've killed its little Shadow Children. That's your signal that the banshee can be targeted. Use your ranged weapon, preferably with the Sub-Targeting ability, and fire straight into its head! It's possible to drop a banshee with a Master-level crossbow in just a few shots, provided you aim for the head! You only have a few seconds before it summons another wave of Shadow Children and covers its face again, so act fast!

Shadow Creatures

VARIETY	HP	HOLY	EVIL	INFERNO	SHOCK	BLADES	CHAOS	VORTEX	FORCE PUSH	BLUNT	CUTTING	BULLET	ARROW
Beetle Facehugger	160	O	X	O	–	–	–	–	–	–	–	–	–
Beetle Spitter	160	O	X	O	–	–	–	–	–	–	–	–	–
Hobbe	310	O	X	O	–	–	–	–	–	–	–	–	–
Bandit	400	O	X	O	–	–	–	–	–	–	–	–	–
Banshee Children	600	O	X	O	–	–	–	–	–	–	–	–	–
Cornelius Grim	1300	O	X	O	–	–	X	–	X	–	–	–	–
Highwayman	1400	O	X	O	–	–	–	–	X	–	–	O	O
Balverine	1600	O	X	O	–	–	–	–	X	–	–	O	O

Shadow creatures are confined to the Shadow Court in Wraithmarsh (except for banshee children) and are essentially stronger, darker, versions of the enemies you face elsewhere. Shadow creatures are all black and semi-transparent, but dreadfully strong and with far fewer vulnerabilities. The best way to handle the various shadow creatures is with the Inferno spell, particularly if you're playing as an evil Hero and have already earned your Evil horns. Inferno is the only attack that any Hero can use effectively against every type of shadow creature.

Ghost Pirates

	VARIETY	HP	HOLY	EVIL	INFERNO	SHOCK	BLADES	CHAOS	VORTEX	FORCE PUSH	BLUNT	CUTTING	BULLET	ARROW
	Crew	600	O	X	O	–	–	–	X	–	–	–	–	–
	Captain Dread	4000	O	X	X	X	X	+	X	X	–	–	–	–

You'll encounter the ghost pirates and their leader, Captain Dread, at the Sinkhole cave. These ghostly assailants are every bit as aggressive as you'd expect the ghosts of dead pirates to be. The standard ghost pirate is vulnerable to Inferno and attacks from Holy Heroes, but they have no other vulnerabilities. Use Time Control and Inferno to thin their numbers, then switch to melee and ranged attacks. Flourishes and headshots will enable you to finish off the remaining ghost pirates while getting some practice for Captain Dread. Their leader is much bigger than the other ghost pirates and is resistant and/or immune to all magic attacks. Nevertheless, you can slow him down with Time Control and tilt the odds in your favor with the Raise Dead spell, particularly if you cast it immediately after finishing off the last ghost pirate.

Quest and Area Index

This is a quick reference index to help you navigate through the guide and find exactly what you're looking for, exactly when you want it. Each entry immediately shows whether it's a quest or area with its color: Orange = Areas and Brown = Quests. There's no linear progression to the quests or even the order in which you visit areas, so take advantage of this index!

FABLE II
OFFICIAL STRATEGY GUIDE

Written by Doug Walsh

©2008 DK Publishing, a division of Penguin Group (USA), Inc.

BradyGames® is a registered trademark of Pearson Education, Inc.

BradyGames Publishing
An Imprint of DK Publishing, Inc.
800 East 96th Street, 3rd Floor
Indianapolis, Indiana 46240

ISBN: 0-7440-1049-7

Printing Code: The rightmost double-digit number is the year of the book's printing; the rightmost single-digit number is the number of the book's printing. For example, 08-1 shows that the first printing of the book occurred in 2008.

11 10 09 08   4 3 2 1

Manufactured in the United States of America.

BradyGames Staff

Publisher
DAVID WAYBRIGHT

Editor-In-Chief
H. LEIGH DAVIS

Licensing Director
MIKE DEGLER

Marketing Director
DEBBY NEUBAUER

International Translations
BRIAN SALIBA

Credits

Sr. Development Editor
CHRISTIAN SUMNER

Screenshot Editor
MICHAEL OWEN

Lead Designer
CAROL STAMILE

Designers
DAN CAPARO
KEITH LOWE

Production Designer
AREVA

Map Illustrators
ARGOSY PUBLISHING

A Sincere Thank You from the Editor

Wow. Closing in on a decade in the strategy guide business and I'm still meeting absolutely extraordinary people. This project was a fantastic experience and everyone we dealt with both at Microsoft and Lionhead Studios was, to put it simply, remarkable. First off, thanks to the whole *Fable II* team. Jeff MacDermot, John Miller, Jeremie Texier, & Jason York went beyond the "extra mile" marker about a week after the process began. Thanks guys. Ryan Wilkerson was 110% behind this thing from the moment his hat was thrown into the ring and all I can say is "Thanks a million." John McCormack is just an incredible person and I feel as if I've become a better person on all fronts just by having worked with him on this amazing project. Lastly, Nancy Figatner, our tireless contact at Microsoft worked non-stop to make sure that this entire project came off without a hitch—and it did. Thank you Nancy, for everything.

Microsoft Game Studios

NICOLLE BLACKWELL	SOREN LAULAINEN
NATHAN BOROUGHS	AMRITZ LAY
JONATHON BRESSLER	ROSS LITTLE
RICH BRYANT	SHANNON LOFTIS
LEIF CHAPPELLE	JEFF MACDERMOT
SEAN COLBERT	RICK MARTINEZ
KEVIN DODD	JOHN MILLER
TIM DUZMAL	BRYCE PINKSTON
NANCY FIGATNER	MIKE RHINE
MATT GIDDINGS	AMANDA SCHNEIDER
CHAD HALE	ANN THOMAS
WHITNEY HILLS	RYAN WILKERSON
WILLIAM HODGE	JASON YORK
JEFF KAFER	MOHAMED ZOWEIL

Lionhead Studio

LOUISE COPLEY	PETER MOLYNEUX
JON ECKERSLEY	JEREMIE TEXIER
IAN FAICHNIE	MIKE WEST
BEN HUSKINS	STUART WHYTE
JOHN MCCORMACK	

Author Acknowledgments

A book of this magnitude doesn't come together without the hard work and assistance of many people, and nobody was more helpful than Jeff MacDermot of Microsoft Game Studios. Jeff painstakingly answered every question I could throw his way and did it with a speed and sense of humor that made working with him a real joy. Of course, Jeff doesn't work alone so I must also thank everyone at Microsoft and Lionhead Studios who helped funnel tips and data through him. Additionally, I also want to thank Jason York and John Miller for their assistance with the *Pub Games* portion of this guidebook. It was much appreciated! A tremendous amount of credit also needs to go to my editor Christian Sumner of BradyGames, one of the hardest working guys in the industry. Christian continually challenges each of us to put out the best guidebook we can and offers a perfect blend of guidance, support, and patience that we authors crave. Thanks Xian! I also want to thank Carol Stamile of BradyGames for the incredible design work she did for this book, and everyone else at BradyGames who contribute to the look and feel—it really would be just a collection of text and screenshots without their talents. Lastly, I want to thank Leigh Davis, Mike Degler, and David Waybright of BradyGames for giving me the honor of writing this guidebook.

About the Author

Doug Walsh has been authoring strategy guides for BradyGames for over eight years and has over seventy books to his credit including guidebooks for *Bioshock*, *Gears of War*, and *Tales of Vesperia* to name but a few. He lives in Snoqualmie, Washington with his wife and two dogs and spends what little free time he has mountain biking in the hills near his home. Doug took a short break during the writing of this book to compete against Lance Armstrong in the hundred mile Leadville Trail 100 mountain bike race high in the mountains of Colorado. Lance beat him—by a lot.